SURRENDER ALL

CHARLES E. CLANTON

I SURRENDER ALL

The amazing story of

Pauline Gruse, Missionary

to Liberia, as told to

Charles E. Clanton.

I Surrender All

by Charles E. Clanton

©Copyright 1979 Word Aflame Press
Revised Edition
©Copyright 1998 Charles E. Clanton
777 SW 19th
Moore, OK 73160

Cover Design by Paul Povolni

ISBN 1-56722-227-7

All Scripture quotations in this book are from the King James Version of the Bible unless otherwise identified.

All rights reserved. No portion of this publication may be reproduced, stored in an electronic system, or transmitted in any form or by any means, electronic, mechanical, photocopy, recording, or otherwise, without the prior permission of Heartland Press. Brief quotations may be used in literary reviews.

Printed in United States of America.

*I humbly dedicate this book
to the many hundreds of fearless
men and women who have so
unselfishly devoted their very best
to the cause of missions.*

Contents

1. Going Home??? 9
2. In the Beginning. 17
3. All Alone 29
4. The Making of a Nurse 41
5. Stones Become Mountains 59
6. He Brought Me Out 81
7. Tulsa Bound. 97
8. Missionary in Training 109
9. Finally!!! 129
10. Learning the Ropes 139
11. The Northern Trek 153
12. The Southern Trek 167
13. Furlough Away from Home. 183
14. Maheh, Bomi Hills, and Quoy Town 191
15. Fassama Mission 219
16. Oh, No—Not Another Furlough 251
17. Dedicated to LaVerne 259
18. Furlough Number Three. 279
19. Raised from the Dead. 285
20. Rediscovering the Will of God 299
21. The End??? 307
    Epilogue 331

ONE

Going Home???

Bzzzzzzzzzzzzzzzzz. . . . .

The harsh, impersonal, toneless buzzing of the clock radio at the head of my bed seemed to fill every cubic inch of the room—needlessly buzzing, as I had been fully awake for some time now. A thousand thoughts of yesteryear had been racing through my mind over the past few hours, but for the life of me I could not seem to recall even one of those thoughts now. I quickly reached over, and after clumsily fumbling with the knobs, finally managed to turn the alarm off. I noticed it was 7:00—just four hours before the plane would depart for my one-way trip to the States.

For a few moments I just lay in bed, staring aimlessly at the ceiling, seeing nothing, and wondering if I could muster up enough faith to face this, certainly the most dismal day of my entire 67 years. I must have become lost in self-pity, for the next thing I knew it was 7:45, and Esther Nigh was knocking at my door.

"Pauline, are you up? It's a quarter to eight, and breakfast will be ready shortly. We'll have to leave soon if we're to make it to Frankfurt in time for your flight."

Without the least bit of enthusiasm I reluctantly crawled out of bed. As my feet touched the floor, I felt a sudden compelling force driving me to my knees:

> *Lord, I can't make it by myself. If You don't help me I just can't possibly go through with it. You and I have been through a lot in the past 35 years, and not one time have You failed me. I can see that You've had Your hand upon me since the day I was born, and I must believe that You will continue to watch over me. Please mend this broken heart, and teach me to accept my return as Your will. And if I have even one selfish motive, please forgive me. Thank You, Jesus.*

With this, I arose, made my bed, and began dressing for the return flight to the States. There was little packing to do, as I had literally crammed my two travel-weary suitcases the night before. Most of my personal effects had been shipped straight from Bomi Hills, Liberia, my temporary home for the past year.

As I prepared to leave the bedroom for breakfast, I suddenly reflected on the many unmatchable friends God had given me over the past thirty-five years. For every "so-called friend" I had been forced to give up in accepting the call of God, I had been given at least a hundred "true friends" in return.

Wayne and Esther Nigh, my hosts for the two weeks in Germany, had to be included in this innumerable family of Christian friends. The Nighs, who were natives of the Great Northwest, had been missionaries for the past few years to the American military personnel stationed in West Germany.

For as long as I could remember, I had harbored a secret desire to visit Germany. While spending a few weeks with the Robert Rodenbush family in Accra, Ghana, I shared this dream for the first time. So, the Rodenbushes contacted their friends, the Nighs, and arrangements were made for me to visit them on my way back to the States.

I had fully intended, upon leaving Ghana, to spend but a few days in Germany—just enough time to see a few of the more spectacular and historical sights—just enough time to be able to say "I've been to Germany." But, upon the Nigh's insistence, which was strengthened by an extremely good time and a reluctance to begin the final leg of my journey, a few days somehow stretched into two weeks.

But now, even the two weeks were over, and like it or not, it was time for me to face reality. I was going home—at least what "they" called "home."

After a hearty breakfast, which was far more than a stomach full of butterflies and tied in knots needed, we loaded my two suitcases and travel bag into the Opel and began the trip to Frankfurt.

Two weeks had not accustomed me to the German brand of driving, but Brother Nigh assured me it was a bit more tame back in the States. Driving, however, would not be one of the many cultural adjustments I would have to make. My recent driving experience was limited to wrecking a missionary pickup in Liberia, and I was sure that if I could manage to have an accident when there was not another vehicle for miles around, it would be certain calamity if I were to attempt to drive in the presence of two or more cars.

The ride to the airport seemed altogether too short. It was as if each completed phase of my return trip severed just a little more of my already-torn heart. The closer I got to home, the more my worst fears and apprehensions were being transformed into stark reality.

Brother Nigh pulled up to the terminal, unloaded my luggage, and drove off in search of a parking place. The day seemed to match my spirits perfectly—gloomy, without even a trace of sun peeking through the damp, cool mist. Esther and I walked slowly towards the Pan Am check-in counter, waiting for her husband to catch up with us.

Checking in, I was further depressed to discover that flight 67 had already arrived, was being serviced, and would be ready for boarding in approximately 25 minutes. By this time Brother Nigh had joined us, and suggested we have a quick cup of coffee before I boarded.

It seemed that we had no sooner sat down than I noticed it was 10:35, and time to board my plane. As we left the coffee shop, and made our way toward the gate, the thought flashed into my mind: "Your only reason for living over the past thirty years is being snatched from you—just like that."

The Missions Board had "requested" that I meet with them, and I knew what the verdict would be. They hadn't actually told me that I would not be reappointed as a missionary, but I hadn't been born yesterday, and I could clearly see the handwriting on the wall. In my heart, and in my mind, too, I guess, I knew I'd never return to Liberia—that this was indeed a one-way trip.

I harbored no resentment, for I had enough faith in the Missions Board to know that their decision would be based solely upon what they felt was best for the work in

Liberia, as well as for me personally. Still, this did not alter the fact that I had absolutely no desire to return to the United States. My heart was in Liberia, and would always remain there. I would live in America as a foreigner.

Before I knew it, I found myself saying goodbye to the Nighs, and preparing to walk up the flight of stairs that would lead me inside the white Boeing 707 that would, without the least trace of compassion, take me back to New York City. A handshake, a hug, a wave, and I was on my way.

I slowly climbed the steps, looked back for a final glimpse, and found myself inside the plane. The stewardess glanced at my boarding pass, and directed me to my assigned seat in the coach section. I walked with my head bowed, fearing that if I looked up someone would see the huge tears that were forming like pools in my eyes and coursing down my cheeks.

Somehow I was able to focus my eyes and locate seat 14-A. Normally I preferred an aisle seat, but this time I had specified a seat by the window. I could pretend I was a novice flyer and direct my attention out the window. This way my broken heart would not have to be shared with my traveling companions.

To the unsuspecting I was watching the two handsome young Germans who were loading the last of our luggage onto the conveyor belt. My tear-drenched eyes, however, were sending only partial signals to the brain, for all I could see was a myriad of black faces—empty, perplexed faces, not exactly sure of what they were searching for, but begging to hear about that man called "Jesus." I could see a million pair of black hands desperately grasping, but continually coming up empty.

Perhaps it was silly of me to wait until I was departing

Germany to show such intense emotion about leaving Liberia. However, I had become quite adept in my 67 years at pushing unpleasant things into the most remote corners of my mind. It was only now that that villain, "Reality," had been successful in setting up roadblocks on all the paths to "Dreamland."

I was completely oblivious to the whine of the jet engines as they were started. My mind was several thousand miles from Frankfurt when the "Fasten Your Seatbelt" light was illuminated. I didn't hear a single word of the pretty young stewardess as she gave instructions regarding the use of the oxygen masks in case of cabin depressurization. I didn't recall her directions concerning the use of the seat cushions in case of an emergency landing over water.

Suddenly, I was jolted back into the "now" by a gentle voice: "Ma'am, we're about ready for takeoff. Would you please fasten your seatbelt and return your seat back to its most upright position?"

For the first time I noticed I was not alone on my row of seats, but was seated next to a young woman in her mid-twenties, with a little girl who appeared to be about three. I was grateful that the mother had chosen to occupy the middle seat. Though I had always been extremely fond of children, I didn't feel up to entertaining a pre-schooler at this particular moment.

I looked at my watch and decided to go ahead and set it for New York time. Remembering that Frankfurt was six hours ahead of New York, I turned the hands back to 5:00 A.M. I had a momentary sense of pleasure, thinking that I had more than likely gotten the jump on the other passengers, and would be one of the few to arrive in New York with the correct time. My moment of egotism would have been smashed to smithereens had I known that due to daylight saving time, it was really 6:00 A.M. in New York.

I could feel the aircraft begin to move, and in a few seconds was pushed back into my seat by the acceleration of the plane taking off. In a matter of moments we were airborne, and I had the sickening realization that the next time we touched down, barring any emergencies, I'd be in New York—like it or not—never to return to Liberia.

TWO

In the Beginning

I glanced at the young child seated by the aisle, and for a moment allowed myself the luxury of wondering what it would be like to have one's entire life before him; how it would feel to be carefree, without a burden or concern in the world. At that moment it seemed impossible that I was once like that child. Suddenly my mind began racing backwards at supersonic speed, not stopping until it reached somewhere in the year 1907.

My first recollection is of sitting on Grandfather Paul's lap. I must have been about three at the time. Grandfather Paul, my mother's father, had descended from a Dutch family that had immigrated to America in the mid 1700s. Sometime after their arrival in Pennsylvania, they Americanized their name "Paulus" to simply "Paul." Although I have hazy memories of Grandmother Paul, I am unable to remember anything outstanding or specific.

Grandfather Shutt, my father's father, died when I was just a toddler, and I was never quite sure if I remembered him or not. Later in life I was told that he had been a Civil War veteran, fighting, I presume, on the side of the North. Grandmother Shutt lived until I was almost twenty, so my memory of her is quite clear.

I entered the world on August 20, 1904, the second child, and the first daughter born to Winfred and Maggie Shutt. I was named Mary Pauline, but quickly became known as "Pauline." My brother, Leland, had been born the preceding year. Mother had come from a large family—nine boys and three girls. Father, on the other hand, had come from a comparatively small family for that day—two girls and four boys.

Like my father, I was born at the old homestead along the Salmone River, near Huntington, Indiana. Following the accepted pattern of the day, Mother and Father set out to raise a large family of their own, and by 1918 had presented Leland and me with two brothers and three sisters, making a grand total of three boys and four girls. In addition, we had seen two brothers die in infancy.

We maintained a small garden, sufficient to supply the table with fresh and canned vegetables. Father's primary occupation, however, was that of a butcher. I can still remember his working from dawn till dusk, six days a week to bring home his meager paycheck from Black and Thorpe's Meat Market.

As far back as anyone could remember, Father's family had been members of the Methodist Church. Father was never one to break with tradition, but with the exception of two funerals, Mother's and his own, I can recall but one time he ever graced the interior of a church building.

Mother, like Grandmother Paul, was a member of the Dunkard Church. She suffered considerable persecution for her fundamental beliefs and modest manner of dress. There wasn't a Dunkard Church in the Huntington area, so Mother seldom had the opportunity of attending services of her faith. Rather than worship in the assembly of another denomination, she chose to practice her religion at home. Her determination that we children grow up to be good Christians was made apparent by her ever-present example of holiness and morality.

I don't recall her ever attempting to persuade Father, or for that matter, any of us children, to her religion. She was, however, quite insistent that we not miss a single session at the Methodist Sunday school.

Sometime prior to my beginning the first grade, the family moved to Warren, Indiana, a community near Huntington. I've often thought it strange that I could remember so well Grandfather Paul, as I can remember no other incidents between then and my first year in school.

What I recall most vividly about the first grade is that we had to pass the local cemetery on our walk to school. From the older and "more experienced" children in the neighborhood I had heard the eerie tales of people who had been buried alive, only to regain consciousness after their burial and claw their way out of the casket and grave. According to those who were much "wiser" than I, these incidents occurred at night, most often on or near Halloween. Even in broad open daylight I was a bit apprehensive when passing the graveyard. When nightfall approached, bringing with it the shadows of uncertainty, apprehension graduated to cringing fear.

It was also during this year that Mother had to

I SURRENDER ALL

"switch" me all the way to school one morning. I had always been a shy child, abhorring the idea of attracting the least bit of attention to myself. This particular morning I had dillydallied around and was not ready for school when it was past time to leave. I couldn't bear to think of arriving late, and having to stand before the entire class as I explained to Mrs. Lucas why I was tardy.

I began making every excuse a six year old could dream up, but Mother would fall for none of them. I even went so far as to suggest that I be allowed to stay home to help her take care of the baby and do the housework. The bribe didn't work, however, and the answer remained a firm "No!"

I can remember, as if it were yesterday, her chasing me all the way to school with her favorite switch. She never did quite catch me, as I managed to stay at least two steps ahead of her. Upon reaching school, the ordeal wasn't nearly as bad as I had thought it would be.

The school in Warren was not the stereotype oneroom schoolhouse that all children of my generation are supposed to have attended. I've always somewhat regretted that I was denied the opportunity of attending classes in such an environment, as I could have no doubt achieved more in life—who knows, perhaps even gone as far as being the first female version of Abraham Lincoln. But, our facilities were strictly first-rate for the early 1900s—a separate room for each grade.

My memories of the second grade are totally nonexistent, and I retain but one memory of the third grade. Although I can't recall the details, I do remember that Mrs. Plasterer, my third grade teacher, took me home to spend the night with her the day my brother, Robert, was born.

The fourth grade seems to hold a few more memories, which might have something to do with the fact that it covers a longer span of time—I failed. The winter of 1913 saw an epidemic of German Measles hit our part of the country. My brother, Forrest, and I became victims, and I was forced to miss several weeks of school. Just when Forrest was about to recover from the measles, he contracted pneumonia. The many days of school missed, coupled with anxiety over Forrest's condition, affected my ability to keep pace, and the teacher felt it wise for me to repeat that grade.

I don't know why I associate this with the fourth grade, but it was about this time that the Methodist Church in Warren lifted its ban on dancing and card playing. Prior to this it had been considered a shame to even dance to the music of the band that played every Saturday afternoon in the town square during the spring and summer.

Card playing had always been associated with the gambling halls and brothels that could easily be located by everyone except the local police.

The midwestern thinking of 1913 still considered public drunkenness as completely scandalous. I recall, as a child, seeing a woman hurriedly leading her intoxicated husband home before the neighbors saw him in his tipsy condition. For a woman to be seen drunk was unthinkable.

Without a doubt, the fondest memory I have of this portion of my life is that of my mother praying for me after she had tucked me into bed one night. I had been playing outside that evening, just before dark, and had decided to become brave and adventuresome. To the side of the yard I spotted a big mud puddle that I was certain

I could jump over if I got a sufficient running start. My calculations were somewhat off, however, and I made it only part way.

I was thoroughly scolded, but to my utter amazement, I didn't get a whipping. After removing my mud-soaked clothes, Mother gave me a bath, and sternly lectured me on using better judgment and taking care of my clothes. After drying me off, she tucked me into bed. As if it were yesterday, I remember her gently kneeling beside my bed and praying this prayer: "Lord, keep Your hand upon my little girl." The prayer was simple and short, but I've never been able to forget those heartfelt words.

The fifth grade, without a doubt, holds more memories than any year in school, for it was in this year that an unforgettable encounter took place—a life-changing and direction-setting encounter that would chart the course for the rest of my life.

It all happened on a lazy summer day, just a few weeks before I would be returning to school for the fifth grade. I was lying in the shade of one of the big oak trees that lined our front yard, daydreaming about the things a typical eleven-year-old girl dreams about. Suddenly, without the least bit of warning, I heard as if it were an audible voice speaking to me:

I want you to become a medical missionary!

There was absolutely no doubt in my mind as to the origin of the voice. Never, not even for a moment, did I entertain the thought that I had allowed my childish imagination to run free. I had heard the voice of God, and I knew it. I was familiar enough with the ways of God from Mother's teaching and the Sunday school lessons to know that God did talk to people in an audible voice. I never shared this visitation from God with anyone, however, until later in life.

Previous to this moment I had never harbored any thoughts of being a missionary. I'm not even sure that I had ever been introduced to the term "medical missionary." I knew no missionaries, had never been in a missionary service, and to the best of my knowledge, had never even seen a picture of a missionary. No doubt I had been taught about missionaries in Sunday school, but I don't recall that either. All I knew was that God definitely wanted me to become a medical missionary—whatever that meant. Adding to the uniqueness of the situation was the strong impression that I was to be sent to a people who were small of stature.

From that moment on, I put all my limited resources to work, doing everything within the power of an eleven-year-old girl to learn exactly what a medical missionary was, what he did, and where he did it. After accumulating and assimilating all the information I could get my hands on, I set out to do a lot of daydreaming about the exciting adventures my adult life held in store. How well I recall that day in the fifth grade when Miss Good whacked me on the head with an arithmetic book for daydreaming at the blackboard when I was supposed to be doing a problem.

I attended my first revival service in the spring of that school year. For several weeks my Sunday school teacher had been reminding us of the revival which would be held, beginning the first week in April. I had heard different ones describe the revivals held in the Methodist Church in Warren—how the women would shout until their hair fell down, and the men would run the aisles and climb the stove pipes. I assumed this was the customary order of services in a Methodist revival.

For reasons which I have never been able to determine, my father, who never attended church, announced at the supper table one Tuesday evening that he thought he'd go down and "check out" the revival. Suddenly bells started ringing in my head—this might be the answer to beginning my preparation to be a medical missionary.

At first Father was insistent—I could not go with him, in no uncertain terms. The answer was a flat "No!" But then he yielded. A man who seldom changed his mind about anything told me that I could go—but just this one time.

We arrived a few moments after service had started. As we stepped through the door, I truly expected to see things in full swing—some of the men running the aisles with the throttle wide open, while the more daring climbed the stove pipes; the women doing their part by dancing until their hairdos became completely disheveled.

I found the service to be a bit more orderly and sedate than I had anticipated. However, I did feel something I had never before experienced. It was a strange and warm feeling, powerful and exciting, yet peaceful and soothing. I assumed this must be the Spirit of God that I was feeling.

The congregational singing, as well as the special singing, was lively and evoked a response of worship from those in attendance. I thoroughly enjoyed the testimonies given, and secretly longed for the day I would be an adult and could participate in this part of the service. The evangelist, a young man whose name escapes me, preached for perhaps twenty or thirty minutes, then made the appeal. There was no mention of receiving the Holy

Spirit, but a strong emphasis was placed on true repentance and conversion.

The aisles were quickly filled with hungry seekers, and I was surprised to see several of the town rowdies and drunks making their way down to the altar. One of the church elders, Brother Drexel, walked back to where Father and I were standing, and invited us to accompany him to the altar. Father had been visibly touched by the sermon, but refused to respond to Brother Drexel's gentle coaxing.

With his jaw firmly set, and his knuckles turning white from grasping the bench in front of us with a death-like grip, Father refused to budge, or for that matter, even look up at Brother Drexel. All the time I was silently praying, "Please, Father—please go to the altar so I can go, too!" It may seem foolish to some, but my strict upbringing had convinced me that a decision this important could only be made with Father's approval.

When Brother Drexel finally gave up and returned to the front of the church, Father grabbed my arm, and said, "Let's go!" This was the last time we attended the revival, and as I have already mentioned, it was the last time he set foot inside a church, except for Mother's funeral.

I was disheartened, to say the least, but I would soon learn that this was but one of the many roadblocks standing between my present station in life and that which God had told me I was to strive for and achieve.

For the next few months my church attendance was once again restricted to weekly visits to the Methodist Sunday school. I continued to harbor my special calling, but grew more and more frustrated at the lack of open doors.

Just before school resumed for the sixth grade, I was

invited by a classmate to spend the weekend. Her family belonged to the Campbellite (Christian) Church in Warren, and on Sunday morning I attended service with them. I remember little of the details of the meeting, except that the minister made a strong appeal in his message for those wishing to have Christ in their lives to come forward and repent of their sins.

It was as if a strong magnet were drawing me to the front of the sanctuary, and before I knew what had happened, I found myself kneeling at the altar, begging Jesus to come into my life. As my weeping eyes caused giant puddles on the altar, the thought came to me: "Finally—I can finally start doing the things God wants me to do so I can become a medical missionary."

A few hours later, when I returned home, I wasted no time in informing my parents of my decision for Christ. I still didn't share with them my calling as a missionary, but I was certain they would be as thrilled as I over my newfound faith. Actually, I didn't feel any different, but I had followed the minister's instructions to a tee, so I was able to convince myself that I had indeed found salvation.

Much to my surprise and dismay, Mother and Father weren't even the least bit thrilled over the news. Mother said I was too young to make such a lifetime decision, and Father added that they were playing with my emotions. Evidently Mother didn't place too much stock in the Campbellite doctrine, and Father, being the lifelong member of the Methodist Church that he was, no doubt felt that if I were going to join any church, it should be the Methodist.

Consequently, I was not allowed to return to the Christian Church, and once more my church attendance was limited to Sunday school at the Methodist Church. I had just experienced roadblock number two in the long journey to my life as a missionary.

The remaining three years of elementary school hold very few memories for me. The outstanding feature seems to have been my reluctant acceptance of the fact that I could never obey the commandment of the voice I had heard under the shade tree. I didn't fail any more grades after repeating the fourth, and was able to finish elementary school without further difficulty.

In the fall of 1919, at the age of fifteen, I entered my freshman year at Warren High School. High School proved an exciting adventure, with the changing of classes for each course and the making of new friends. My favorite subjects that year, and for that matter, throughout high school, were English and history.

The days were long and full that fall, as Mother was expecting again, and began having complications towards the end of her pregnancy. Her being confined to bed much of the time made it necessary for me to rise early each morning to fix breakfast for Father and the children. Of course, it was also my duty to make sure everyone had something to wear that day. As soon as I returned from school in the afternoon, it was time to begin supper and squeeze in what housework I could manage. It was usually at least 10:00 before I had finished the chores and put the younger ones to bed. Then, it was time to tackle the mountains of homework that each teacher had assigned as if theirs was the only course I was taking.

On December first of that year Paul was born, but died a few hours later. For two-and-a-half weeks Mother lay in a semi-conscious condition, expected to die any moment. Her death on December nineteenth was one of those experiences that no amount of anticipation and forewarning can prepare you for. Mother had been my lighthouse in the stormy sea of life, and every dream, every hope, every aspiration, and every desire for life itself seemed to be lowered into the ground and covered with dirt.

It had always been a simple matter to maintain the true spirit of Christmas at the Shutt house, seeing that excessive wealth had never been one of our problems. This Christmas, however, even the spirit appeared to be missing. Somehow it didn't seem that a family who had just lost its mother and a baby brother had much to be thankful for, especially when you considered the fact that this would more than likely be our last Christmas together.

After the holidays were over, and Father had a chance to clear his mind a bit, he began to fear that he could not support the family, as well as pay someone to look after the younger children. So, after exploring all possible avenues, and with the advice of two of our aunts, it was decided that adoption or placement in foster homes was the only logical solution.

Robert, who was nine, was adopted by a family named Tibeals, who lived near Chicago. Ruby Jane, who was eighteen months old, was adopted by the O'Neils, a family who lived near Lancaster, Ohio. Leland, my older brother, who was almost seventeen and working a fulltime job, struck out on his own. The remaining children were taken into foster homes. I spent the rest of the school year with the Tamms, a local family in Warren.

After seeing that we were all placed into homes, Father left Warren and moved to Toledo, Ohio. Years of struggle had finally convinced him that it was impossible to make a decent living working for Black and Thorpe. Perhaps he would fare better in a larger city like Toledo.

THREE

All Alone

A sudden lurching of the plane snatched me from the year 1919 and planted me firmly into 1971. A voice was speaking to us over the intercom—"This is your captain speaking. We have encountered some unexpected turbulent weather, and it appears we'll be flying through it for the next ten minutes or so. For your own comfort and safety would you please see that your seatbelts are securely fastened?" I made it a practice to keep my seatbelt buckled throughout a flight, but looked down to double-check anyway.

After we had been unmercifully tossed to and fro for what seemed like an hour, but was in reality, five minutes or less, I began to fear that New York City might not be our next landing after all. The captain came on the intercom again: "It looks like this severe weather pattern is a little more extensive than we had anticipated. We have received permission to descend to a lower altitude, and feel the flight will be considerably smoother there. Please continue to keep your seatbelts fastened until instructed that you may do otherwise."

After a few more minutes the ride did seem calmer, and I was able to once more lean back and attempt to relax.

By the time school resumed in mid-February for the second semester, I was reasonably settled in my new home with the Tamms. Our family had never been personal friends with the Tamms, and I had known Mr. Tamm only as the pharmacist at the local drugstore. Somehow he and Mrs. Tamm had heard of our plight through the grapevine, and contacted members of my family about the possibilities of my staying with them—at least until the school year was over.

In return for my total support, I was to assist Mrs. Tamm with the housework and care of their two small children. I was given my own room, a first for me, which was tastefully decorated and even included a desk and bookcase. Mrs. Tamm decided that my wardrobe could stand some replenishing, so we made a shopping trip for some material, and together made several new dresses. The amount of work expected of me was actually far less than I had grown accustomed to at home, so I was able to devote more time to study and still get to bed at a decent hour.

I tried to stay as busy as possible, leaving no time for reflecting upon my sadness and loneliness. Often, however, after the last algebra problem had been solved, the lights had been turned out, and I was in bed, I would suddenly remember just how alone I was—how much I missed Mother, Father, and my brothers and sisters.

I was afraid that I might never see some of my brothers and sisters again. I guess I was most concerned with Ruby Jane who had moved to Florida with her adoptive parents. In the months prior to Mother's death, I had become more or less a mother to Ruby Jane. It was almost as if my entire family, not just Mother, had died. My daily schedule normally included crying myself to sleep at night.

I did occasionally see Leland, my older brother, who had remained in Warren when Dad moved to Toledo. From time to time he would drop by the house, and we would sit on the porch and chat about small things. Several times we walked down to the drugstore where Mr. Tamm worked, and had an ice cream soda. Two or three times over the next few months I received a brief, hastily-scrawled letter from Father. Reading between the lines, I could detect that the grass was no greener in Toledo. He never returned to Warren, however.

My stay with the Tamms lasted until mid-May, when school was dismissed for the summer. The trauma of Mother's death, coupled with the breakup and scattering of our family, evidently created a mental block, as I am unable to recall with a great deal of accuracy the events that transpired during that five month period.

I do remember, however, that although the Tamms were good, moral people, they never attended church—at least not while I was living with them. To the best of my knowledge, I didn't attend services during that period of time either—not even the usual Sunday school class at the Methodist Church. I often reflected upon my shade tree encounter with God, but by now "fate" had done a thorough job of convincing me that this was one dream that would forever remain just that—a dream. I was foolish to think that I could ever become a medical missionary. There was just no way.

Around the first of May I had received a letter from two aunts living in Chicago, inviting me to spend the summer with them. Tiny Gamble and Stella Heiny, both widowed, were older sisters of my father. I mulled over the decision for several days before giving them my answer. On the one hand, the situation didn't promise much in the way of excitement, but on the other hand, the opportunity of staying with some blood relatives did have something to offer. So, I decided to tell them I would be happy to come. A few days later I received another letter from them containing my fare. The following Monday morning found me bidding the Tamms goodbye and boarding the train for Chicago.

As I had expected, the summer was anything but eventful. Even a shy, small-town, sixteen-year-old girl found it difficult to get excited about sitting on the front porch and watching the cars go by. Upon my arrival in late May, there had been some talk of making my stay in Chicago a permanent one, but as the summer progressed, Aunt Stella and Aunt Tiny decided I would be better off if another foster family could be found for me. Somehow they were able to locate some people in Moreland, Indiana who were looking for a teenage foster daughter.

The Kerschners had but one child, a son who was in college. Their lifelong dream of having a daughter had never been realized. Imagine my enthusiasm upon learning that Mr. Kerschner was the minister of the Christian Church in Moreland. To say that I became excited about moving to my new home would have indeed been the understatement of the year 1920.

Could it be that God had His hand in this move? Could it be that this was the open door I had been waiting for all my adolescent life—the opportunity to begin preparing for the task I was sure God had called me for—that of a medical missionary? Suddenly, hopes that had been pushed back into the darkest corner of the closet of my mind, were quickly brought out, carefully dusted off, and placed once more in their rightful place of prominence.

I arrived in Moreland on a Friday, three days before school was to start. Mr. and Mrs. Kerschner met me at the train, and from their instant warmth my hopes and aspirations took another leap forward. Here was a good Christian family that wanted a daughter and a sister, not a housekeeper and a babysitter. I was certainly grateful for all the Tamms had done, but being a daughter was far better than being an employee.

The Kerschner's son, Warren, had already left for the fall semester at college, so I would not meet him until he came home for Christmas break.

The remainder of Friday and all day Saturday were spent in becoming adjusted to my new home. Sunday I accompanied the Kerschners to church—the first service I had attended in almost nine months. I admired the eloquence and forcefulness with which my new foster father delivered the morning message. The congregation, which had in excess of 200 members, was quite a bit larger than the one in Warren.

I became adjusted to my new high school environment with surprisingly little difficulty. My favorite subjects continued to be English and history, and despite my extreme shyness, I developed a keen interest in public speaking. Later that year I entered a contest, speaking on the subject "American Immigration." After being crowned school champion, I advanced to the district finals in New Castle, Indiana, but that was as far as I got.

The next year, which was my junior year, I had an English teacher who seemed to bring out the best in me as a writer. Towards the end of the term, she encouraged me to pursue training in the field of journalism, assuring me I could make it as a professional writer. However, I was certain that the course for my life had already been charted—I was to be a missionary—a missionary to a people who were small of stature.

With this in mind, I did everything possible to become involved in the activities of the Moreland Church. Seeing my intense desire to participate, my foster father appointed me to conduct the "Christian Endeavor" meetings, services led by and aimed at the youth in the Church. However, it seemed that the more I did, the less fulfillment I felt. Try as I might, I just couldn't capture that contented feeling that would assure me I was headed down the path which led to the goal God had selected for me.

Perhaps I should have shared these thoughts with the Kerschners, but being the introvert I was, I found it impossible to expose my inner-feelings to them, or for that matter, anyone. They were constantly praising me for my involvement, and I was sure they'd find these feelings hard to understand. But there was no denying it—something was missing—there was something more to serving God—a more intimate relationship that would prepare me for my purpose in life—but what?

Continuing to feel unfulfilled, I remained as active as possible, making sure that my mask of contentment remained securely fastened.

The Kerschners, knowing that I had made a commitment at the Christian Church in Warren, had just assumed that it had included baptism. For some reason, the thought had never occurred to me that I needed to be baptized.

One night, in the early spring of 1922, I was having trouble sleeping, and decided to get up and read for awhile. Suddenly, as if hit by a bolt of lightning, it dawned on me: "I've never been baptized! That's it! That's why I've felt so depressed lately! I needed to be baptized! Why didn't I think of that before?"

My foster parents were more than a little taken back upon hearing the news the next morning, and strongly insisted that I be baptized the following Sunday, at the close of the morning service.

The next few days were filled with mixed emotions. Being shy, I dreaded the entire Sunday morning congregation watching me. I just knew that the more critical ones would question my having been so active in church prior to baptism. Yet, at the same time, I was excited about the completion of my Christian commitment. I was well along the road of convincing myself that this was the missing link in my experience with God. I fully expected instant transformation upon coming out of the water.

Sunday morning, at the conclusion of the service, I was immersed in water by my foster father. The *new Pauline* I had expected to rise from the water, came out, instead, a cold, wet, *old Pauline*. What a disappointment—absolutely no change—none whatsoever. I was completely let down to say the very least.

In August of 1922, right after my eighteenth birthday, and just before beginning my senior year in school, I moved with the Kerschners to New Castle, Indiana, where my foster father had been called to serve as minister. The church membership was about the same as the Moreland

Church, but the congregation was evidently a bit more affluent, as I distinctly remember the parsonage being somewhat nicer.

I found the switch to the high school in New Castle to be more difficult than the transition from Warren to Moreland had been. Two years in Moreland had afforded me the opportunity of cultivating a few close friendships among both students and teachers. I didn't leave behind what you would call a steady boyfriend, however.

That winter, as usual, the Kerschner's son came home for Christmas. Warren was now in his junior year in a small college sponsored by the Christian Church. Several times during the next week or so, and without being too obvious in sharing my life's calling, I coaxed Warren into describing the missionary-oriented courses offered at his college. In relating these details, Warren mentioned that often, during chapel services, they would have a missionary speak who was home on furlough. Right then and there I decided what I wanted to do after graduating the next spring—go to that college. There I could receive the professional training that would prepare me for my calling as a medical missionary. No doubt this was the ingredient in my life that would bring fulfillment.

I knew that the Kerschners cared for me, and I was positive that if I hinted strongly enough and often enough they would get the message and offer to send me to college that following fall. So, the next few months were spent in rising above my shyness, offering both subtle and not-too-subtle hints about how nice it would be to attend the college Warren attended.

Evidently the subject was the farthest thing from their minds, as even my best efforts proved completely fruitless. They seemingly never got the message. No doubt I was ahead of my day, and forgot that concepts like *ERA* and *Womens Lib* were still years away. I stopped just short of saying, "I want to go to college where Warren goes, and I want you to pay my way!"

I was extremely hurt by the Kerschner's failure to offer to send me to college. I was quite certain they could well afford it. Apparently they didn't care as much about me as I had been led to believe. Earlier I had thoroughly convinced myself that God had placed me in this home for the express purpose of preparing me for the calling I had received seven years earlier. I would later see that God truly did have His hand on my staying with the Kerschners. He was using them to train me. The problem was that I had no idea what lessons I needed to learn. Oh, the blessedness of hindsight. But in 1923, all I could see was one more gigantic roadblock.

In May of 1923 I graduated from New Castle High School. I knew I would have a home with the Kerschners for as long as I wanted, but other than that, the only thing New Castle had to offer was a low-paying job, unfulfilled participation in the local Christian Church, and perhaps later, marriage.

So, several days after commencement exercises were over, I said goodbye to the Kerschners and boarded a train for South Bend. Aunt Stella, one of the aunts with whom I had spent the summer of 1920, was now living in South Bend with her brother, Uncle Albert. While I had been living with the Kerschners, Aunt Tiny had gone to live with her son in Springfield, Illinois.

I had left New Castle feeling that the future there held nothing in store for me—nothing I would be interested in at least. I arrived in South Bend with the promise of an even more bleak future staring me in the face. I had been unable to give a logical explanation to the Kerschners for my hasty departure, and I'm sure it must have hurt them. In fact, it made little or no sense to me. All I knew was that for some strange reason I felt an undeniable force compelling me to leave. I had no choice.

After living with Aunt Stella and Uncle Albert for a few weeks, it became apparent that I would have to find a job. Even if they had been willing, their meager incomes could not continue to support an extra mouth at the table, not to mention the clothing that would be necessary once my wardrobe began to wear out. Thus, my mornings became devoted to scanning the want ads and my afternoons were taken up with interviews, employment tests, and "we'll call you if anything comes up."

After a few days I was able to detect a definite pattern developing—no one wanted to hire me. The answer was always the same: "What we're really looking for is someone with experience or perhaps vocational training in high school." I had neither. But, they always assured me, "we'll call you if anything comes up."

One day, after having been turned down the normal amount of times, I returned home completely dejected, knowing for sure that I was a useless parasite to society, and that it would be better for all parties concerned if I were to suddenly die of some mysterious disease. I went straight to my room, without even telling Aunt Stella I was home, and threw myself across the bed.

Evidently she heard my footsteps, and sensed something was wrong, for within seconds there was a rapping at the door. Reluctantly I told her to come in. She could tell from my face that the story was the same, but she asked anyway.

"Did you have any luck today, Pauline?" I told her no.

"Well," she said, "I just may have something. I was talking with Mrs. Berry, the lady next door, today, and she mentioned that Epworth Memorial accepts applications for nurses training about this time every year. Maybe you ought to check it out. Mrs. Berry said they don't charge you any tuition, and provide free room and board. At the end of three years you graduate as a registered nurse."

I had been half listening to Aunt Stella, and politely thanked her for the information, assuring her I'd give it some serious thought. For a few minutes I continued to lie across the bed, thinking the most negative thoughts I could possibly call up.

All at once I sat straight up in bed: "Pauline—you big dummy! This is the break you've been waiting for since you were eleven years old. This is the chance to become what you've wanted to be for the past seven years." How foolish I felt, not realizing until now that I'd need medical training before I could become a medical missionary. How blind I was, not recognizing at once that this was the hand of the Lord working in my life.

Suddenly a dying ember was reignited, and a dream that I had long ago labeled as just that—a dream, once more began to take on reality. I leaped from the bed, bolted into the living room where Aunt Stella sat knitting, and excitedly informed her of my decision.

The next morning I paid a visit to the administration office of Epworth Memorial Hospital, and filled out the required forms for taking the entrance examination to be given the following Monday. As I returned home that afternoon, I had the sensation of truly walking on cloud nine. The people I passed were more friendly, the sky appeared bluer, the breeze felt more gentle, the sidewalk seemed softer and cooler, and the trees and flowers were

I SURRENDER ALL

more pleasing to the senses. I inventoried my many rediscovered blessings, and whispered a heartfelt "Thank You" to Jesus, then suddenly realized that I had not attended church even one time since leaving New Castle.

FOUR

The Making of a Nurse

"Excuse me . . . Ma'am, excuse me. Will you be eating lunch with us today?"

I looked up, a bit embarrassed, at the stewardess, hoping she hadn't been attempting to gain my attention for too long. I nodded "yes" and proceeded to let down the tray table. Glancing at my watch, I thought to myself: "7:00 A.M. New York time . . . let's see, that's 1:00 P.M. Frankfurt time . . . guess it is time for lunch."

The food arrived, and proved to be the typical airline meal: a small piece of meatloaf, green peas, cubed potatoes, a small green salad with a container of French dressing, a none-too-fresh dinner roll that was no doubt once warm, a small piece of cake which I was unable to identify, and, of course, the proverbial lukewarm coffee which tasted like a drop of quinine had been added. The cuisine didn't bother me, however, as my stomach continued to churn like the ocean several miles below us, and absolutely nothing seemed appetizing at that moment.

I dabbled with the food for a few minutes, managing to take a token bite every now and then, and waited impatiently for the stewardess to return for my tray. As I waited, I stared out the window, watching the billowy clouds that seemed to extend forever, and ever, and ever, and. . . .

I was awakened early Monday morning by the very first beam of sunlight that filtered through my bedroom window. I hopped out of bed, feeling for the first time in many weeks that the day actually held something worth getting up for. From the busy sounds and smells coming from the kitchen, I could tell that Aunt Stella was already in the middle of cooking breakfast. The sizzling sound of frying bacon seemed to play a waltz in my ears.

I carefully brushed my hair, selected my prettiest dress, and glided into the kitchen. I quickly gulped down breakfast, not even minding Aunt Stella's chiding remarks about my eating like a pig. After brushing my teeth carefully enough to please even the most discriminating dentist, I checked myself in the mirror, grabbed my purse, gave Aunt Stella a kiss and an affectionate hug, and bounded out the door, down the steps, and toward the hospital.

I knew that quite a few girls would be taking the exam, and that not all of them would make it. I was certain, however, that divine providence was on my side, and that come September I would be one of those wearing the uniform of a student nurse. I was the epitome of self-confidence as I strolled up to Epworth Memorial.

I arrived at the hospital about 8:45, and was directed by a huge sign to a room on the second floor. Entering the room, I was surprised at the number of girls present. There were already at least 80 seated, and I was sure more would come in before 9:00. I had expected no more than 35 or 40 to compete for the 25 available slots. Doing some hurried mental arithmetic, I calculated that no more than one fourth of those present would be selected. My once-indestructible faith was beginning to waver—just a little.

At exactly 9:00, a nurse, who I judged to be an old maid in her mid-fifties, entered the room and smugly announced that she was to administer the test. She seemed to take great delight in reminding those of us present that only 25 applicants would be selected. After she had succeeded in making us sufficiently nervous, she explained that the test would be given in three parts, each 45 minutes in length. We would be notified, she continued, within two weeks of our test results.

Test booklets, answer sheets, scratch paper, and pencils were passed out. After carefully reading the instructions and filling in the personal data, we were directed to proceed with part one.

The first few questions were quite simple, and as I breezed through them I somewhat regained my confidence and composure. As I got further into the test, however, I detected the questions becoming increasingly more difficult. The time required for me to select what I felt to be the proper answer became longer and longer. More often than not I proceeded to the next question not sure of my wisdom in the last one. I had begun the test confident that I'd have ample time to retrace my steps and double-check my answers, but I had gotten no more than three-fourths through when we were told "time's up!"

After standing to stretch for a few moments, we were told to sit down and begin part two. The second phase of the test was identical to the first: it started relatively simple, but became progressively more difficult. The third phase was a carbon copy of the first two—I was unable to get past the three-quarter mark.

I was completely crushed as I left the hospital. There was not a shadow of doubt in my mind—I had failed and failed miserably. I wanted to cry, but my eyes couldn't seem to call up any tears—just that sickening feeling down in the pit of my stomach.

I began the long walk home without the least ray of hope. I was in no condition to face Aunt Stella. I wasn't quite sure whether I had failed God and the world, or the world and God had failed me. Time completely eluded me, as I aimlessly wandered about the neighborhood. The first thing I knew I was shocked back into reality by the ringing of the bells from the Catholic Church in the neighborhood.

Bong . . . Bong . . . Bong . . . Bong . . . Bong . . . I couldn't believe it: it was already five o'clock, and Aunt Stella was probably worried sick. After I got home, her worry would quickly change to anger, and justifiably so. I had told her I'd be home no later than two.

She could evidently sense from my look of total dejection that something had gone wrong, as she didn't so much as mention my whereabouts that afternoon. After we had eaten supper, and the dishes were done, she calmly asked me to tell her about it.

"I'm a flop, Aunt Stella—a great big miserable flop," I sobbed.

"What do you mean, child?" she asked.

"I failed the test . . . I just know I failed the test! What am I going to do?"

She looked at me rather pensively for a few moments, and asked, "How do you know you failed? You told me the other day that it would take two weeks to get the results."

"I know . . . I know!" I stammered, "But I've never done so poorly on a test in my whole life. There were over a hundred girls there, and I'm sure that all of them did better than I."

"Well," she said, after a momentary pause, "let's just wait until we get the results. I'm sure that you are only one of about a hundred girls who are feeling this way now. We may just get a pleasant surprise in the mail in a few days."

I appreciated her sincere desire to cheer me up, but I really felt there was not a semblance of a chance I would be one of those selected.

The next two weeks were surely the longest I had ever spent. Part of me kept saying: "Pauline, you're a big fool! Quit dreaming! Forget it!" Another part of me retorted: "Have faith! God has His hand in this! You're going to make it!" How perplexing not to know which voice to believe.

"Pauline, there's a letter here for you. It's from the hospital." I slowly rose from the chair by the window where I had been reading, and reluctantly walked into the living room. Was I prepared for the death-like blow I was certain the letter would deliver? I took the envelope, and for a moment just held it tightly between my hands, debating whether or not I should even open it. Gingerly I did open it, but before daring to look, I closed my eyes and silently prayed: "Jesus, please let the answer be 'yes' . . . please, Lord." I opened my eyes:

Dear Miss Shutt:

Congratulations!
Based upon your application and test scores you have been selected to begin nurses training as a member of the graduating class of May, 1926. Please notify this office of your intentions within ten days of your receipt of this letter. You will receive full instructions regarding registration at that time.
We look forward to hearing from you.

Sincerely,

Ruth B. Franklin
Supervisor of Nursing

I couldn't believe it! I read the letter again, running my finger over every word. I read it a third time before I finally allowed the good news to sink in.

"Aunt Stella . . . I made it . . . I made it . . . I really and truly made it!" I shouted to the top of my lungs.

"I made it . . . I made it . . . I really did make it . . . I've been accepted for nurses training!"

After hugging Aunt Stella, kissing the letter at least a dozen times, and lovingly allowing Aunt Stella to say, "I told you so," I retreated to the privacy of my room. I carefully unfolded the letter once more, savoring each word as I read it. In vain I searched for words to express my appreciation to God, but all I could come up with was "Thank You, Jesus." At that moment I was certain that never again would I doubt God. I would be that pliable clay that He could mold at will, and I would forever trust in His love and ability to take care of me.

There was no doubt about it—the detours and roadblocks were finally over. From this point on the sailing would be as smooth as glass. Oh, the folly of youth. Had I only known—had I only known that before my dream finally materialized I would witness the stones in the road of life becoming mountains—mountains that could not be humanly traversed.

For the next four weeks time seemed to come to a complete standstill. I was sure that September must be strapped to the back of a lame snail. Aunt Stella and Uncle Albert had agreed that it would be senseless for me to try and find a job just to work for a month, so I was allowed to continue as a parasite until school started. Days filled with nothing, and nights devoted to the same, made the waiting just that much longer.

Upon notifying the hospital of my intentions to begin training, I had been given several mimeographed sheets which contained instructions regarding registration. About midway down on page three was a paragraph I certainly hadn't expected:

> Students will be required to supply their initial set of uniforms. Through special arrangements with "Worthmore Uniform Center" the standard wardrobe may be purchased for slightly under $10.00. Replacement items, of course, will be paid for from the $15.00 monthly allowance given to students for incidentals.

This unpleasant surprise left me in a quandary to say the very least. Not only was I lacking the $9.25 that I discovered the uniforms would cost, but I was so broke that I would have found it necessary to float a loan to become part-owner of a postage stamp.

I guess I was still riding somewhat on the coattails of my previous miracle, however, as after I got over the initial shock, I was able to muster up enough faith to believe that somehow God was going to provide for the need. If God was truly in this thing, He wasn't going to be stopped by $9.25. I returned home, convincing myself that I was confident that somehow God was going to supply the need.

When I got home, I shared the predicament with Aunt Stella, not suspecting for even one moment that she was the one God had selected to come to my rescue.

"I just happen to have a little money stuck back for a rainy day, Pauline. I don't expect it'll ever rain much harder than it's raining right now. This is just a loan . . . I'll expect you to pay me back as soon as possible."

With that she went into her bedroom, where I could hear her rummaging around in the closet. After a few minutes she reappeared with a handful of well-worn one dollar bills.

"Here's ten dollars, Pauline. You can keep the change, but I'll need you to pay me back the very first chance you get."

I assured her I'd repay the entire amount as soon as I drew my first $15.00 paycheck. I never did repay her, however. On several occasions I attempted to pay her part of the money, but she always told me to wait until I had the entire amount. To tell the truth, I don't think she expected or even wanted me to repay her.

So, with $10.00 in my purse, I went shopping at the uniform store the hospital had recommended. You would have thought I was trying on wedding gowns the way I fussed over the selection of my uniforms. Everything had to fit just right. Finally, after completely taxing the patience of the sales lady, I made my purchases and started home with my prized bundle. I felt like the prettiest, luckiest, wealthiest, and most blessed girl in the whole world. I couldn't wait to get home and model my uniforms for Aunt Stella.

As soon as I arrived home, I rushed straight to my room, closed the door, and tried on one of my new outfits. Looking into the mirror, there was no doubt about it—I was absolutely stunning in my white dress, white stockings, white shoes, and cute little cap. After smoothing out a few wrinkles that had developed on the trip home, and adjusting the cap to the position I thought correct, I took one final glance at myself, and tripped into the kitchen to model for Aunt Stella.

She looked me over from head to toe, and then with a twinkle in her eye, said, "Well, if you don't look like a beautiful Florence Nightingale." From the look of pleasure on her face, I could tell that Aunt Stella considered her $10.00 "loan" a wise investment.

Finally! The big day finally arrived! I must have awakened at least 25 times during the night, only to be disappointed that it was still dark. At last I heard the 5:50 church bells tolling for 6:00 Mass. Heretofore I had been infuriated at being awakened from a deep sleep, but this day the bells seemed to be inviting me to step out and begin an exciting journey that God was taking me on. Why, in just three short years I would be a medical missionary—at least I thought I would.

I bounced out of bed, and in no time at all had brushed my hair, dressed, and crammed a few last-minute articles into the battered cardboard suitcase Uncle Albert had given me. Aunt Stella had outdone herself in fixing breakfast this morning, feeling, perhaps, this would be our last chance to have a meal together for some time.

Nurses training proved to be a heavy schedule: classes in the morning, sweeping and dusting and emptying bedpans in the afternoon, and mountains and mountains of homework in the evening. In between we were treated to nutritious, but hasty, meals. The days normally began with breakfast at 6:50 and ended with the lights going out at 10:00 before we had finished our homework.

Except for our heavy workload, there were no requirements that we remain on the hospital premises during the evening. To most, however, this proved to be ample restrictions. For those few times that we did chance a visit to the "outside," there was an 11:00 P.M. curfew.

Classes met on Monday through Friday, but we were required to work an additional eight-hour shift on either Saturday or Sunday. On my day off each week I would visit Aunt Stella and Uncle Albert, go window shopping, or perhaps take in a movie.

My roommate that first year was Doris Burke. Although she would later quit school to get married, and we would lose contact for several years, we would eventually renew our acquaintance and become lifelong friends.

A couple of the girls in my class were already married, and lived at home rather than in the nurses quarters. The rest of us, however, had entered training single, and were instructed that we must remain so if we expected to stay in the program. If it was real love, they assured us, it would last until after graduation. We were warned against getting any bright ideas of becoming secretly married. This had been tried before, and the guilty parties had paid the consequences. The hospital administration, we were informed, had ingenious ways of uncovering even the best-hidden secrets.

Over the next few months I seemed to never possess a spare moment. The few nights that I did manage to escape the drudgery of homework, I was too exhausted to do anything but sleep. On several occasions classmates offered to "fix me up" with a blind date, but I always managed to have an excuse. In addition to being too tired, I was a little reluctant to date someone I had never met. Also, I really felt that I should refrain from any relationships that might not leave me free to follow the plan of God for my life.

It was really quite strange—I felt certain that my attending nurses training was in the definite will of God, and many times found this to be the determining factor in my decision-making. Yet, not one time during my three years at the hospital did I attend church. And, while I did occasionally read the Bible and pray, you certainly couldn't say that my devotion resembled that of someone who was sacrificing three years of her life to train for missionary work.

Often, on my day off, I would pass the Methodist Church near the hospital and catch myself thinking: "Oh, how I wish I could attend that church." I really don't know why I didn't, as I had every other Sunday off. But for some reason I never seemed to feel that strong compelling force drawing me there. Perhaps attending that church did not fit into God's training plans for me.

Towards the end of the first school year, the proverbial spring fever caught up with me, and I finally gave in and agreed to accept a blind date which was arranged by a classmate across the hall. Kathy told me his name was

I SURRENDER ALL

Frank Moneer; he was from Lima, Ohio, had a very good job as an electrician, was 24 or 25, and quite handsome. I decided to take a chance—just this once. Surely one time couldn't hurt anything.

I can't say it was love at first sight, but Kathy was right—Frank was handsome. He was also thoughtful and courteous, and much more mature than the boys I had dated back in Moreland and New Castle. It was kind of nice having someone pay so much attention to me, and I found myself, without the least hesitation, telling him "yes" when he suggested we go on a picnic the following Sunday, my next day off.

After the picnic, I didn't see Frank for the next two weeks or so. The spring semester was drawing to a close, and this meant burning the midnight oil in preparation for year-end exams.

Classes were dismissed for the summer, but training continued, as we were assigned to regular shifts on the floor. By now I had graduated from the bedpan brigade, and was allowed to perform the more simple duties of patient care. For the next three months I had two days off each week, and most of my evenings were free. I began to date Frank on a regular basis.

The summer seemed to literally fly by, and before I knew it, I was once more in the grind of full-scale nurses training. I continued to see Frank, but our dates were now limited to one or two a week. I still tried to see Aunt Stella at least every other week, but if I missed occasionally, she didn't seem to mind. She had met Frank, and didn't appear the least bit jealous about sharing my affections with him.

I was nearing the end of my second year of training at Epworth, and had been dating Frank steadily for almost a year, when he surprised me one night with a proposal of marriage. I guess I shouldn't have been shocked at all, but in my naive way the thought of marriage had never so much as entered my mind.

From the tone of his voice I detected he meant right away, not next year after graduation. I tried to explain to him the strict hospital regulations concerning marriage prior to graduation, but this didn't seem to discourage him. Something inside of me seemed to be shouting: "Tell him the real reason—that God wants you to be a missionary and marriage would stand in the way of His plans!" For some reason, however, I couldn't bring myself to share this with Frank. Perhaps it was because I had grown to really like, maybe even love, him and I just couldn't bear to think of how it would be not dating him anymore. If ever anyone had been in a dilemma, I was in one.

"We could get secretly married," Frank said. "It's done all the time. Lots of the student nurses have done it. Nobody would ever know. I promise you."

"I can't afford to take the chance, Frank," I finally managed to tell him. "I really care for you, but graduating from school is very important to me. I'm sorry, but I just can't afford to take the chance." I still didn't tell him why graduation was so important.

After several pensive moments, Frank replied, "Well, Pauline, you think it over. I'll give you a few days to think about it. But while you're making up your mind, remember . . . I love you very much."

The next three days were spent cramming for finals, and I was unable to see Frank. The day classes let out, he called, saying he had to go to Lima for a few days, and would call me as soon as he got back. His last words, just before he hung up, were, "I'll be expecting an answer to my question when I get back."

I returned to my room, certain that I had but one answer to give Frank—I could not marry him. Frank Moneer had become someone really special in my life, but if the choice were between marrying him or giving him up, I'd have to give him up. Upon entering the room, I was surprised to see Doris, my roommate, packing her things. Although classes had been suspended for the summer, practical training would continue as it had last year.

"I . . . I guess I should have told you sooner, Pauline. I'm dropping out of school to get married."

"Doris Burke, you've got to be crazy!" I assured her. "Surely you're not serious about quitting with just one year to go."

Doris convinced me, however, that she was dead serious. She had carefully weighed the decision, and there was no changing her mind.

The news was a real blow to me, as Doris and I had been best friends for the past two years, making it a practice to share everything. At least, I thought we had been sharing everything. Several days later, upon paying a visit to Aunt Stella, I received some more news—news that put the finishing touches on my already-shattering world.

"Pauline, several weeks ago I received a letter from my daughter in North Carolina, asking me to come down and live with them. They've built a new house and she assures me there's plenty of room. I think the warmer climate will be better for my health. I guess I'll leave sometime early next week."

I pretended to be happy for Aunt Stella, as she seemed so excited about her move, but deep down inside I was sick. Already I was feeling completely stranded. Although

Uncle Albert would still be living in South Bend, he and I had never really been close. After a few minutes of small talk, I kissed Aunt Stella goodbye, assured her I'd write, and thanked her for all she'd done over the past two years.

Somehow I managed to block the tears until I had left the house, but as I reached the sidewalk I could hold them no longer. My tear ducts seemed to erupt like a volcano, and no sooner would I wipe my eyes, than they would fill up again. I elected to walk back to the hospital, not wishing to share my grief with anyone.

It seemed like a dream. I couldn't believe all this had happened to me in such a short period of time. One moment I had felt reasonably secure, and the next I was completely distraught. I'd lost Doris, I'd lost Aunt Stella, and in a few days I'd have to give up Frank. What was I to do?

My mind was a million miles away as I approached an intersection near the hospital, and began to cross the street without even looking. The next thing I knew, a car had rounded the corner and come so close to hitting me that I could feel the fender scrape against my skirt. The driver, certain that he'd struck me, slammed on his brakes, and ran back.

"Are you alright, Miss?" I assured him I was.

With a sigh of relief, he said, "if you want to keep on living, you'd better be more careful in the future."

I told him I was sorry, and muttered that I would be more cautious from now on. I wasn't too sure, however, if I was that interested in continuing to live. I didn't think much more about the incident at that time, but later in life I recognized the occurrence of that day as just one more of the many examples of God's protecting hand upon my life, and not some quirk of nature.

Upon reaching the hospital, I hurried straight to my room, fell across the bed, and cried like a baby for what must have been several hours. The next thing I knew, the room was completely dark except for the streetlight shining through the window. I rolled over, totally cried out, and stared at the beam of light coming into the room. It was at that moment that I decided to make a deal with God: I would give up my plans of becoming a missionary, marry Frank, and become a good Christian wife and mother like my mother had been.

The next day, shortly after supper, Frank called. The only telephone in the building was in the first floor reception area. As I walked down the stairs to answer the call, I found myself shaking uncontrollably. I knew full well what my answer to Frank would be, but at the same time I couldn't convince myself that God was pleased with the decision.

"I just got back in town, Pauline, and I'm anxious to see you. Can I pick you up in about an hour?"

I assured him I'd be ready.

Frank arrived on time, and as we walked to the car, I tried to think of all the reasons I had for marrying him. As soon as we were in the car, and without even pulling away from the curb, Frank "popped the question."

"Pauline, I love you. Will you marry me?"

"Yes," I whispered after pausing a few seconds.

"I knew you would!" Frank shouted jubilantly. "Somehow, I just knew you would. You'll never be sorry, Pauline. I promise you—you'll never be sorry. I'll make you the happiest girl in the whole wide world."

The remainder of the evening was spent making wedding plans. Frank agreed that it would be best to keep our marriage a secret so I could finish training. The only ones needing to know would be our friends who would serve as witnesses.

Frank and his partner had been awarded an electrical contract for a building project about a hundred miles from South Bend, and it would be necessary for him to be out of town, except on weekends, for the next six weeks or so. Therefore, it was decided that we would get married sometime in mid-August. The only sensible thing to do was have a civil ceremony performed by a justice of the peace in one of the adjoining counties. We would ask some married friends, Bert and Alice Stephens, to serve as witnesses.

FIVE

Stones Become Mountains

The excruciating pain shooting up and down my leg was almost unbearable. No doubt the swelling had begun several minutes before, but I had been too deeply engrossed in my reminiscing to notice it. For the past several years I had suffered from a severe case of phlebitis, making it impossible to keep my leg in the same position for an extended period of time. The doctors in Liberia had admonished me, telling me a woman of sixty-plus had no business taking day-long treks into the bush, but I had ignored their warnings. Since the day of my arrival in Liberia, the spreading of the Gospel had come first, and at that stage of the game it was a mite late to rearrange my priorities.

Asking the young mother in the center seat to please excuse me, I made my feeble way to the aisle. Several trips to the rear of the plane and back restored the circulation and eased the pain somewhat. Upon returning to the seat, I glanced at my watch and noticed it was 8:45 A.M. New York time—I'd be arriving in the States in less than five hours.

The next six weeks went neither fast nor slow. Doubts about marrying Frank had begun to work their way to the back of my mind, but I had to admit I was not fully persuaded I was doing the right thing. I felt it was too late to change my mind (I really didn't want to anyway), but I just couldn't feel that God was pleased with my decision.

I began to notice that I no longer approached my nursing duties with the usual spark of enthusiasm. I had looked forward to this summer, knowing that I'd be permitted to perform many of the tasks normally assigned only to registered nurses. I just couldn't become as excited about preparing to be a wife and mother as I had been about training to be a medical missionary.

Finally, the big day arrived-Friday, August 14, 1925. We had discussed last minute wedding plans that Monday, and had decided that since Saturday was my day off that week, Friday night would be the most logical time. I would request an overnight pass, under the pretense of spending the night with my aunt. This would give us the chance to have a brief, one-night honeymoon.

I still didn't have that deep-settled tranquillity that told me I was doing the right thing, but as we entered the office of the justice of the peace, I knew I was too far down the road to turn back. The ceremony lasted no more than eight or ten minutes, and I got the idea the justice was trying to stretch it out, hoping he'd impress Frank and get more money from him. The brief ceremony was over, Frank slipped the man five dollars, and we walked out as Mr. and Mrs. Frank Moneer. I'd still be known in most circles, however, as Pauline Shutt.

I have no way of really knowing, so I'll just have to assume that the next three weeks were quite typical for a young student nurse who has gone against the dictates of her conscience in becoming secretly married, is deathly afraid her secret will be discovered, and is forced to continue "dating" her husband.

Marriage did have its advantages, as Frank proved to be a kind, loving, and terribly understanding husband. He was constantly surprising me with little gifts, and always made certain I had more than enough spending money. He never once seemed to be jealous of my responsibilities at the hospital. My heart was beginning to win the battle with my mind, and I was feeling more and more comfortable being Frank's wife.

Three weeks passed and classes resumed for my final year of training. Once more I was thrown headfirst into the morass of an almost impossible schedule, and my time with Frank was again limited to one or two nights a week and part of either Saturday or Sunday. Frank was very accommodating, however, and not one time did I have reason to suspect him of being unfaithful.

In justifying my decision to marry Frank, I had determined to channel my efforts into the domestic circle, and scrap my plans of being a missionary. After all, I reminded myself, a woman's rightful place was in the home: cooking, washing, sweeping, changing, and hanging: not traipsing through the jungle, swinging a machete with one hand and swatting mosquitoes with the other.

In my one-sided compromise with the Lord, I had determined to be not just a wife and mother, but a *Christian* wife and mother . . . like my Mother had been.

But, as the semester began to wear on, and I began to feel more like a wife and accept and enjoy the responsibilities of that position more fully, even my aspirations of being a good Christian began to wane. My Bible was being opened less and less, and my knees seldom touched the floor anymore. In later years the words of Paul, as found in I Corinthians 7:34, would have real meaning

> *The unmarried woman careth for the things of the Lord, that she may be holy in body and in spirit: but she that is married careth for the things of the world, how she may please her husband.*

As seniors we were granted a ten-day Christmas vacation, and I was able to spend a few days with Frank and be a real housewife. But all too soon the New Year rolled around and I had to trade in my apron for a nurse's uniform.

Finally, after four-and-a-half more months, it was mid-May and time to graduate. Frank and I immediately set up housekeeping in a small, but tidy house he had rented in Mishawaka, a town adjoining South Bend. Prior to my graduation, Frank had been living in a furnished garage apartment, so for the first few nights, until we could make the rounds of the second-hand furniture stores, our household goods consisted of a pallet and several contemporary cardboard boxes. I wondered at the time why it was necessary for us to shop at second-hand stores, as I knew Frank made good money. Surely he would have no trouble getting credit if for some reason he was short of cash.

Job opportunities for newly-graduated nurses didn't

prove as plentiful as I had been led to believe. The openings were there alright, but they were all for the evening or night shift—certainly not the storybook situation for a recently-married couple that had spent the first ten months of married life dating. So, I settled for doing private duty nursing three or four days a week. The pay was no where near what it would have been had I been working for a hospital, but with just the two of us expenses weren't really that much.

During the fall of that year Frank decided to sell his share of the electrical business, and take a job as an electrician with the City of South Bend. Frank's partner had grandiose ideas about expanding the firm into a full-scale construction company, and Frank was quite leery of making the investment required on his part (hindsight reveals he couldn't have made the investment had he wanted to).

His salary as a city employee was considerably less than what he had been making as a partner in the business, but the sale gave us a small nestegg to put back for emergencies. By early January it became apparent what that emergency would be—I discovered I was pregnant.

On August 17, 1927 our son, Robert (Bob), was born. He was without a doubt the most beautiful human being that had ever lived, and certainly the pride of Mama and Daddy. As in most cases, the birth of our baby added a new dimension to our lives and marriage. As the soft, warm, helpless bundle was placed into my arms for the first time, my mind shot back to a scene approximately two years earlier, one in which I had made a pact with God:

Lord, You know I really can't go through with my plans to be a missionary. But, if You'll let me marry Frank I promise to be a good Christian wife and mother . . . just like my mother was.

I had found it impossible to continue doing private duty nursing during the final trimester of my pregnancy, as the job I had been assigned to required me to do a lot of lifting in addition to being on my feet most of the day. With time on my hands, something I certainly wasn't accustomed to, I struck up an acquaintance with Sally Mallory, a young woman about my age who lived a few doors down. She and her husband, Dave, had been married just a few months longer than Frank and I, and were expecting their firstborn also.

Sally and Dave were members of the Methodist Church in Mishawaka, and on several occasions she had asked if Frank and I would like to attend Sunday service with them. Every time Sally would extend these invitations, deep spiritual hunger pangs would seem to gnaw at my stomach. But knowing Frank's aversion to organized religion of any type, I felt it best to not even mention the subject to him.

But as that precious, priceless, tiny, totally dependent human being was placed into my arms that day in the hospital, I suddenly was made aware that no longer would my decisions affect only me. Each time the nurse would bring Bob in for feeding, my mind would spin into a state of turmoil. I knew what I had to do, but how to do it was the unanswered question.

Several days after I had returned home, Sally came over to see the baby. I explained my apparent dilemma to her frantically hoping she might be able to offer some wisdom.

"Pauline, what you need to do is have Bob baptized.

When you feel up to it, why don't you and Frank bring Bob and come with us to a Sunday morning service? I know what you're thinking, Pauline, but you may just be surprised. Becoming a father often makes a man change his attitudes about some things. Why don't you ask Frank? You may get the shock of your life."

"Okay, I'll give it a try," I promised her, "but I really don't expect him to like the idea."

That evening, when Frank came in from work, I gave him a chance to unwind a bit, then approached him with the proposal. His moment of hesitation made me wonder about the wisdom of my decision, but then the shock of shocks:

"You know, Pauline, I've been thinking about that myself. With Bob here we probably should be going to church somewhere. That church where Dave and Sally go is probably as good as any."

The following Sunday morning we attended service with the Mallorys. Sally had already notified the pastor of our intentions concerning Bob, and Reverend Combs had agreed to baptize him at the conclusion of the service. Upon arriving, we were conducted to an empty pew near the front of the sanctuary. As we were seated, the usher handed Frank a visitors card.

"He must really mean business," I thought to myself, as Frank wasted no time in borrowing a pen from Dave to fill out the card. My heart skipped a beat as I looked out of the corner of my eye and saw Frank check "yes" to the question that asked, "Are you interested in becoming a member of this church?"

I'm quite sure I didn't hear more than a couple of words of Reverend Combs' message, as I spent the entire service daydreaming about all the churchy things I would be able to do—the church clubs I would be active in, the hours I would spend praying, the times I would read my Bible, how dedicated I would be in setting a godly example for Bob to follow, and how meticulous I would be in getting our clothes ready for service each week.

At the conclusion of his sermon, the pastor asked the congregation to stand, and motioned for Frank and me to bring Bob up to the front near the altar. He then took Bob, spoke a few words to the congregation about the importance of raising a child in a Christian environment, then prayed over Bob. Afterwards, he sprinkled some water on him and said another prayer. As we left the church that morning, I whispered a heartfelt "thank You" to God for His many blessings to me: a wonderful husband, a beautiful, healthy baby, and a happy home. Evidently God was pleased with the decision I had made. Yes, my place was in the home.

Towards the end of the week we received our first communication from the church, a letter thanking us for expressing a desire to become members. Along with the letter was a card requesting personal information such as our name, address, ages, etc. At the bottom of the form was a section asking the amount of financial support we could pledge each month. I had planned to throw the card away before Frank got home, but in the hustle and bustle of cleaning house, cooking supper, and taking care of Bob I left it lying in the open.

Wouldn't you know it? That was the first thing Frank noticed when he came home that night. He nearly exploded when he read the pledge card. I can't remember ever seeing anyone so angry.

"That church is just like all the rest!" he screamed. "All they want is your money!"

With that he tore the letter and card into dozens of tiny pieces and threw them into the wastebasket.

"I'm not gonna set another foot inside that church, or for that matter, any church!" he shouted.

To the best of my knowledge, this was one of the few promises he kept in later years.

To say I was crushed would be tremendously understating my reaction. I couldn't really blame Frank for feeling the way he did, as I, too, had felt the pledge card was not only in extremely poor taste, but unchristian as well. Once more my world had been shattered—this balloon had just been blown up, and already it had popped.

Receiving the pledge card seems to have marked the turning point in Frank's life. Evidently he had been fighting a fierce battle with himself over whether to overcome his carnal desires or give in to them. Apparently he had tried to conquer them for the sake of Bob and me, but receiving the pledge card from the pastor and elders of the Methodist Church had made him give up and wonder, "What's the use?"

From that moment on I detected a definite change in Frank. At first it was subtle, but like a snowball rolling down a steep incline, it began to pick up momentum and grow with each successive day. Soon, he was drinking heavily and staying out until all hours of the night. While I had no definite proof, I was sure he was being unfaithful to me, as well. He became increasingly irresponsible, and would stay away from his job for days at a time.

The next few months saw the rapid transition from what was once a relatively happy life to what can only be described as basic survival. I quickly saw a new side of Frank—at least a new side to me. The man who had once been loving, kind, and understanding, was now violent, impatient, and totally apathetic. It was as if Bob and I were nothing more than excess baggage that was cramping his lifestyle.

Although the stock market crash of '29 was still almost two years away, depression had already taken up residence in the Moneer household. Frank's already meager paychecks were reduced even further by his increased taste for liquor, and only God knows what else. The situation was made even worse by the fact that he only worked when he felt like it.

With an infant son to care for, going back to nursing was out of the question. I have often thanked God for the companionship Bob provided during these ominous hours. Without him, there is absolutely no telling what course of action I might have pursued. All the friendships I had cultivated had been as Mrs. Frank Moneer, and now that our social life was nonexistent, I suddenly found myself friendless, except for an occasional visit from Sally.

One afternoon, while returning from the grocery store several blocks from our home, I bumped into a girl with whom I had attended nurses training. In the ensuing conversation, I learned that Doris, my roommate the first two years, was still living in the South Bend area. After locating her address, I paid Doris a visit. Before parting company, we promised each other we'd keep in touch, but I made no attempt to get together with Doris after that visit. We just didn't have that much in common anymore. She was enjoying a successful marriage with all the frills of happy middle-class America, and here I was suffering from a marriage on the rocks, and was the epitome of misery and self-pity.

Several weeks later, Frank came in from a night on the town and announced we were moving to Lima, Ohio, his hometown. A few months earlier he would have discussed the matter with me, but things were different now—a whole lot different. He was dissatisfied with his job, he hated the neighborhood, his friends had all turned against him. I was beginning to see Frank's adroitness at placing the blame everywhere except where it rightfully belonged.

In keeping with his recent behavior, Frank saw no need to give his employer the customary two weeks' notice, so within a matter of a few days we were packed and on our way to Lima. For the first month or so we lived with Frank's sister, Bertha. His parents had been dead for several years, and Bertha was all the family he had in Lima.

Frank was finally able to land a job working in a local electric shop, and we set up housekeeping in a small run-down cottage. I did all within my power to transform the place into a tidy and cheerful home—a place Frank would look forward to returning to in the evenings. I was determined to forsake all pride and do everything I could do to save our marriage. As it turned out, however, even my best efforts were in vain, as Frank's drinking problem only worsened, and many times he didn't even come home at night.

We could have lived comfortably on Frank's pay, but less and less of his weekly checks were finding their way home. On more than one occasion I had nothing to feed Bob but biscuits and gravy—certainly no diet for a growing toddler. But against my better judgment I refused to give up. With the exception of my son, Frank was all I had, and I'd had more than my fill of being lonely. I couldn't bear to think of being alone. If only I could somehow rekindle the flame of love that had once burned so brightly. I tried—God knows I tried—but always to no avail.

The next three years saw bad become worse and worse graduate to worst. I was finally reaching the point of accepting the fact that it was a hopeless dream. Our marriage was beyond repair. Frank had no desire to rebuild our relationship, and I was sure he'd be relieved if I left him. But how did one approach the subject of divorce? Where would I go? What would happen to Bob? These and other questions kept me hanging on, hoping, wishing, even praying for a miracle.

I discussed my plight with Bertha, Frank's sister, and she sympathized with me completely. We had become quite close in the few months Frank and I had been living in Lima.

"Frank has always been an extremely selfish person, Pauline. He's never been one to accept responsibility, and I don't expect he'll ever change. You do what you want, but if I were you I'd leave him in a minute—while you've still got your sanity and pride."

In May of 1931 I got a surprise letter from my father. He was still living in Toledo, but it had been several years since we had visited. In fact, Bob was almost four years old now, and his grandfather had never seen him. In his letter, Father said he was planning to take a week or so off in early June and if it was okay with me, he'd like to come down for a few days and see us. I shot back a quick reply, assuring him we'd anxiously await his visit.

Bob and his grandfather never did get to meet, as Father was killed in an automobile/train accident on the way. He had left Toledo after work on a Friday evening, planning to make the two-hour drive before nightfall. About an hour out of Toledo, however, he was hit broadside by the Toledo-Lima Inter-Urban, as he crossed an unmarked track. From the best reports we could get, the train had failed to signal when approaching the crossing. Judging from the appearance of the wreckage, Father never knew what happened.

The trauma surrounding the funeral was almost more than I could stand. We had never been really close, especially over the past twelve years or so, but he was still my father. Several brothers, sisters, aunts, and uncles were at the funeral, but time and distance had erased the closeness that had once existed, and they afforded little consolation. At a time when I truly needed the strong, dependable shoulder and comforting and reassuring words of a husband, I found neither.

The only reaction at all from Frank was that of resentment and jealousy towards my family. Through sheer industry some of my relatives had become reasonably successful in life, and Frank felt they should have offered to share their "wealth" with us. Evidently it never occurred to him that a little incentive on his part would have provided the cure for most of our problems.

Frank's inexcusable behavior at the funeral was the straw that broke the camel's back. I had been pushed and shoved to the outer limits of toleration, and I was finally able to muster up the courage to tell Frank I was fed up and wanted out. He didn't argue, he didn't try to get me to change my mind, and he acted neither surprised nor regretful. In fact, he showed no sign of emotion whatsoever. His response could only be described as that of total apathy.

Within a few weeks final arrangements had been made for the divorce, and I was ready to leave Lima. I was penniless, and had no idea where I would go. All I knew was that I had to get away from Frank Moneer.

For days I pondered the dilemma of what to do with Bob. He was all I had left in the world—the only thing I could call my own. I couldn't bear the thought of parting with him, but I was broke, and had absolutely no leads on a job. How would I be able to provide food and shelter for us? And, even if I was lucky enough to land a job, who would take care of Bob while I was working? On the other hand, if I did force myself to give Bob up, who would take him? It was evident that his father would never accept that responsibility.

When I was about to reach my wits' end, Bertha suggested that I allow her and her husband to raise Bob. They had grown to love him in the time we had lived in Lima, and perhaps they also felt a little guilty about Frank's behavior. Bertha and her husband had a nice home and could offer Bob all the advantages, but the very thought of leaving him behind made me deathly sick.

My immediate reaction was a resounding "NO!" The more I thought about it, however, the more I began to realize my thoughts were selfish. Bob had his entire life before him, mine was ruined. He needed a home and plenty of wholesome food, things I could not provide him. So, with an aching heart that had been crushed into a million tiny pieces, I kissed my son goodbye, and gave him to my sister-in-law. I had been assured that I could visit Bob anytime I wished, but at that moment I felt that this was the final kiss.

I left Lima alone—all alone. I had nothing in this world that I could claim as mine—no material possessions, no friends, no family, no hopes, no dreams, no desires. Nothing. I was lower than low, but still had not reached the bottom of the pit.

Using most of the few dollars I had managed to scrape together, I bought a train ticket for South Bend. Why South Bend? I couldn't explain it. There was nothing there for me to return to: no family, no relatives, no friends, no job, and certainly no memories that I wished to recall. Still, as if some powerful magnetic force were drawing me, I felt compelled to return to South Bend.

Some years later I would discover that the overpowering force I had felt back then was none other than the stubborn love of God. In charting my own course, I had drifted far from the path God had selected for me that day under the shade tree. But, in His patience He had not given up on me and was preparing to place me back on that path.

Upon my arrival in South Bend, I went immediately to the local Nurses Registry, where I inquired about possible openings in either hospital or private duty nursing. My fears became reality, however, as I was told that there were absolutely no jobs available, not even on the evening or night shift. For several days I walked the streets in a state of bewilderment and near panic, my limited funds running dangerously low. At best I had enough for two more nights at the Y.W.C.A. and three or four meals.

On the fourth day, as I was aimlessly wandering, trying to collect my wits, I was approached by a rather sinister-looking character, who began keeping pace with me and going to great lengths to strike up a conversation.

"What's your name, Baby?" he asked. I tried to ignore him, and kept on walking.

"Where you going?" he asked. I continued to ignore him, and quickened my pace, hoping he'd get the message.

"You're awfully pretty, Honey," he continued, obviously thinking this would surely evoke a positive response.

I SURRENDER ALL

Once more I pretended not to hear.

"Listen," he said, "I've got connections. With looks like yours, I could get you into pictures in Hollywood. What about it, Honey, would you like to take a trip to Hollywood with me?"

By now I was beginning to get more than a little scared. So, as we passed a department store, I made a sudden unannounced left turn and entered the store. I waited inside until I was completely satisfied that my "suitor" had given up and left. From that moment on, I was overly cautious when walking the streets alone even in broad open daylight.

Finally, just as I was getting down to my final few cents, I managed to find a job as a nurse for a rather well-to-do family that had recently adopted twin newborn baby boys. I saw the job advertised in a discarded newspaper I found lying on a park bench. The paper was several days old, so I was quite surprised to find the job still open upon applying. As I look back on it now, I realize that it was the hand of God that kept the job vacant until I had the chance to answer the ad.

My primary responsibilities in working for the Engles consisted of acting as a mother to the two boys. The twins, who were Jewish, had been adopted through an agency in Chicago. The Engles were able to adopt the boys because Mr. Engle, himself, was Jewish. At the time of my arrival, Marvin and Irvin were three months old.

Jerome Engle owned a drug store and served as a bail bondsman on the side. His heavy, varied, and totally unpredictable business schedule made for long days and short nights. He seldom joined the family for supper, and frequently did not return home until well after midnight.

Ethel Engle and I seemed to "hit it off" right from the

start, and within a matter of weeks she was treating me more like a sister than an employee. Unlike Mr. Engle, who was a native of the Chicago area, Ethel had been born and raised somewhere in the South—Texas I think.

The pay I received was nothing to write home about—that is if you had a home to write home to—but I did have a comfortable, well-appointed room of my own which was adjacent to the nursery, and I ate all my meals with the family. In addition, Ethel would occasionally surprise me with a gift or some extra money with which to treat myself to a shopping trip.

But oh, how I missed Bob. I tried my very best to remain detached from my heart, but someone else had my son—my son, my only son, the only thing I had in this world—and it was killing me. At naptime, as I would be rocking one of the twins, my thoughts would race back to a scene in a hospital room some four years earlier—a hospital room right there in the South Bend area—a scene in which my baby boy was placed into my arms for the very first time.

"Oh, Bob," I'd sob, "I love you. I miss you so much my heart is about to break."

How I longed, oh how I longed, to feel the tenderness of my four-year-old wrapping his arms around my neck, and in his sweet little voice, saying, "Mommy, I love you." But someone else was Mommy now, and I'd never hear those precious words again.

Many were the nights I'd cry myself into a state of fitful sleep, one in which I'd dream that I had Bob back with me. How empty I'd feel upon waking and finding that my son was not lying there beside me.

Deep down, within the innermost recesses of my heart, I knew Bob was better off living with his Aunt

Bertha, but the rest of my heart, the part that I could feel, constantly throbbed from the loneliness this forced separation was causing. Nothing can be more lonely than loneliness.

Memories of my first year with the Engles are limited to rocking, feeding, changing, and crying. I tried to stay as busy as possible, realizing that the less I thought, the better I felt. I was entering into my second year with the family when I met John Gruse, the man I would later marry. John was a police officer with the South Bend force, but did carpentry work on the side to supplement his income.

The twins were growing by leaps and bounds, and Mr. Engle decided a spare bedroom should be converted into a playroom for the boys. John, whose patrol beat included the block where Mr. Engle's drugstore was located, was hired to do the remodeling.

I was usually home in the evenings when John came over, and within a week or so we had become pretty good friends. I would usually brew a pot of coffee, and after John had completed his work for the night, we would sit at the kitchen table and chat. The last night he worked, we had our usual coffee, and munched on some chocolate chip cookies I had baked earlier in the day. Before he left I agreed to go out with him that following Saturday night if I could arrange to get off.

I dated John several times a week for the next few months, and by the late fall of 1932 we were married. I was able to keep my job with the Engles, working on a 9:00 to 5:00 basis Monday through Friday. In return for the room and board I was no longer receiving, my pay was raised.

I continued to work for the Engles for about a year,

but in the latter part of 1933 the Depression finally caught up with them also, and they were forced to let me go. In the meantime John had quit his job with the police force and had gone to work for the Bendix Corporation. Our standard of living was modest, but we never lacked for the basic necessities of life.

I had been amazed at the reckless abandon with which I had agreed to marry John. You'd think my experience with Frank Moneer would have left me with absolutely no confidence in the male species, but once again my heart overruled my head. John, in being aware of the trauma I had gone through with Frank, seemed to go well out of his way to restore my lost confidence, and prove to me that Frank had been a lemon.

John and I never had any children of our own, but during those first few years of marriage he was extremely understanding about my love and concern for Bob. On three or four occasions he arranged for Bob to come to South Bend to spend a week or so with us. In addition, he drove me back to Lima to see Bob several times.

John had been raised a Roman Catholic, but hadn't attended Mass in years. From past experience I determined that it would be in the best interest of our marriage to refrain from even mentioning the subject of religion to him. The subject wasn't on my mind that much anyway. Over the next few years, as I would drift even farther away from God, I would reflect little, if any, on the special calling God had given me some twenty years earlier.

I was sinking deeper and deeper into the pit from which God would later dig me, but I was tenaciously determined that this marriage was not going to go bad. I was fully prepared to do anything and everything to solidify our relationship. Even if I had a desire to serve God at that time, I wouldn't have been able to fit it into our schedule, as our nights and weekends were crammed with card parties and nights on the town. To please my husband and to be socially acceptable, I learned all the latest dances and began to drink and smoke.

But once again my best efforts were in vain, as I witnessed our marriage beginning to crumble. John had started drinking quite heavily and was making absolutely no attempt at concealing the fact that he was being unfaithful to me. He seemed to take delight in going to great lengths to make sure I knew he was seeing other women.

Evenings that only a few short months before had been spent "painting the town" were now spent alone at home—staring at the four gray walls. For the first time in several years I had time to reflect on the mess I had made of my life. It seemed ironic, but it was only yesterday that I had avoided the subject of religion, fearing it would be the ruin of my marriage. Now I was beginning to look upon it as the only possible savior. I had done all I could do. Maybe, just maybe, God would look over my many faults and failures and come to my rescue.

There was a Christian Church several blocks from our house, so I determined to give it a try the next Sunday morning. It had been in a Christian Church that I had made my first commitment to God, and Mr. Kerschner, my foster father for three years, had been a minister in the Christian Church. My first visit was my last, however, as I left the service with the same empty, sick feeling I had come with.

Next, I tried the Methodist Church in the neighborhood. My father had been Methodist by birth, and I had attended the Methodist revival with him. In addition, it had been in a Methodist Church that Bob had been baptized as an infant. The story was the same, however. I left the service feeling just as depressed and bewildered as when I had entered. I didn't return to the Methodist Church either.

Then, on the spur of the moment, I decided to make a really bold move and try the Catholic Church. My only real knowledge of Roman Catholicism was the ear-rending church bells that robbed me of precious sleep at precisely 5:50 each morning. Heretofore, I had not even considered Roman Catholicism to be included in the broad definition of "Christianity." But why not? I'd tried everything else, and nothing had worked. John had been raised a Catholic. Maybe this would prove to be the answer. Yes, why hadn't I thought of that before I had wasted my time going to the other churches?

Through a Catholic neighbor I made arrangements to see a priest at the local parish. After talking with him for a few minutes, explaining the domestic problems I was having, he suggested I attend a week-long series of classes scheduled to begin the following Monday morning. The classes, which were designed exclusively for women, were taught by the priest, and touched on such topics as Christian living, the raising of children, and managing the household budget.

"This will give you some exposure to the Church," I was told, "and you'll be better prepared to make the decision about becoming a Catholic."

I attended the classes as recommended, and at the end of the week had my second "audience with the Pope." After asking me numerous questions, many of which were quite personal to say the least, I was informed that an application would be forwarded to the Vatican. If my request was approved, I would be permitted to join the Church. I was cautioned, however, that the entire process usually took several weeks—perhaps even a couple of months or so.

As I heard these words, something within me said, "Pauline, they aren't the least bit interested in your soul. You could die and go to hell before that letter was ever approved and returned."

I politely thanked the priest for his time, telling him I'd get back with him after I'd given the matter some more thought. I left his office more empty than I'd ever been. I had just witnessed my final hope being swiftly washed down the drain.

SIX

He Brought Me Out. . . .

Transatlantic flights were no longer considered "Moments to be remembered." True, I had looked forward with a great deal of anticipation to my first commercial flight when returning to the States for furlough in 1947, but since that time I had become a veteran flyer, and now considered these lengthy confinements to be boring at best. In addition, the excitement of "really flying" in the small missionary planes we had been provided with in more recent years made commercial flying too tame.

On previous return flights I had been certain my Timex was running backwards, as my restless spirit had been anxious to land in New York the very moment we took off. After all, the sooner I got back to the States, the sooner I could begin and end my furlough, and the sooner I could return to Liberia for another term.

This time was different, however. This time there would be no return trip. This trip was one way. This time the hour hand on my watch seemed to be spinning at the speed normally assigned to the sweeping second hand. In a little more than three hours I would be landing at New York's Kennedy Airport.

Although Doris Klapp, my roommate in nurses training, had been living in South Bend the entire time I had been back, I had made no attempt to look her up. It had been a full-time job just trying to hold my marriage together and keep my sanity at the same time. Besides, I had been the one who for no apparent reason had broken off our friendship before moving to Lima some six years earlier. But now I had more than enough time on my hands, and in my desperate condition, I was grasping for any help I might possibly receive. I had to have someone to share my problems with.

Finding Doris' number, I gave her a call. She seemed more than a little surprised to hear from me, but insisted that we get together right away. She had heard I was living in South Bend, and that I was married again, but had assumed that for some unexplained reason I was not interested in resuming our friendship.

Several days later I paid Doris a visit, and ended up spending the whole day with her. I did most of the talking, sharing all my problems with her, and pouring out my soul for the first time in what surely must have been years. When she could squeeze in a word edgewise, she casually mentioned that she and her husband were attending Christ Temple in South Bend, a Pentecostal Church pastored by Brother Charles Taylor. This, however, was all she said about the matter. I had heard the word "Pentecostal" somewhere before, but I couldn't remember exactly where.

For the next month or so Doris and I exchanged visits at least once a week. Each therapy session was the same: I would talk and Doris would patiently listen. Occasionally, in rehearsing the latest details of my rapidly deteriorating relationship with John, I would have to stop to catch my breath. This would give Doris the opportunity of making some nonchalant comments about church. It was not until later, however, that she actually invited me to attend. I can't remember her telling me even once that if I were serving God I wouldn't be having all these problems. What I didn't know at the time was that Doris was spending many tireless hours on her knees in intercessory prayer. God had strongly impressed her that in the case of Pauline Gruse this would be the most effective means of soulwinning.

One afternoon, in the course of conversation, Doris mentioned that their church was currently having a revival with a Brother Bibbs, and that she and her husband would be more than happy to pick me up for service if I wanted to go with them some night. I made a feeble excuse, one which I can't even remember now, and turned down the invitation.

Sometime later I learned that on the last night of that revival Brother Bibbs asked those in attendance to write the name of an unsaved friend or relative on a slip of paper and drop it into the offering pan when the collection was taken. Doris wrote "Pauline Gruse" on her slip of paper.

Later in the service, just before Brother Bibbs preached, those who had turned in a name were asked to come to the front. The offering pan was placed on the altar and those participating were instructed to file past and take out a name. When this had been accomplished, Brother Bibbs asked those present to set aside some time each day to pray that the person whose name appeared on their slip of paper would give his heart to God. A dear saint, Sister Frick, had drawn my name.

The following week I paid my normal visit to Doris, and as we sat at the kitchen table drinking coffee, she asked me once again to go to church with them. Before I could catch myself, I had answered "yes." It was as if some uncontrollable force within me were answering Doris, and I was completely powerless to recall my answer. Evidently Sister Frick had been faithful in following Brother Bibbs' instructions. I'm sure Doris must have been joining her, in addition to praying for the name she had drawn.

So, the following Sunday night found me seated next to Doris on the right hand side of the church, about three-fourths of the way back. From the moment I entered the door, I sensed a warm, strange, and wonderful feeling of expectation. I couldn't understand this spine-tingling sensation, but for some unexplained reason I began to wonder if perhaps I might find the answer to my myriad of problems in this church.

As I witnessed the spirited song service, I was reminded of the time I had visited the Methodist revival with my father some 25 years earlier. The complete freedom of worship and the manner in which so many participated in the testimony service recalled a feeling I had not experienced since that night back in Warren. By the time Brother Taylor, the pastor, had entered the pulpit, there was a burning desire within my heart to do something. I just didn't know exactly what.

At the conclusion of the sermon, as the invitation was given, the congregation was asked to stand. As I rose, my mind again raced back to the night I had attended the Methodist revival with my father, and once more I had the sensation of a twelve-year-old standing next to her father, desperately wishing he would go to the altar with Brother Drexel so she could go.

This time, however, the decision was completely mine. But as badly as I wanted to go forward, and as much as I knew I needed to go, I could not seem to marshal enough courage to take that first bold step. I shall be eternally grateful to Sister Knight, the lovely Christian lady who understood my dilemma perfectly, and gently placed her arm around me, and said, "Come on, Honey, I'll go down to the altar with you."

Even with Sister Knight's company I felt that every eye in the building was sharply focused on me, sizing me up, and determining just how great a sinner I was. It seemed like the walk, which couldn't have been more than thirty feet, took at least ten minutes. I was relieved to finally reach the front where I could kneel and partially hide from what I thought was the stare of the congregation.

I neatly folded my hands into a sanctimonious position, and very piously began to "say my prayers."

"Honey, forget about everyone around you," Sister Knight whispered in my ear as she knelt beside me. "Forget about everything but your need for God. Just pour your heart out to Him. Tell Him you know you're a sinner, that you're sorry for those sins, and that you're determined to not sin anymore. If you really mean it, He'll forgive you."

It was quite obvious that my ritualistic method was

getting me nowhere, so I decided to try to follow Sister Knight's instructions. After all, I had everything to gain, and certainly nothing to lose. For the first time in my life I decided I wasn't going to be steered by the attitudes of others. If God was pleased with what I was doing, that would be sufficient. So, I opened my heart to God with absolutely no reservations, and presented myself to Him completely unrestrained. As the floodgate of tears burst from my eyes, I could feel a gentle cleansing taking place throughout my being.

Since then I've seen scores of people repent of their sins on the way to the altar, receiving the Holy Spirit almost instantly. I would not for one moment argue the validity of such an experience, as the changed lives of the recipients, as well as Scripture, attest to the genuine character of such an encounter with God.

This was not the case with Pauline Gruse, as I was so alien to God that it took some contrite repenting to get me to the broken place God wanted me. With bitter tears of remorse I cried out to God for better than an hour. By then I was completely exhausted, but felt clean and refreshed. I was certain God had forgiven me of every sin I had committed.

Those praying around me were quick to share in the joy I felt for having repented, but urged me to continue on and seek for the baptism of the Holy Spirit. But all I felt like doing was thanking the Lord for being so merciful to a sinner such as I—for allowing me to feel so clean and free from the burdens of life. Besides, I was too weary to keep pace with the enthusiastic praying of the saints around me.

As I left the church with the Klapps, I had the sensation of stepping on air. I was positive that my feet weren't even touching the pavement as I walked to the car. There was no doubt in my mind: Through this experience God was going to solve all my problems. The method He would choose, however, wasn't exactly the one I had in mind at the time.

It was around 11:00 when I got home from church, but John had not yet returned. In a way I was glad he wasn't home, as this would allow me time to pray and work up enough courage to tell him about my experience that night. He finally staggered in about 2:00 A.M., but from the reel in his walk and the smell of his breath I could tell this would not be the proper time to break the news to him. He wouldn't remember a word I had said to him in the morning anyway.

The next three days were devoted to Bible reading and prayer. I had gleaned enough from the Sunday night service to know there were three basic steps to salvation. By repenting, I had taken the first one, but I still needed to be baptized in water and receive the Holy Spirit.

The more I prayed and read my Bible, the more intensely hungry I became for all that God had in store for me. On several occasions I attempted to share with John what God had done for me, but he always managed to cut me short or divert the conversation to something that interested him. He made it quite plain—there were things more important to him than me and what I was doing.

Before parting company the previous Sunday night, I had made arrangements with the Klapps to pick me up for church on Wednesday night. I was relieved when John finished his supper and left for his night on the town before Doris and her husband arrived.

Once again I found the spirit of the service overwhelming. It was as if the power of God hit me full force the moment I walked through the door. The burning desire within my soul to go all the way with the plan of God was burgeoning with each passing moment. This was only my second service at Christ Temple, but already the warmth of the saints was making me feel at home. I found myself easily joining in the congregational singing, and even managed a short, stammering testimony when called upon by the pastor.

I'm quite certain Brother Taylor didn't preach any longer than usual, but I didn't think he'd ever get through so I could go to the altar. This time I responded to the invitation without the least bit of prodding. I knelt at the altar completely oblivious to everything and everyone. I had one thing, and one thing only, on my mind—receiving the baptism of the Holy Spirit.

I prayed with all I had for several minutes, but it seemed as though my petitions to God were rising no more than a fraction of an inch above my head. It was as if I was talking to a brick wall—or so I thought. Discouraged, and in a state of confused bewilderment, I stopped seeking. Some of the ladies, upon noticing that I had quit praying, began to talk with me. After several minutes of discussion they suggested I be baptized. They went on to explain that while it was possible for a repentant person to receive the Holy Spirit prior to baptism, the universal promise was made only to those who had been baptized in water as well.

I had been reading almost exclusively from the Book of Acts the past three days, so the things they were telling me were familiar and made sense. By this time Brother Taylor had joined the group. After telling him I wished to be baptized, he took several minutes to explain to me the purpose and power of water baptism in the name of

Jesus. His final instructions, as I left to change clothes for the baptismal service, were, "Sister Pauline, you should fully expect to come out of the water speaking in tongues."

As I was getting ready, the two women assisting me repeated the words of the pastor, reminding me that it was fully scriptural to rise from the waters of baptism speaking in other tongues as an initial sign of the indwelling of the Holy Spirit.

I went into the baptistery fully expecting to burst forth speaking in a strange language the moment my head popped out of the water—at least I thought I fully expected to. Instead, I had another visitation of enraptured joy, much like I had experienced three nights before when I had repented. I refused to become discouraged, however, as I knew I had satisfied the first two steps in the plan of salvation. The promise was mine, and I was sure that any moment I would lose the ability to speak English. Until then I would be content to bask in the liberating presence of God.

Later in the week I took a bus downtown to do some shopping, and quite unexpectedly ran into Ethel Engle, the lady for whom I had worked several years before. After an exchange of small talk, she suggested we continue our conversation over lunch.

I felt very strongly that I should share my new-found experience in the Lord with Ethel, but she had never known me as a religious person, and I was experiencing great difficulty in determining just how to break the news to her. Imagine my surprise when she "beat me to the punch" and informed me she was now attending a Pentecostal church in the area. She couldn't have helped but notice the total look of surprise that swept across my face.

I SURRENDER ALL

Ethel went on to mention that her church was in the middle of a revival, and that she'd love for me to accompany her some night. I assured her I'd really enjoy going, then went on to tell her that I had been attending Christ Temple for the past week. I detected a rather startled look on her face at the mention of Christ Temple, but I thought nothing of it at the time. Being a novice to the "World of Pentecost," I assumed all Pentecostal churches believed and taught the same message.

As we continued to talk, I filled Ethel in on my current marital problems. The night I repented I was sure I had discovered a cure-all for my many problems. As the days wore on, however, and John continued to openly display his total contempt for me, I became less and less convinced of the possibilities of changing my husband.

After sympathizing with my situation, Ethel suggested I consider returning to work for them. She said things were looking up now and that my job and room were waiting for me to return. I assured her I would consider the offer and let her know. I still maintained hopes of salvaging my marriage, but it was comforting to know I had this opportunity as a safety valve—just in case.

The following night, about 7:00, Ethel picked me up for the revival at her church. As the service got under way, I saw little difference between the way the people worshipped in her church, and the manner in which they worshipped at Christ Temple. There was the same spirited song service, and the saints were quite active in the testimony service. The evangelist was quite demonstrative in his presentation, just like Brother Taylor, but I was rather confused by his reference to water baptism "in the name of the Father, and of the Son, and of the Holy Ghost." This certainly wasn't the manner in which I had been baptized at Christ Temple. Had I been baptized incorrectly?

I whispered to Ethel, "Where in the Bible does it tell us to be baptized like he's saying?" She opened her Bible to Matthew 28:19 and pointed to it:

> *Go ye therefore, and teach all nations, baptizing them in the name of the Father, and of the Son, and of the Holy Ghost.*

I read the scripture over very slowly several times. There was no denying it—it was there. Why hadn't Brother Taylor baptized me this way? Perhaps this was the reason I had not received the Holy Spirit yet. I had been baptized incorrectly, and the promise was not yet mine. I determined in my mind to correct the mistake that very night.

As soon as the evangelist was through preaching, and the altar call had been made, I told Ethel I wished to be rebaptized according to the way her church taught. It was easy to see that the idea pleased her, and after quickly introducing me to her pastor, she led me to a room behind the baptistery where she helped me change into a baptismal robe. Once again I expected to rise from the water speaking in a strange language, but I felt absolutely nothing. Words cannot accurately describe my utter surprise and disappointment. What had I failed to do this time?

I dried and changed back into my street clothes. Still in a daze, I returned to the sanctuary and began to pray. I was desperate now, and in great earnest I sought the Lord for the baptism of the Holy Spirit. I must have been praying for thirty minutes or so when I felt my tongue beginning to grow heavy. Almost instantly I was knocked to the floor, completely slain by the power of the Spirit. I remained in that state for more than four hours. Upon coming to, I knew for certain that I had had an experience with God, but in my heart I knew there was more to come before I would have a complete relationship with Him.

Several days later I received a call from Doris, inquiring as to why she hadn't seen or heard from me in the past few days. At first I made a barely plausible excuse, not wishing to tell her the real reason was that I felt she had misled me on the subject of water baptism. But then I decided to go ahead and tell her about attending the revival with Edith and being rebaptized. There was a hushed silence on her end of the line for what seemed like several minutes, and when she did speak, I could tell that Doris was more than a little disturbed over what I had done.

After regaining her composure, Doris went to great lengths in explaining to me that Matthew 28:19 was not the formula for water baptism, but a commandment given by Jesus to His disciples regarding world-wide evangelism. She went on to assure me that it was necessary to go to the Book of Acts to discover how the apostles carried out this commandment. She stated that in every example of Christian baptism recorded in the Bible, the candidates were immersed in "the Name of Jesus," or some synonymous phrase such as "the Name of Jesus Christ." I certainly couldn't argue with her on that point, as my intensive reading of the Book of Acts substantiated every word she was saying.

By the time Doris had finished her telephone Bible study, I was thoroughly confused to say the very least.

Friday of that week I attended a special service with Doris and her husband in Mishawaka. The speaker for the evening was Brother Joseph Urshan, and his message concerned the importance of water baptism in the name of Jesus. He spoke of his missionary experiences in Russia, and described in great detail the manner in which baptism in Jesus name had been suddenly revealed to him and a fellow missionary. He went on to relate how that upon receiving the enlightenment he had rebaptized his friend and his friend had in turn rebaptized him. Then, the two of them set out to find and rebaptize all the Russian converts they had incorrectly baptized previously.

Brother Urshan then launched into the scriptural basis for water baptism in the name of Jesus, and ended his message by asking how many would like to be baptized in the name of Jesus. As he held out his arms, beckoning those interested to step forward, it seemed as though his hands were ten times their normal size.

"Lord," I whispered under my breath, "I've got to know the truth. I've come too far and I've burned too many bridges to fall short of true and complete salvation now. If water baptism in the name of Jesus is the correct way, please reveal it to me right now."

Once again Brother Urshan said, "Now, who would like to be baptized in Jesus name tonight? If you'd like to be baptized tonight, stand up."

Completely unconscious of what I was doing, I found myself rising to my feet. I looked around the vast congregation to see who else was standing, but found to my utter amazement that I was the only one. I continued to stand for a few moments, certain that others had been touched by the message and would soon join me. I remained the only one, however.

Overcome by embarrassment, I was about to sit down, when I felt something literally lift me up and set me in the aisle. I had been standing at the other end of the pew, next to the wall, one moment, and the next thing I knew I was standing in the middle of the aisle. In later years I have compared this experience to the translation of Philip from Gaza to Azotus.

Seemingly helpless to do otherwise, I obeyed the instructions of Brother Urshan and proceeded to the front of the church where I was directed to the room where I would change clothes for the baptismal service. Before baptizing me Brother Urshan made sure I fully understood the scriptural validity of water baptism in the name of Jesus. There was no longer any doubt in my mind, as the events of the last few minutes had left an indelible impression upon me.

I explained to Brother Urshan that I had been baptized in Jesus name by Brother Taylor only a week or so earlier, but he agreed that I should be baptized again, seeing as how I had been rebaptized using the "trinitarian" formula.

This time I decided I would neither present God with an ultimatum nor put any undue pressure upon myself. If God wanted me to come out of the water speaking in tongues, that was okay with me. If, on the other hand, He had another plan for my life, that was okay also. As it was, I did not receive the Holy Spirit that night. Instead, I had another warm, glowing visitation of the Spirit.

Several nights later I attended a service with Doris and her husband at Christ Temple. At the conclusion of Brother Taylor's message, I lost no time in going to the altar to once again seek for the Holy Spirit. I had prayed but a few minutes when I saw as if it were a gigantic ball of fire descending from heaven and falling towards me. The very instant the ball touched me I began speaking in other tongues. It was an hour or more before I regained the ability to speak in English.

I was completely exhausted as I got up and sat on the altar. One of the sisters who had been praying nearby placed her arm around me and said, "The Lord has a special work for you to do, Sister Pauline." The others nodded in agreement, saying that as I spoke in tongues, my face was shining as if it were translucent glass.

That night, after I had returned home, I went into the bedroom and once more began to pray. I wanted to speak in tongues again, to make sure I had *really* received the Holy Spirit. After I had prayed for perhaps five minutes I again lost command of the English language, this time speaking in tongues even more fluently than I had in church.

Just as I was getting up from my prayer meeting, John stumbled in the front door in his usual drunken manner. Even if he had been interested, there was no chance to discuss the events of the night, as he went straight to bed and fell into a deep, snoring sleep the moment his head hit the pillow.

Up until now John had not had much to say regarding my frequent church attendance. I got the idea that he considered this a good way of keeping me out of his hair. Oh, he'd make an occasional snide remark about religion in general, but he never really tried to hinder my participation.

As I began to attend Christ Temple on a regular basis, I started noticing the difference between the way the ladies dressed and the manner in which I was accustomed to dressing. Upon discussing the matter with Doris, she explained to me what the Word of God taught concerning a definite standard of holiness. Wishing to do all I could possibly do to please and serve the Lord, I began lowering hems on my long sleeved dresses, as well as getting rid of my makeup and jewelry. I had already quit smoking and drinking, and John's complete lack of attention had taken care of my dancing and card playing.

Evidently my modest manner of dress began to embarrass John, making him take notice of the other changes I had made in my life style as well. Suddenly he took a renewed interest in me, asking me to go places I knew a Christian had no business going. I tried to explain to him that I could not do these things and remain a Christian, and countered his offer by inviting him to church.

As you might imagine, this idea went over like a lead balloon.

SEVEN

Tulsa Bound

Rummaging through the pocket in the back of the seat ahead of me, I found a copy of "Clipper Magazine," Pan Am's version of the very best in inflight reading. Thumbing through the pages, I spotted an article on vacationing in "beautiful, exotic, inexpensive Haiti." As with most travel articles, there was an abundance of pictures—pictures of black faces—boys and girls and men and women— very similar to those I had left in Liberia. It seemed that no matter where I went, what I saw, or what I did, I was somehow reminded of my people—the ones I had left forever. I continued to read the article, but the words were not getting past my eyes. My wandering mind had me in another place and at another time.

It was obvious that John had serious doubts regarding the sincerity with which I approached my new commitment to God. It was easy to see, from his constant efforts

I SURRENDER ALL

at persuading me to rejoin him in his night life, that he thought he could "turn on the charm" or shower me with phony affection, and I would quickly abandon all thoughts of serving God and jump right back where he wanted me. After a few weeks, he saw he was getting absolutely nowhere, so he began to resort to less subtle tactics.

One Wednesday evening, as I was getting ready for church, John bounded in the front door all excited: "Pauline, come outside quick . . . I've got something real special I want to show you!"

Grabbing me by the arm, and half-dragging me out the door, he proudly pointed to a sleek, new Chrysler—my favorite model. I've yet to figure out how John was able to purchase such an expensive automobile, especially in 1939.

"Isn't she a real beauty? I knew you'd like it," he continued, not giving me a chance to respond to his question. "Come on out to the curb . . . I want to show it to you. Come on . . . we'll go for a little spin and I'll show you how she rides."

I tried my best to act excited, yet at the same time, explain to John that I needed to finish getting ready for church. I told him I was expecting Doris and Virgil to be by in just a few minutes, but the words I spoke didn't seem to register with him. I repeated what I had said, and he mumbled something about, "Oh, we'll just take a quick ride around the block." I saw it was useless to argue, so I told him okay.

Just before we drove away from the curb, John reached over and pulled out a built-in bar that had come as optional equipment on the car. "And if this isn't enough," he said as he pointed to the flasks of liquor, "we can drink that case of beer in the back seat."

For a few moments I was speechless, no doubt causing John to feel he had penetrated my defense and was beginning to break down my resistance. When we reached the first intersection, John continued going straight rather than circling the block as he had promised.

"John," I said rather sternly, "you promised me we'd just go around the block! Now I've really got to get back and finish getting ready for church. It's after 7:00 and the Klapps will be by any minute!"

I could sense the anger welling up. John slammed on the brakes, and almost flipped the car as he made a sharp U-turn in the middle of the street and began speeding like a madman back towards our house.

As I got out, John said, "Don't bother waiting up for me tonight, or for that matter, any night!" When I returned home from church a few hours later, it was quite clear what John had meant by that statement, as he had taken all his personal belongings and anything else of value he could load into the car. A few days later I learned he had moved in with his mother who lived across town.

Later in the week I went to the neighborhood grocery to pick up a few items and discovered that John had closed our account. In the days that quickly followed, my worst fears became vivid reality, as I discovered that all our charge accounts had been closed. I was left penniless and completely destitute. If Doris had not come to my rescue with the offer of a place to stay for as long as I needed it, I have no earthly idea what I would have done.

Several days after moving in with the Klapps, I received a letter informing me that John was filing for divorce. Up until that moment I had maintained a ray of hope that somehow God was going to untangle my marital problems.

But upon receiving the letter from John's attorney, I felt strongly impressed that this was God's will for my life, and that I should make no attempts to contest John's efforts.

Still, John seemed obsessed with the idea of making my life as miserable as he possibly could. This was such an ironic twist for a man who had just a few short weeks earlier considered me "in the way." On several occasions he drove his new car past the church during service, gunning the engine and honking the horn for all it was worth.

His devious scheme reached a climax the night he threatened to kill me. That particular Wednesday night he was waiting for me when service let out. Meeting me at the back door, he told me he had something very important to discuss. At first I was reluctant to accompany him, and Doris warned me I'd better stay with her and her husband. "It looks and smells like he's been drinking," Doris added. But wishing to avoid the public scene that I knew would follow if I refused John's request, I agreed to accompany him.

We got into the car, and for the next few minutes John rambled in drunken small talk. When the lights had been turned out, and the last car had left the church, the climate changed drastically, however. Reaching into the glove compartment, John pulled out what I instantly recognized as a .38 revolver.

"Do you know what this baby will do?" he asked. Scared out of my wits, I nervously nodded that I was fully aware of the capability of the weapon. Then, with a surge of emotional strength that could have come only from the Lord, I looked John straight in the eyes and boldly told him: "John, you can kill me if you want to, but you cannot touch my soul!"

At these words John froze as if he were paralyzed. For several moments he remained motionless and without expression. Then slowly he lowered the pistol to the seat between us, then shouted, "Get out . . . Get out of this car, and don't let me ever see you again!"

This was one invitation that didn't need repeating. I barely had time to slide out before John had revved the engine and sped into the night. Three weeks later our divorce became final.

Feeling that I could not possibly continue to impose upon the Klapps, I set out to look for a job, no easy task in 1939. Finally, after seemingly exhausting all possible leads, I found employment caring for an elderly lady who was struggling with what appeared to be terminal cancer. In exchange for the around-the-clock care that I administered, I was given room and board plus a small salary for personal effects.

In the early afternoon, on Mondays, Wednesdays, and Fridays, Mrs. Brinkley's son would take her to a nearby hospital for treatment. So, after assisting him in loading his mother into the car, I had a couple of hours or so to myself. I gladly spent this time in prayer and Bible study.

One Friday afternoon, as I was earnestly seeking the Lord for guidance in my life and future, I fell into what would best be described as a semi-trance. There, as I lay in the middle of the living room, I had a vision of the continent of Africa. In the center of what appeared to be a huge map of Africa, was the figure of Jesus holding His arms out in a beckoning fashion. I'll never forget, even if I could live to be a thousand years old, those loving and compassionate eyes that were looking straight at me.

The vision continued, but the scene slowly changed, as the image of a young girl sitting under a large shade tree came into focus. In the background I could hear a voice saying, "I want you to become a medical missionary!"

With that the vision was over and I was once again Pauline Gruse sitting in the middle of the living room floor. For a moment my mind refused to function, but when I was finally able to collect my wits I was powerless to do anything but weep. Was it possible? Was it really possible that God had not given up on the call He had placed on my life almost 25 years earlier? Could it be that God still had a special work for me to do—after all these years of running and doing my best to circumvent His will and replace it with my own? I could barely contain myself with the excitement of this thought. Just to think that God would have this much faith in the likes of little old insignificant me was more than I could comprehend.

The following Sunday night Mrs. Brinkley's son came over for a few hours, relieving me from duty and allowing me to attend church for the first time in several weeks. After service, I asked Brother Taylor if I might speak with him a few minutes. I was absolutely sure of the vision I had received, but I hadn't the least idea how I would go about getting to Africa. Surely Brother Taylor would be able to give me some sound advice in this area.

Brother Taylor listened attentively as I described the calling I was certain God had placed on my life.

"Well, Sister Pauline," he responded after pausing several moments to gather his thoughts. "I appreciate your desire to do a real work for God, but let's not try to evangelize the whole world just yet. Why don't you start out by becoming more active here in the local church? We'll try to use you to a greater extent in leading song service and testimony service."

In later years I was able to see the wisdom of Brother Taylor in helping me apply the brakes, but that night I was completely crest-fallen, as I felt God wanted me to "catch the next train out to Africa." For some reason leading testimony service at Christ Temple didn't seem like a suitable substitute for being a missionary to Africa.

While Brother Taylor's apparent failure to share my excitement had caused initial discouragement and despair, the vision I had received was far too real to be permanently pushed aside and forgotten by just one roadblock. My next course of action was to write W. T. Witherspoon, General Chairman of the Pentecostal Assemblies of Jesus Christ (P.A. of J.C.), asking his organization to sponsor my going to Africa. His answer, that the organization was not presently dispatching new missionaries, was not exactly the answer I had been expecting, but I was not going to allow this to turn me aside either.

In his letter, Brother Witherspoon said, "If you are ever able to go to Africa, Sister Gruse, it will be by your faith." Upon reading this, I pondered the statement for a few moments, then decided to do as Hezekiah had done—I spread it before the Lord and placed the problem in His hands. God had called me and I was certain that He would provide a way.

Several weeks later, during a ladies prayer meeting, I shared my calling and burden with those present, asking them to help me find God's will in this matter. As we were leaving, I overheard one of the sisters whispering to another, "Huh, just what makes her think God would send someone like her?" I assumed she was referring to my recent conversion, as well as the life of sin I had led before coming to the Lord. At that moment, my soul was strengthened by the words spoken to Peter, as recorded in

I SURRENDER ALL

Acts 10:15: "What God hath cleansed, that call not thou common."

About this time a woman evangelist, Emily Taylor, held a two-week revival at Christ Temple. During the course of the meeting, I became acquainted with Sister Taylor and shared my vision with her. Knowing that I needed the opportunity to get out and do some preaching and personal work, bless her soul, she invited me to return with her to Rockwood, Tennessee and assist her in the Gospel work there. At first I was uncertain of what I should do, but then Mrs. Brinkley suddenly passed away, leaving me homeless and unemployed. So I took that as a sign that God was leading me to Tennessee.

The next few months were spent with Sister Taylor, working not only in the Rockwood church, but in surrounding towns as well. Preaching opportunities proved numerous, and within six months I had received ministerial credentials with the Church of Jesus Christ, a small southern organization to which Sister Taylor belonged. I remained a member of this group until joining the United Pentecostal Church in 1947.

In the summer of 1939, after having spent almost nine months with Sister Taylor, I began to feel strongly impressed that the Lord wanted me to make a move. I didn't know where or what, but something told me this move would prove a positive step in preparing me for my calling to Africa.

Upon leaving Tennessee, and spending a week or so with the Klapps in South Bend, I continued on to Toledo, Ohio to see my older brother, Leland. I hadn't seen him since our father's funeral, some eight years earlier. For the life of me I could not explain the overpowering, magnetic force that seemed to be drawing me to Toledo. Years of separation had caused Leland and me to have little, if anything, in common. And, while Leland did do his best to be hospitable and courteous, I could easily detect that my new Christian life style made us even more distant. In the intervening years Leland had become quite successful, despite the Depression, and to him everything a man could ever hope to acquire and attain was right here on earth.

Years of toil, heartache, and disappointment had taught me to be less discriminating in the type of employment I held, so within a week I was busily engaged in my new job as a housekeeper. Through my employer, I became acquainted with an elderly Pentecostal lady, and we were soon spending several nights a week together in prayer and Bible study.

One evening, as I was sitting in the living room waiting for her to return with some coffee and homemade doughnuts, I noticed a copy of the *Pentecostal Outlook* lying on the coffee table. Casually leafing through the magazine, a full-page advertisement caught my eye. Listed in the ad were the three Bible Colleges endorsed by the P.A. of J.C.: Apostolic Bible Institute in St. Paul, Minnesota, Apostolic College in Tulsa, Oklahoma, and Southern Bible and Vocational College, located in Rising Star, Texas.

I carefully scrutinized the curriculum by each school. Then, as if being divinely directed, my eyes became focused on the portion of the ad devoted to Apostolic College in Tulsa. Something far too powerful to be my imagination told me this would be the next step in my going to Africa.

As I was preparing to leave that night, I asked Sister Bishop if I might borrow her copy of the *Outlook*. When

I SURRENDER ALL

I got back to my room, I opened to the page with the school ad, and as before my eyes were drawn to Apostolic College. I was confident that I could receive excellent training at any of the three schools, but for some reason God wanted Pauline Gruse to attend Apostolic College. Although I was weary from the long and tiring day, I felt the Lord would not have me go to bed before I had written a letter of inquiry to the school.

I began the letter by sharing my vision and burden for the people of Africa. Next, I mentioned my reasonably recent conversion, and described my Gospel work experience with Sister Taylor in Tennessee. I went on to explain that I would not be financially able to enroll before mid-year, the following January.

About ten days later I received a reply from Mary Williams, wife of the founder and President of the college. In her letter, Sister Williams told me to forget about my "lack of finance" and make plans to enroll for the fall semester. "The expenses will be met by faith," she assured me. Wasn't this exactly what Brother Witherspoon had told me in his letter? The letter went on to say that I would more than likely receive academic credit for my Gospel work, enabling me to graduate in just two years.

I read the letter over several more times, carefully savoring each word, and assuring myself that I was positively the most blessed individual in the whole wide world. I slowly sank back into the arm chair in which I had been sitting. As I closed my eyes, my wandering mind carried me back to a scene some seventeen years earlier, the afternoon I received a letter informing me I had been accepted for nurses training. In some ways that day seemed as only last week, but in many more ways it seemed at least a hundred years ago.

So much had happened: a disastrous marriage, a forced separation from my son, a second marriage on the rocks, and a host of other misfortunes and disappointments far too numerous to mention. As I continued to reflect upon my tragic past, I felt a resurging loneliness for my son begin to sweep over me. While it had been almost four years since I had seen Bob, and I had long since resigned myself to the fact that he deserved far better than I could ever offer him, right at that moment I would have given anything just to hold my little boy. He was twelve years old now, but in my mind he was still my little boy.

Before I could travel too far down Melancholy Lane, I was suddenly jolted back into the present and reality, and my attention was drawn once more to the letter lying on my lap. My thoughts quickly shifted gears, and I fully realized, I think for the first time, that in less than two years I could easily be in the very heart of Africa, satisfying a lifelong dream and fulfilling an eternal calling upon my life. I pinched myself to make sure I wasn't dreaming. No, it was true—I really was going to Bible College in Tulsa. And yes, I could very easily be a walking, breathing missionary in Africa by this time in 1941. Nothing could stop me now. Nothing. Absolutely nothing.

The housekeeping job I had taken a few days after my arrival in Toledo had been on a week-to-week basis, so I felt under no obligation to give the normal two weeks notice. There would be barely enough time to gather my things together and catch a bus to Tulsa in time for pre-registration for the fall semester, but the tight schedule didn't pose any problems. I needed no time to make arrangements for my personal belongings, as I would take them all with me—tucked very neatly into my battered cardboard suitcase. It would not be necessary to plan a preschool shopping spree, as no one in Tulsa had seen me wear the three dresses already hanging in my closet. And, like most of America in 1939, I would require no time for transferring my savings account to a bank in Tulsa.

While I'd almost rather hitchhike than ride a bus today, I assure you that bus service has improved greatly over what it was in 1939. However, the adventure of traveling west of the Mississippi for the first time in my life, coupled with apprehension of going to the "Wild West," was sufficient to keep my mind off the inconveniences of a long, bumpy, and extremely hot bus ride. Believe it or not, I was naive enough to wonder if those wild, gun-totin' cowboys had been tamed yet, and I sincerely hoped the Indians were still observing the treaties they had signed. After all, I reminded myself, Oklahoma had not even become a state until 1907, three years after I was born.

EIGHT

Missionary in Training

I felt badly about having sat next to the young woman and her child for almost four hours, and saying nothing more than "excuse me" the entire time. I really didn't feel like carrying on a conversation, but at the same time it wouldn't be Christian to totally ignore her. Who knew—God might have arranged for me to sit next to them so that I could witness to her.

"Have you and your little girl been visiting relatives?" I asked her.

"No, my husband is an Air Force officer, and we've been stationed in Germany the past three years. He recently received orders for California. The movers picked our furniture up last week, so Jennifer and I decided to leave a few weeks early and spend some extra time with my folks in Minnesota. My husband will join us there shortly."

"Oh, how nice," I commented, trying to act genuinely interested.

> *"And, what brought you to Germany?" she asked me. "Visiting relatives or just vacationing?"*
>
> *"Well," I told her, "I'm a missionary, or should I say ex-missionary, from Liberia, and I just stopped over in Germany for a couple of weeks on my way home."*
>
> *"Oh, how interesting. I don't think I've ever met a real live missionary. What's it like?"*
>
> *"Well," I began rather pensively, "that's a question that can't be answered in a few words."*

The letter from Sister Williams had been received on Friday afternoon. By 6:00 P.M. the following Tuesday I was boarding a bus for St. Louis, my intermediate stop enroute to Tulsa. I located a seat by the window, about halfway back, and settled down for the scheduled eighteen-hour trip.

I was hoping I wouldn't have anyone sitting next to me, but such was not my lot for the trip, as I was soon joined by a cigar-smoking, middle-aged man who appeared to be a traveling salesman. My characterizing proved to be right on target, as he wasted no time in telling me he was a sewing machine salesman on his way to a sales convention in St. Louis. By the time we made our first stop some two hours later, I knew far more about sewing machines than any mortal had a right to know. I was more than ready to get out and stretch my legs and give my clothes and lungs a chance to air out.

The original eighteen-hour trip evolved into more like twenty hours, and seemed like every bit of a week. Upon arriving at the St. Louis station, I claimed my lone piece of luggage and set out to get information on the next bus for Tulsa. As I feared, my two-hour delay had caused me to miss planned connections. There would not be another bus leaving for Tulsa until 7:30 P.M., some six hours away.

I wasn't exactly crazy about the idea of sightseeing the downtown section of a strange city, but at the same time I wasn't excited by the prospects of spending the next six hours admiring the furnishings of the bus station either. So I decided to splurge and treat myself to a good meal, the last one I might get for quite awhile. After all, I was getting dangerously close to total bankruptcy.

Carefully counting the money in my purse, all I had to show for 35 long years here on earth, I discovered my assets to total $7.76. Why not make a real meal of it and spend all my change? This would leave me with $7.00 upon arriving in Tulsa.

By the time I had located a reasonably clean restaurant and had eaten a leisurely meal, it was almost 3:30. I had about three-and-a-half hours to go. I went back to the bus station, located an empty chair in the corner of the waiting room, and spent the remaining time reading my Bible.

Finally, at a few minutes after 7:00, I boarded the bus and soon departed on the fourteen-hour trip to Tulsa. For the first hundred miles or so I had the seat to myself, and was able to catch a quick nap. When we made our first stop in Rolla, Missouri, a dozen or so passengers boarded, and I was joined by an elderly woman on her way to visit a sister in Oklahoma City. Fortunately she didn't smoke foul-smelling cigars and had little to say, thus making the second leg of my trip much more pleasant.

At last, after traveling all night, and well into the morning, we arrived in Tulsa. We had been in Oklahoma for almost four hours now, and I had yet to see a single teepee or even one gun fight. I felt safe in my assumption that actually Oklahoma was not too different from the rest of the Midwest. (Two years in Tulsa convinced me that this was a dangerous statement to make in the presence of a proud Okie).

Eight hours out of St. Louis my will power had been victimized by the smell of freshly brewed coffee and the sight of a fat piece of apple pie, and I had been "forced" to break the vow I had made to myself about not eating until I had arrived in Tulsa. So, I got there with $6.75, and not the $7.00 I had fully intended to have.

As I stepped from the bus, I hopefully looked around, carefully searching for a face that resembled someone who might have come to meet me. But that was absurd. How would anyone know when I was arriving?

Reason would have dictated that I grab a taxi and head out to the school, but a strong, unexplainable feeling came over me, urging me instead to go to the Williams' home. So, after retrieving my luggage, and locating their address in the phone directory, I hailed a taxi outside the bus station.

The trip, which was three or four miles, took about ten minutes. The driver pulled up to a large three story brick house, assuring me it was the one that matched the address on the slip of paper I had given him. I handed him a dollar bill—seventy-five cents for the fare and a quarter for a tip. As the taxi pulled away, leaving me standing at the curb with just my suitcase, a sudden fear came over me. I didn't see a car in the driveway. What if no one was home?

I slowly made my way up the walk and onto the porch. Taking a deep breath I hesitantly rang the doorbell. I could hear footsteps in the hallway, and shortly a tall, rather stately woman came to the door.

"Hello . . . My name is Pauline Gruse. Is Sister Mary Williams home?"

"Well, praise the Lord, Sister Gruse," she answered. "I'm Sister Williams. It's so good to see that you've made it. I trust you had a pleasant trip. Why don't you come in and make yourself at home? Brother Williams is out making calls, but should be back any minute. When he returns we'll take you out to the school and get you settled. You must be bushed after that long bus ride."

After we had chatted for a few minutes over a cool glass of lemonade, Brother Williams returned and we left for the school, which was two or three miles from their home. Pulling up to the curb, Brother Williams pointed to a large two-story building adjacent to the church. "There's where you'll be living, Sister Pauline."

While Brother Williams waited in the car, Sister Williams accompanied me to the second floor, which served as the girls dormitory. I was quite surprised to discover I would have my own room. I had naturally assumed I would be living in open-dormitory style.

After helping me find an empty room, Sister Williams introduced me to a couple of dorm-mates. "They will show you around," she assured me. "Be in my office at 9:00 tomorrow and we'll take care of getting you all registered."

After Sister Williams left, Susan, one of the girls to whom I had been introduced, mentioned that supper would be served at 5:00, which was about two hours away. This would give me a chance to unpack my suitcase, a task that should take no longer than ten minutes, freshen up a bit from my almost two-day bus ride, and possibly catch a short nap. The next thing I knew, I was awakened by the bright rays of the morning sun as they filtered into my room.

I was so intensely groggy that I felt as if I'd been drugged. It took me almost a full minute to get my bearings and realize where I was. The last thing I could remember was lying across the bed to rest my weary eyes for a few minutes. Evidently the girls had peeked into my room and decided to have mercy and allow me to sleep straight through.

As I jumped out of bed, I could hear the voices and footsteps of several of the girls going down to breakfast. Glancing at my alarm clock, I saw it was ten till seven, and that I had no time to waste if I wished to eat. As I scurried about, trying to brush my hair and put on a dress at the same time, I suddenly realized just how terribly hungry I was. I gave little or no thought as to what the menu would consist of. If it was edible, my stomach would be most appreciative.

I was the last to enter the dining room, and I felt more than a little conspicuous as I looked around trying to figure out what I should do and where I should go. I became even more ill at ease when it dawned on me, I guess for the first time really, that I was most likely the oldest student that would be enrolled. Why, I was almost old enough to be the mother of most of these students.

Evidently Susan had detected my total look of bewilderment, as about this time she came up and filled me in on the dining room procedures. She told me they were saving a place for me, and pointed to a table in the far corner.

Breakfast that morning consisted of milk, hot biscuits, and plenty of gravy. To the empty stomach, however, it couldn't have tasted better if it had been two eggs over easy, a thick slice of ham, and several pieces of hot buttered homemade toast. I would be eating many, many more biscuits in my two-year tenure at Tulsa, and each time my stomach would be grateful for that special touch the Louisiana girls had with biscuit dough.

As we were finishing breakfast, one of the girls at the table reminded us of the prayer meeting that was scheduled from eight until nine that morning. She went on to explain to me that we normally had chapel service each morning at eight, but that they wouldn't begin until classes started on Monday. So, after cleaning the table and disposing of our dirty dishes, we made our way to the church which doubled as the Bible college.

After singing a few songs, and asking for special prayer requests, each of the fifteen or twenty students assembled found a place to pray. The Spirit of the Lord seemed to descend in a very special way that morning, a way in which I desperately needed, confirming that I was indeed in the center of God's will, and providing much-needed spiritual refreshment for a travel-weary soul.

As soon as the prayer meeting was over, and I had gotten directions to Sister Williams' office, I left for my nine o'clock appointment. When I stepped into the outer office, I saw there was another student with Sister Williams. Nevertheless, she motioned for me to come in. Handing me an application, she said, "Here, fill this out. I'll be with you in a few minutes."

In fifteen minutes or so, the student who had been with her left, and Sister Williams called for me to come in. Handing her my application, I accepted the chair she offered, and tensely waited as she meticulously scrutinized

everything I had written. Finally she looked up.
"Do you definitely feel a call to Africa, Sister Pauline?"
I assured her I did.
"What part?"
I told her I wasn't sure yet.
"Why did you choose Tulsa?"
I had shared this with her previously, in the letter of inquiry I had written, but I repeated the story of having seen the ad for the Bible College in the *Outlook*, and how the Spirit of God had impressed upon me so strongly that I should go to Tulsa. I went on to tell Sister Williams that I really felt that in addition to gaining the insight into God's Word that I so desperately needed, I would discover here the exact details related to my call to Africa. She didn't answer, but her nod of approval was sufficient.

There was a slight pause, and she could no doubt tell I was frantically searching for the best way to phrase what I was about to say. "I . . . I wrote in my letter that I would not have the finances for attending this semester." Up until now there had been no mention of the subject.

"And, what was my answer, Sister Pauline?"

"You said the finances would be met by faith," I meekly answered.

"Then, don't you think it's about time we started exercising that faith?"

I nodded yes.

"For the time being you will be expected to get up at five each morning to help with breakfast. From time to time there may be some other kitchen-related duties that we'll call upon you to assist with. Other than that we ask that you apply yourself one hundred percent to your studies."

From the gentle, yet firm tone of her voice, I could tell that Mary Williams meant business. I thanked her several times, each time feeling that mere words were not adequately expressing the deep gratitude I felt. As I walked out the door and back to the dorm I felt as light as a feather, like I was walking on billowy puffs of clouds.

The events of the weekend don't stand out in my memory at all. Evidently my mind had raced ahead of my body, and I had started living in Monday as soon as I left Sister Williams' office.

At 5:00 A.M. Monday, however, my body caught up, as I was jolted back into reality by the clanging of the alarm clock. Jumping from bed, in an attempt to stop the ringing before I had awakened everyone in the dorm, I noted that it was still night outside. I had barely thirty minutes to get dressed and down to the kitchen to assist with breakfast. As I stepped outside, I was greeted by a cool, gentle morning breeze that let me know that summer was getting ready to step aside and make way for fall.

Breakfast that morning was a special treat. In addition to our usual fare of biscuits and gravy, there was freshly smoked bacon that had been brought in by a man in the West Tulsa church. Those of us working in the kitchen ate first so that we'd be ready to handle the stampede of hungry students that would descend upon us at 7:00. After breakfast had been served, the dishes washed, and the kitchen restored to order, I, along with the other two student helpers, left for registration.

In addition to Sister Williams, who taught most of the Bible courses I would be taking, my teachers that first year were Ruth Pardue, who taught Bible Geography and Tabernacle, and Lucille Stewart, who taught business related courses. Sister Stewart later served as a missionary to Brazil and the Philippines. While Brother Williams taught an occasional class, his primary duties were that of pastor of the church, as well as President and Administrator of the Bible College.

While I had possessed an intense burden for the continent of Africa for some time now, I had to be the first to admit that I was very weak in my knowledge of the Word of God. It was therefore with great enthusiasm that I attacked my Bible courses, especially Homiletics.

Each day, at the close of Homiletics class, Sister Williams would write a verse of scripture on the board. Our assignment for the following day was to write a sermon, using this verse as the text. I would spend several hours each afternoon and evening on this assignment, doing my best to develop a sermon that would cover every angle and aspect of the verse and include as many supportive scriptures as I could possibly find.

All too soon the month of March rolled around, and I knew it was time to start making plans for the summer. It was about this time that I received a letter from Sister Taylor, asking if I'd like to spend the summer with her, assisting in the work in Rockwood. This sounded like a definite answer to a prayer that I hadn't even prayed yet, so I rushed her a letter by return mail, assuring her I'd be delighted to come. I was itching to get out into the real world and preach some of my sermons to live people.

The thought of how I'd finance my trip to Tennessee didn't occur to me until several days after I had mailed my reply to Sister Taylor. A few days later, however, this answer came by mail too—in the form of cash for a bus ticket and expenses.

The first Monday of April saw me boarding a bus for Tennessee. (The school year in Tulsa lasted only from the first of October through the last of March in those early days of the college.) The trip, which covered approximately 600 miles and carried me through Little Rock, Memphis, and Nashville, took a little more than 24 hours. The bus station in Rockwood was really nothing more than a gas station that sold bus tickets, but at least there was someone there to meet me when I arrived.

I spent the next five months with Sister Taylor, doing much of the preaching in the Rockwood church, and holding several revivals in neighboring towns in that part of eastern Tennessee. Before I knew it, September was approaching and it was time to start making plans to return to Tulsa. But the more I thought about it, the less liberty I felt to leave Tennessee. I still felt that deep burden for Africa, and I was certain that somewhere down the road in God's timetable I would be returning to Tulsa to finish that last year. But, as for the fall of 1940, I felt very strongly that God wanted me to stay right where I was.

I shared these feelings with Sister Taylor, and she reassured me by saying that God had been dealing with her along the same line. Thus my tentative plans became to spend a year in Rockwood and return to Tulsa in the fall of 1941. I was aware that this would delay my going to Africa for a year, but there was something I was to learn in this next year in Tennessee that God considered vital to my composite Christian character.

The next nine months sped by as quickly as the preceding summer had, and before I knew what had happened May was sliding into June. One morning, in the early part of June, I awoke with the feeling that God had accomplished His purpose in my staying in Tennessee, and that it was time for me to move on in preparation for my return to Tulsa. I still wasn't quite sure why God had directed me to stay with Sister Taylor for an additional nine months, but I was confident that I was leaving better prepared for the role God wanted me to fill in His Kingdom.

While school wouldn't be starting for another three and one-half months, I felt strongly impressed that the Lord wanted me to leave Tennessee then, rather than wait until just before it was time for classes to resume. Doris Klapp had written several times while I was in Tennessee, inviting me to come spend a few days with them. So, I determined to go to South Bend and wait for further instructions from the Lord. As it turned out, I stayed with the Klapps until time for school to start.

While in South Bend, I had the opportunity to preach several times in Christ Temple. In addition, I traveled around a good deal, ministering in the neighboring churches.

Several weeks before leaving for Tulsa, Brother Taylor told me he'd like to have me preach the last Sunday night I was there. That evening, just before turning the pulpit over to me, Brother Taylor told the congregation that he felt led of the Lord to ask the church to help with my expenses for the coming school year. He then asked for those who would pledge some amount for the next six months to stand. To my surprise, a total of ten dollars a month was raised—no small sum in 1941. This was in addition to the love offering given me for preaching that night. Each month, when I received the ten dollar check from the church, I immediately endorsed it and gave it to the school to apply toward my room and board and tuition.

The following morning saw me heading west for the second and final year of Bible College. The bus ride was no more eventful than the first one had been two years earlier. This time, however, I felt I knew my way around well enough to go straight out to the school from the bus station.

Upon my arrival, I noticed several changes from when I had left 18 months earlier. For one, the girls dorm had been completely remodeled to make room for increased enrollment. What had once been several private rooms was now an open dorm. I would be sharing one corner of the large room with LaVerne Collins, who would later join me on the mission field. A second change I noticed right away was the uniform requirement for women students, which consisted of blue skirts and white blouses.

Of the approximately 60 students enrolled that year, 14 were seniors. Homiletics continued to be my favorite course, and as in the first year, occupied most of my study time. As a senior I became more active in student affairs, and was elected Editor of the school yearbook, *The Standard*, as well as Secretary-Treasurer of the Senior Class. Towards the end of the year, I was also chosen for the position of Secretary-Treasurer of the Alumni Association.

A month or so before graduation, Porter Davis, a missionary to Liberia, who had been forced to return to the States due to World War II activity, visited the school for several days. Learning of my burden and call to Africa, he encouraged me to make myself available to Liberia when the country was reopened to missionary activity.

For some time now I had felt impressed that God was sending me to a people who were small of stature. I had strongly suspected this meant the Pygmy people of Nigeria or what was then the Belgian Congo. In sharing these feelings with Brother Davis, he informed me that many of the Liberians were comparatively small. No sooner had he said this than a feeling of absolute certainty came over me. I was going to Liberia—wherever that was.

The following weeks of school seemed to come and go with one sunset, and before I knew it, it was cap and gown time. The Baccalaureate Sermon and Commencement exercises for the Class of '42 were held Wednesday night, March 31. The annual State Bible Conference, which had been in progress all week, was scheduled to run through Friday night, so I made plans to attend, then stay over the weekend for services at the First Apostolic Church there in Tulsa. I would leave for South Bend early Monday morning.

As we had promised each other, Doris and I had corresponded regularly during my second year at Bible College. As graduation time approached, I received a letter from her, asking me to stay with them until I had made arrangements for my departure to the mission field. Once more my good friend, Doris, not to mention her ever-understanding husband, Virgil, had come to my rescue in the time of need.

Bright and early Monday morning saw me doing my best to wedge my way up to the ticket counter. American involvement in the War was in full swing now, and the bus station was swarming with servicemen trying to get home for that last furlough before going overseas. Somehow the elbows and shoulders didn't bother me nearly as much as the ache in my heart as I looked into the sad eyes of men, both young and middle-aged, some of whom were going home for the last time.

The major commercial bus lines had commissioned additional buses into service, but still the demand far exceeded supply, and schedules were about as dependable as a campaign promise. In the past there had been that possibility of having a seat to yourself, but on this trip one was fortunate to even get on a bus. The next task was to

Missionary in Training

locate a seat to share with someone.

I arrived in St. Louis, where I was to have changed buses, only to discover that the next available bus to South Bend would not be leaving for at least seven hours. Already it had been more than twenty hours since I had entered the Tulsa bus station. By the time I finally reached South Bend I had been on the road almost 48 hours.

Several days after my arrival in South Bend I wrote a letter to Robert Hancock, who was Director of Foreign Missions for the Church of Jesus Christ, the organization to which I belonged. About the first of May I received a reply from him, assuring me he would submit my request to the Executive Board of the organization, which was scheduled to meet the first week of June.

About the middle of June I received a second letter from Brother Hancock, informing me that my request had been approved, and that I had been appointed to a three-year term in Liberia, commencing as soon as I could get there. The letter went on to say that in addition to my fare to and from Liberia, the organization would provide me with a $50.00 per month salary . . . if funds were available. I was told that the first thing I should do was apply for a passport.

My heart was pounding like a big bass drum as I lay the letter down. I had been expecting it all along, but still it was hard for me to believe that the last mountain had finally been traversed, and the dream of a lifetime was finally coming true. After years of tears, heartache, and bitter disappointment, I was finally fulfilling the call of God delivered to a girl of eleven some 27 years earlier.

I suddenly felt very small and unworthy, and became fearful that I could not stand up to the responsibility of the many souls that had been placed squarely upon my shoulders. Just then the sweet and reassuring presence of the Lord came over me, and I had the utmost confidence that if I could remain humble the Holy Spirit would produce greatness through my smallness.

The next morning I went to the local post office and obtained an application for my passport. A few days later I mailed it, along with my birth certificate, two recent photographs, and my diploma from nurses training to the State Department in Washington. I anxiously waited two weeks, four weeks, six weeks. Finally, after two months, I received a reply from the State Department. I could tell by the size of the envelope that it contained nothing but a letter. The form letter was short, not too sweet, and to the point: Due to wartime conditions and the low priority of my request, my application was being denied at the present time. I knew this answer was not from God, and I wasn't about to sit back and accept it. My Uncle Sam might be strong, but my Heavenly Father was stronger.

I wrote to Brother Hancock, telling him of my denial. A week or so later I received a note from him, informing me he was going to Washington to make an appeal before the State Department officials. About a month later I received a letter from him stating that he had been successful in his efforts, and that my passport would be forthcoming. About three weeks after this, around the first of November, I received a large brown manila envelope which I knew was large enough to contain my passport, as well as the birth certificate and diploma I had submitted.

I immediately began making plans to depart for the East Coast where I would book passage for Liberia. Upon the insistence of Doris and Virgil, however, I decided to stay in South Bend through the end of the year. The

Missionary in Training

Klapps, as well as the saints in the South Bend Church, did their best to make Christmas of 1942 a memorable one. It would be several years before I'd enjoy another Christmas in the States.

On January 3, I boarded a train for New York City. The congestion I had encountered on my Tulsa to South Bend bus ride the previous April was nothing compared to the confusion I experienced on this trip. Everywhere I turned I encountered wall-to-wall soldiers. It seemed like the whole world was going to war. And, I guess they were.

Finally, after what had developed into a 24 hour nightmare, I found myself in the middle of the total pandemonium of Grand Central Station. After a delay of more than two hours I was able to locate my luggage. I had been given the names and addresses of several people in the New York City area whom I could contact, but right then the only thing I wanted to do was get away from that mad house and find a quiet place to get some much-needed sleep. Securing the services of a Red Cap, I got my bags out to the curb where I hailed a taxi. Having absolutely no idea where I was or where I should go, I instructed him to take me to the nearest Y.W.C.A. I figured I could stay there for a few days until I could locate a ship bound for Liberia.

The next morning, after eating breakfast at a restaurant down the street, I got a quarter's worth of nickels and began calling some of the ship lines. I got change for another quarter and continued to call. Before long I detected a trend developing: nothing available now . . . perhaps not for months. I continued to live at the Y for a week or so, then finally accepted the fact that I might be in for a long stay and had better secure other quarters.

Through the references Brother Hancock had given

me, I was able to make contact with a Black Pentecostal woman who pastored a church in Harlem. Arrangements were made to stay with her until I could find a ship going to Liberia. A day or so after moving in, I was able to find a job working as a sales clerk for Woolworths. My support from the organization would not begin until I was on location. As it turned out, I spent almost six months living with Sister Johnson.

Those six months were spent on pins and needles, desperately hoping that each day would be the last, and anticipating that each ring of the telephone was a call from one of the shipping companies, informing me that a steamer would be departing in a few days. The wait was shortened as much as possible by working six days a week at the store and preaching occasionally for my landlady, as well as some of the other churches, both Black and White, in the New York City area.

One evening, in the early part of July, I received a completely unexpected call from Porter Davis, informing me that he and his wife were in Philadelphia. I had just assumed that the Davises were already resettled in Liberia, as it hadn't dawned on simple-minded me that they would have encountered the same problems I was experiencing.

"Do you still have plans to go to Liberia?" he asked me teasingly.

"What do you think?" was my quick retort.

"Well, in that case, can you be in Philadelphia by two tomorrow afternoon?"

Without hesitating to consider what would be involved, I assured him I could and I would. Brother Davis went on to explain that he had been able to locate a Portuguese liner that was returning to Lisbon. Company officials had assured him that upon reaching Lisbon, we could encounter no problems in obtaining passage on to Liberia. Having already anticipated what my reply would be, he had taken the liberty of making a reservation for me.

I stayed up all night—washing, ironing, selecting, discarding, stuffing, and cramming—but at 1:00 the next afternoon I was walking up the gangplank of the *Maritimos*.

My first photograph—about age two

Mother, Forrest, Robert, Martha, and me (standing in the rear)—taken about 1918

Aboard the *Del Viento* in 1948—en route for my second term in Liberia

Joining Gladys for a few moments rest at the Bomi Hills Mission Station—taken in 1949 (I had malaria when this was taken)

Treking with Georgia (I'm the short one)

Gladys demonstrating the proper way of riding in a hammock

Our first missionary truck—the one I wrecked

Frontal view of the home Geneva Bailey and I built

Geneva Bailey (Jean)—my first co-worker at Fassama

Bomi Hills girls beating palm nuts to make palm oil

LaVerne Collins (on right) and a friend, Maxine Wood

Frontal view of Fassama Mission Station

Standing with the Cupples family in front of our *Sheaves for Christ* plane—taken in 1957

My "special friends," Doris and Virgil Klapp, along with Doris' sister, Leatha

That's me—standing on the Fassama Mission grounds—taken in 1963

My "Official" photograph made in 1960

An aerial view of Fassama Mission Station

Fassama Mission Station—a view from the rear

1969 Missions Conference held at Fassama

Evangelist Gruse preaching to the Fassama congregation

Native workers attending the dedication of Fassama Mission

The "Play Devil" entering a village near Fassama

"Yours Truly" delivering a dedication message in April, 1971

Brother Sam Latta and some of the native boys standing beside a later *Sheaves for Christ* plane

"Boys" from the Fassama Mission, now pastoring churches in other villages

Standing in front of the Monrovia church with the Boltons, Ena Hylton, and several of the native preachers

Services in Belle Baloma, a village near Fassama

Brother Basil Williams taking off in a *Sheaves for Christ* plane

Picture taken in 1974, shortly after my 70th birthday

NINE

Finally!!!

For the past thirty minutes or so I had done all the talking, describing my childhood, and how that God had called me to be a missionary when I was barely eleven years old. Without going into the heart-rending details, I had described my two disastrous marriages, as well as my decision to give up Bob. I had just gotten to the point where I had landed in West Africa, when we were interrupted by the stewardess asking if we would like some coffee or tea.

I soon discovered that most of the passengers aboard the *Maritimos* were either departing missionaries or returning British refugees. Among those refugees were the wife and family of Anthony Eden, successor to Sir Winston Churchill as Prime Minister of Great Britain. Including the Davises and myself, there were fifteen missionaries, sponsored by various missions organizations, bound for Liberia.

While my cabin wasn't exactly a first-class stateroom, the accommodations were quite comfortable, and I sincerely enjoyed the company of my roommate. Gladys, who was a Baptist missionary, was returning to Liberia for her third term. In the days that followed, she did her best to give me a cram course in Liberian geography and culture. The only thing that stuck with me, however, was her warning that I should take extreme precautions against offending the natives in any way, as they were constantly searching for ways to "sue" the foreigners. As it turned out, I had to walk the trails for myself before I learned what Liberia "was all about."

The food and service aboard the *Maritimos* was excellent. Although this was my maiden voyage, I surprisingly didn't get seasick even once. All-in-all the entire trip was quite pleasant—that is until I got my "atrocious" sunburn. Having never been exposed to the effects of salt air, I had no idea how quickly a person could get roasted. One day I decided to sit out on the open deck and catch up on some of my long-overdue correspondence. Before I knew what had happened, my legs had turned a beet red. For the remainder of the trip I suffered the consequences. Believe you me, this was one lesson I learned, and learned well, the first time around.

Upon our arrival in Lisbon, Brother Davis, along with John Bowers, a Lutheran missionary who was returning to Liberia, made arrangements for us to book passage on a Portuguese freighter scheduled to leave later in the day for the seaport city of Bissau in Portuguese Guinea. An hour or so later, in the turmoil of seeing that my baggage was transferred from the *Maritimos* to the freighter, I became separated from the Davises. After making several futile trips up and down the dock, and being assured by the captain of the freighter that absolutely no passengers had boarded as of yet, I resigned myself to the fact that I was just going to have to wait until they returned. I'll admit the thought that the rapture had taken place did run through my mind, but I quickly dismissed it as a trick of the devil.

Finally, after I had been sitting on my suitcase, staring at the open sea for almost an hour, I heard someone call my name.

"Pauline, where have you been? We looked everywhere for you, and finally decided you had gone on ahead to the police station."

"Police station?" I asked.

"Sure . . . you know . . . to get a clearance to leave the Lisbon harbor. Didn't we tell you?"

"This is the first I've heard about it," I assured them.

Hurriedly glancing at his watch, Brother Davis said, "the rest of you go on aboard. If we hurry, Sister Gruse and I can make it to the station and back before time to leave."

After frantically waving for a taxi for what seemed like half an hour, one finally stopped. As we climbed into what appeared to be a World War I vintage cab, we managed to convey to the driver where we wanted to go and that we would make it worth his while if he got us there "*Pronto*." Evidently experience had taught our driver where every bump and chuck hole was, as I can assure you he didn't miss a single one of them.

After driving at breakneck speed, weaving in and out of traffic, and honking his horn at everything that got in his way, the driver suddenly slammed on his brakes, stopping just inches from a slow moving freight train that was blocking the road. After seesawing back and forth for close to half an hour, the train finally cleared the road, and we were off to the races again. I was sure that the next bump would be all it would take to loosen the final bolt that was holding that piece of junk together. I could just visualize Brother Davis, myself, the driver, and several hundred pieces of rusty taxi lying in a giant heap in the middle of the road.

At last we screeched to a stop in front of a rather rundown, three-story building with a sign in front that said "a Policia." I assumed that meant police station. We told the driver to wait, that we'd be back "Pronto." An hour later, when we returned, I knew what the sly grin on his face had meant when we told the driver we'd be back shortly.

The police evidently detected right away that we were in a hurry, as they seemed to go out of their way to insure we had a nervous breakdown. Men who only a couple of hours earlier had taken great pride in their ability to converse in English had suddenly forgotten every word they had ever known. After being shuffled from desk to desk, no one quite sure of the procedures for passport clearance, we were finally rescued by an officer who appeared to be in command. The clock above the door showed that we had exactly 25 minutes before the freighter left.

Racing down the steps, we jumped into the taxi, once more placing our lives into the hands of our daredevil driver—and God, too, I'm convinced. We breathed a momentary sigh of relief as we approached the train tracks and discovered they were still clear. It was a good thing—we could never have stopped this time.

As we neared the dock, however, our hearts sank as we saw that our ship had lifted anchor and was already a half mile or so out to sea. Not really knowing what course of action to take, we instructed the driver to take us to the office of the Port Authority. Somehow he seemed to know where we meant.

The man on duty proved to be much more helpful and understanding than the police. After explaining our predicament to him, he radioed the freighter captain, telling him that he was bringing two passengers out by motor launch. When the ordeal was finally over, and we stepped aboard the freighter, I was too exhausted to do anything but be led to my room where I fell across the bed.

I had honestly expected to sleep at least a day, but after three or four hours I was awakened by a not-too-gentle tossing of the ship. Glancing at my watch, I saw that I still had time to join the others for dinner. One meal was sufficient to convince me that the fare aboard the freighter would not begin to measure up to that which we had enjoyed on the *Maritimos*. While the chef of the *Maritimos* had been trying to please the discriminating palates of his passengers, the cook assigned to our freighter was interested only in filling the hungry bellies of the merchant seamen attached to his ship.

The main course that night consisted of what could perhaps best be described as a "spinach souffle." It was literally swimming in olive oil. This, added to the choppy waters that tossed the smaller freighter to and fro like a toy boat, brought on a genuine case of acute seasickness. The happiest day in my life, up until that point, had to be the day we finally docked at Bissau, and I was able to plant my wobbly legs onto terra firma.

After making certain our baggage had been unloaded and was securely stored, we got directions and set out for the British Consulate. The run-down, weatherbeaten building in the heart of Bissau was identified only by the proud Union Jack flapping in the breeze. The sparse,

I SURRENDER ALL

barely-adequate furnishings of the crude office seemed to match perfectly the thin, worn-out Officer-in-charge, who looked as if he should have been relieved of duty months before.

We entered the office with hopes of catching a military plane from Bissau to Roberts Field, a U.S. Army installation some 50 miles outside Monrovia, the capital of Liberia. For more than a week the British Consul tried pulling every string he had at his disposal. Each morning, however, when we would report to his office, the answer would be the same: "Nothing yet . . . come back tomorrow."

So, back to the town's leading, and only, hotel we would go, to sit and wait for another sunrise . . . and hopefully some good news.

I evidently lived in a state of culture-shock the entire time I was in Bissau, as the only outstanding feature I remember about the city is the ever-present vultures that lurked overhead, seemingly waiting for death to claim its prey so they could swoop down for the spoils.

At last, after we had been in Bissau for more than a week, the Consul admitted that every conceivable avenue had been explored and exhausted. Our only hope was to go by truck from Bissau to Bathurst, a seacoast town that was the capital of Gambia, a British protectorate. He went on to say there was a large British airbase there, and he felt certain that arrangements for a flight could be made there.

With the assistance of the Consul we engaged the services of a native driver who owned a large canvas-covered flatbed truck. After considerable dickering back and forth, a fee was agreed upon, our baggage was loaded, and we were on our way. The roads between Bissau and

Bathurst, a two-day trip, were nothing more than well-worn ruts. An hour or so out, it started to rain heavily, not letting up until our arrival in Bathurst.

After we had been on the "road" for an hour or so, the driver, who had been reluctant to take the job in the first place, became quite temperamental and erratic. As the rains continued, and the ruts advanced to mudholes, his irritability became downright violent. Several times over the next few hours he threatened to return to Bissau. When we would remind him that he had been well-paid in advance, and that he had agreed to take us to Bathurst, he would respond by pushing the accelerator all the way to the floor.

Immediately after one of his tantrums, the driver drove under a low-lying tree branch, all but completely ripping the canvas top from the truck. Had any of us been standing in the back at that particular time, we, too, would have most likely lost our heads.

Towards evening, after having traveled most of the day, we stopped for the night at a small settlement in which there was a French military outpost. Early the next morning, as we were preparing to leave for Bathurst, our driver flatly refused to go any further. We had our choice, he informed us: we could either return with him to Bissau or we could remain where we were and take our chances. We were about to give up hope when the French commanding officer, overhearing our conversation, came to the rescue. Evidently he gave the driver a choice: either take us to Bathurst or spend some time in jail.

The torrential downpour continued throughout the second day, making traveling conditions miserable. With the tarp ripped off, we were fully exposed to the blowing rain, as well as the mud being thrown from the rear wheels of the truck. By the time we had finally reached our destination, we were completely soaked and caked with mud from head to toe.

Upon our arrival in Bathurst, we went straight to the British Army headquarters. Shivering from the rain, and covered with several coats of mud, we must have looked a sight as we approached what we assumed to be the desk of the commanding officer. Brother Davis introduced himself, informing the officer that we desired to secure a flight to Roberts Field. The Major looked us over very carefully, finally shaking his head in disbelief at our appearance as well as our request. "Has anyone informed you we are at war?" he asked wryly.

After a few more minutes of reprimanding us for returning to Liberia while the world was still at war, he informed us a U. S. Army transport would be leaving for Freetown, Sierra Leone the next morning, and that he would do his best to get us aboard. That night we were housed in the visiting officers quarters and ate supper in the officers mess.

The next morning, shortly after breakfast, a driver picked us up to take us to the airfield. We were told that due to limited cargo space on the plane, we could take but one suitcase each aboard the aircraft. The driver assured us he would see that our other baggage was placed aboard the next ship leaving for Monrovia. He went on to say we could expect our baggage to arrive no later than a week from then.

My maiden flight was quite an initiation into the field of aerodynamics. The seats were the web-type, in long rows along each side and down the center. There was no temperature control in the passenger area, and the stewardess was a husky staff sergeant with a .45 strapped to his waist. After we had climbed to a few thousand feet it got extremely cold. I was certainly grateful to the young soldier seated next to me who came to the rescue by loaning me his fatigue jacket. Had I been able to get my mind off how cold I was, I might have been a bit more apprehensive about the method in which I was flying.

After a bumpy flight of perhaps thirty minutes or so, we landed at another British base near Freetown, the seaport capital of Sierra Leone. After checking with the army officials there, we learned that we could most likely get a flight for Roberts Field in the next few days, but that the schedule was totally unpredictable and we'd just have to be patient and ready to go at a moment's notice. We were informed that there were no quarters available on the base, and that it would be necessary for us to find accommodations in town. The officer in charge gave us directions to what he described as the best hotel in Freetown, one operated by a European woman.

The reception we received from the proprietor was anything but inviting. "We don't have any rooms!" was her curt reply, as she turned her back and slammed the door in our faces.

At a complete loss as to what to do next, we sat on our suitcases and prepared to pray and make plans. Evidently the landlady looked out the window about this time and the Lord made her heart to soften, as the next thing we knew she was calling out to us. It seemed she had just remembered that she did have one room available . . . and I could sleep on a cot in her room. Reverend Bowers was given the name and address of a Baptist missionary family that gladly put him up for a few days.

Later that afternoon we had a visit from an Assemblies of God missionary. He had heard there were some American missionaries in town, and came over to invite us for supper that night. Several years later the Kennedys came to Liberia as missionaries.

After three days in Freetown, we received word that a U. S. Army plane would be leaving for Roberts Field in about four hours. A couple of hours later a jeep came to pick us up. After another flight of approximately 30 minutes I was finally in Liberia, my home for the next 28 years. The date was August 13, 1943.

TEN

Learning the Ropes

Upon Nancy's insistence, I continued to tell my life's story as we sipped our coffee. I could see her eyes get big when I described some of the earlier treks. Her mouth dropped open as I told her of my many encounters with the natives—especially the Devil Bush people. About a half hour later, however, I had brought me back to the present, and there was no more to tell.

"I really don't think you should feel badly about having to return," she consoled me. "After all, anyone who has devoted as much of her life as you have deserves a rest."

I appreciated Nancy's attempts at comforting me, but I didn't want to rest. For years my plan had called for me to be busily engaged in the Lord's work—in Liberia—when I drew my final breath. But God, in His infinite knowledge and wisdom, had somehow seen fit to do things differently.

I SURRENDER ALL

Immediately after landing at Roberts Field we were escorted to the Base Commander's office where we were instructed to fill out several U.S. government forms regarding our entry into Liberia. While there had been no actual conflict within the borders of Liberia, it was easy to see, from the tight security that prevailed, that the Allied Forces were on the alert and that the world was indeed in a state of war. After an hour or so of filling out the forms and answering questions, we evidently satisfied the curiosity of the Army officers, and were permitted to hire a taxi for the forty mile trip into Monrovia.

I remember very little of the taxi ride, except that it was bumpy, and that the vehicle seemed overly crowded and stuffy with five adults and several pieces of luggage. I honestly wondered if the automobile had 40 miles left in her.

On the way, Reverend Bowers did his best to fill me in on a few of the major details concerning Monrovia, Liberia's capital. It had derived its name from James Monroe, the fifth President of the United States. It had been under his administration that the first American Negro slaves had been permitted to leave the U.S. and settle in what was now the independent nation of Liberia.

Currently Monrovia had a population of approximately 50,000. This was composed of elected officials and government workers, all of whom were Liberians; a noticeable contingent of English, French, and Lebanese merchants; and a small group of missionaries, mostly North Americans. The remainder of the populace, he continued, was made up of the laboring class of Liberians, most of whom traced their ancestry back to the American slaves.

Monrovia proved to be the very typical West African

city, with its wood-frame and zinc buildings. There were precious few of the modern conveniences that I had grown accustomed to, and even in this capital city I found it necessary to boil my drinking water.

The red-tape we had encountered at Roberts Field was nothing compared to what we experienced in Monrovia. By the time we had fully satisfied the proper officials in the appropriate departments within the Liberian government, we had spent the better part of two weeks in Monrovia. Seemingly everyone within the Department of the Interior with enough rank to warrant having his own desk had to take his turn in closely scrutinizing our passports and visas, as well as placing his stamp of approval and affixing his signature in the correct place on the specified form. My, how well they had adopted American ways!

Next, it was necessary for us to clear the Department of Education where our academic credentials were examined with great meticulosity.

As is still the case, the Liberian government of the 1940's was aggressively promoting a program of nationalism, self-improvement, and self-pride. For this reason, President Barclay was opening his arms to those missionaries who could provide much-needed educational skills and health care. Having graduated from Bible College, as well as Nurses Training, would serve to place me in favorable light with the Liberian officials.

President Barclay's successor, William Tubman, the man who served as President of Liberia during most of my tenure there, was even more receptive to the Christian missionaries. His successor, William Tolbert, the current President of Liberia and an ordained Baptist minister, carried on in this fine tradition.

I SURRENDER ALL

Finally . . . the last thread of red-tape was cut away and we were free to travel, live, and work in Liberia. So, the early morning sun of the next day saw us striking out for Beahjah Mission Station, where I would be working with the Davises for the next two years or so.

The first leg of our journey found us taking a four-hour boat trip up the St. Paul River in an open motor launch, referred to by the natives as the "Chug-chug." We arrived in Arlington, a small Syrian trading post, shortly before noon. After a brief visit, we parted company with Reverend Bowers, obtained the services of some government porters, and headed further inland towards Beahjah.

We had taken but a few steps out of the clearing when it began to rain. At first it was no more than a few scattered splatters which found great difficulty working their way through the dense foliage overhead. Within moments, however, it had graduated with honors into a full-scale, no-holds-barred downpour. Needless to say, I was tremendously encouraged by the words of Sister Davis, assuring me that I could look forward to this on a daily basis from now until the middle, or possibly the end, of November. The natives called this the "Rain Time," and it was during these months that Liberia received most of her annual 70 to 180 inches of rainfall (the amount determined by how closely you lived to the coast).

Mentally, in the past month or so, I had taken numerous treks back into the Liberian Bush, but I had to admit that even with my imagination working overtime I had been unable to dream up what I was currently experiencing. Here I was, Pauline Gruse, a reasonably intelligent 39 year old American woman, slipping, sliding, and wading ankle deep in mud, swatting the giant Mango flies that swarmed incessantly about my head, all the time fighting with every ounce of strength I had to keep my balance on the narrow, uneven trail.

To be very honest, I was beginning to have some reservations about my decision. Had I bitten off more than I was prepared to chew? I was actually trying to devise a plan for leaving Liberia on the next boat out, when I happened to turn around and found myself looking squarely into the strained face of the porter who was struggling with the front end of my heavy trunk. Right there, in the middle of the rain, mud, and Mango flies, I felt a surge of compassion like I'd never known. Yes, I'd go on. I'd stay, and if necessary, I'd die so that he, and thousands more like him, could hear the saving message of Jesus Christ. Yes, the price seemed almost too small to pay when one allowed his mind to revisit Calvary.

Several hours after nightfall, after wading through the sticky, mucky Liberian mire for more than ten hours, we reached Maheh Mission Station, where the Haneys, fellow Pentecostal missionaries, were laboring. After a late night supper of chicken and rice, we gladly retired for the night. I was certainly grateful for the tin roof over my head that kept out a fair amount of the rain that continued to fall on through the next day. But not even the constant pelting upon the metal roof could drown out the strange, unfamiliar sounds of the black African night. And, I just couldn't seem to get the porters off my mind. I wondered if they had found shelter from the rain.

We awoke early the next morning to continue our trek on to Beahjah. If we made good time we could reach our destination by midafternoon. Rain continued to fall as we said goodbye to the Haneys and disappeared into the Bush. The trail on this leg of our journey didn't prove to be any better than that on which we had traveled the day before. By the time we arrived at Beahjah we were soaked from head to toe, and must have looked as if we had just stepped out of a mud bath. Our welcoming party consisted of 20 or 25 natives from the surrounding area, and I got my first look at those whom I would be serving for the next two years or so.

That evening, after I had had a chance to partially unpack, I joined the Davises for the evening meal. After supper we sat in the makeshift living room, rehearsing the events of the past few weeks, and making plans for the future operation of the mission. In the course of the conversation, Brother Davis asked if I'd like a little history lesson on Pentecostal missionary efforts in Liberia. I assured him I would.

According to his account, the first missionary to Liberia had been Sister January. No one seemed to know much about her background, but almost anywhere a missionary would travel in Liberia, he would meet someone who remembered Sister January being in those parts.

The senior missionaries in Liberia at this time were Aaron and Pearl Holmes, a Black couple working at Zoradee Mission. Pearl, who had been born and reared in Little Rock, Arkansas, had migrated with her mother to Liberia in 1896. Soon after her arrival, although still a teenager, Pearl became so burdened for the native Liberians that she offered her services to a Baptist missionary society working there. In the course of her missionary work, she met and married Aaron Holmes, a native of Haiti. Several years later Brother and Sister Holmes came into contact with Sister January and were converted to the Pentecostal faith. Working as a team, they continued to engage in missionary work, establishing the Zoradee Mission in 1924.

Their devotion and total commitment was so keen that they seldom, if ever, took furloughs together. Instead, one would remain in Liberia while the other returned to the States to rest and promote the work. Sister Holmes took her first furlough in 1939, almost 40 years after beginning to do missionary work. The Holmes were to continue to work at Zoradee for 15 years after my arrival in 1943. After Brother Holmes' death in 1958, Sister Holmes would remain at Zoradee an additional six years. She would finally leave Liberia, shortly before her death, with a total of 63 years of service to her credit.

Needless to say, the all-out and totally unselfish dedication of missionaries like the Holmes made me to realize that I was stepping into the company of some mighty tall people.

Earlier, Brother Davis had promised me that with the arrival of the dry season steps would be taken to build me at least a reasonable facsimile of a house. Until then, however, it would be necessary for me to take up residence in an existing hut there on the mission grounds.

One look was all it took to assure me that I'd have plenty of tales to share with the folks back home if I ever made it back for a furlough. My quarters were strictly native in every sense of the word. The walls of the hut, which had been constructed by driving sticks into the ground and dabbing them with mud, had already begun to wear away from the onslaught of several rainy seasons. Before long, I was told, the "bugabugs" would begin to make a meal of the sticks. The next step would be a total collapse of the thatched roof from a lack of support. Fortunately I was able to move out before that fateful day arrived.

My meager household furnishings consisted of an

army cot, my trunk, the contents of the trunk, a mosquito net, a makeshift chair, and some crude wooden boxes I had managed to scrounge.

It took but a few missionary meals to show me at least one reason Liberia was often referred to as the "White man's graveyard." Wartime conditions had made it even more difficult to obtain provisions, and it proved necessary for us to pretty well live off the land. We considered ourselves blessed, indeed, if an occasional meal included a canned good. What flour we did manage to purchase had to be carefully sifted to remove the worms. Thus, our diet consisted mainly of rice, chicken, eggs, and native fruit. Quite often we were presented with the weighty decision of whether we wanted the chicken or the egg.

The cassava plant, a tropical shrub with thick roots, provided the mainstay of the native diet around Beahjah. These edible roots, which are extremely high in starch content, served as the Liberian answer to our potato. The leaves of the cassava plant, when mixed with peppers, made a rather spicy green salad. There was, of course, an ample supply of palm oil on hand for cooking the native meals.

At certain times of the year, when the bugabugs would come out of the ground in swarms, the natives would add this delicacy to their diet, eating them either raw or roasted. Occasionally someone in the village would bring home some wild game such as monkey. The natives didn't seem overly concerned if the meat was rotten or filled with worms. Although I did join the villagers on several occasions, I made certain that anything I sank my teeth into was neither rotten nor wormy. I'm quite sure I never ate any monkey meat, as it has a most unique smell and is not something that can sneak up on you.

No doubt the natives would have enjoyed more rice in their diet, but it was a favorite practice of the village chiefs to sell what rice was available to the Mohammedans who ran the ore mines in Liberia at that time. Needless to say, what revenue was realized from these sales was not distributed among the households in the village.

While many of the Liberians living along the coast could trace their ancestry to the freed American slaves who had immigrated in the first part of the nineteenth century, the majority of those natives living inland were natives of that part of West Africa. Generally speaking, the natives living in the interior, such as those around Beahjah, were darker and shorter than those living along the coast. But, while they were not as tall, they were muscular, rugged, and capable of working long, hard hours if necessary.

One quick trip to the adjoining village was all it took. It would be some time before I could feel at ease with the native manner of dress. I had been duly forewarned of this condition, but like so many other things, I had shoved it to the back of my mind until I was forced to actually face it. While those living on the mission grounds had pretty well adopted a dress code acceptable to North American Christians, often wearing clothing given them by the missionaries, those in the village still "went native."

For the women this meant a loose-fitting skirt wrapped around the waist, leaving the upper body completely bare. A simple loin cloth was often the sole attire for the native men. It was a common sight to see a group of children playing in the nude. No doubt the hot, humid climate was a contributing factor to this lack of clothing, but something had to be done. With each passing day the job loomed larger and more complex.

Other than employment as porters, there was little work available for the villagers near Beahjah. The accepted duties of the man of the house were to clear the farmland, serve as the family tailor, and strange as it may seem, do the cooking. Most of his time, however, was spent in "palaver," a favorite Liberian pastime. The wives, on the other hand, were expected to do the actual farming, in addition to rearing the children.

From the very start I made it a practice to do nothing that would upset the Liberian way of life—that is as long as it didn't conflict with Scripture. Although it really upset me to see the women doing the difficult farm work, while the men sat around and talked, I quickly learned to bite my tongue and control my emotions. I had come to Liberia to evangelize, not Westernize.

I found the marriage contract to be a very binding relationship among the natives. While a Liberian man might not marry until well into his twenties, it was common practice for the girls to be given in marriage by their sixteenth birthday. Additional wives meant more farm hands, so polygamy was quite prevalent among the natives. Once they were converted to Christianity, however, there was little difficulty in accepting the Christian requirement of a monogamous relationship. This was one area of Liberian culture that was out of step with Scripture.

Making friends and being accepted among the natives proved to be a relatively easy task in most cases. While many of them were not fully familiar with the finer details of what we hoped to accomplish as missionaries, they were well aware that the presence of the missionaries spelled hope—if not for them personally, at least for the next generation. Those around the mission with whom I came into contact soon began to refer to me as "Mother," "Ma," or "The Old Lady." I'll have to admit that my initial reaction was to look unfavorably at that last term of endearment, but I quickly realized that nothing derogatory was intended.

Soon after my arrival, several of the village people came to present me with their "white thing." A "white thing" was anything white, such as an egg, a cola nut, or a simple piece of cloth. It served as a welcoming present of friendship. Until the natives were spoiled by the influx of mines in the country, they did not expect reciprocation in their gift-giving.

I also learned, after only a few days on the mission station, that the natives were easily offended if you failed to greet them in passing by. In addition, you were expected, without fail, to say "thank you" if you passed by and observed them working. Even if they were repairing their own hut, or clearing the brush from their own land, you were expected to thank them for doing the task. Although you might pass them several times that day, they would feel hurt if you did not stop each time and say "Thank you for working."

During my first few months at Beahjah I seldom left the station for any length of time, as I was kept hopping from sunup till sundown, acting as both teacher and nurse. At that time the mission concept was one of a combination church, orphanage, and school; a policy that was readily endorsed by the Liberian government in its requirement that a gospel mission offer secular education through the sixth grade. Hopefully the children would find salvation while living on the mission, and would return to their people with the message.

I SURRENDER ALL

While some of the children on the mission were truly orphaned, the majority were simply children who had been "given" to the mission by their parents. This was an accepted practice in Liberia at the time. The parents, in shifting the burden of feeding, clothing, housing, and educating their children to the mission, genuinely felt they were offering them their only chance in life.

After laboring morning, noon, and night for almost six months, I finally took my first preaching trip. Actually, it wasn't much of a trek, as I traveled only to the next village, a walk of an hour or so. But, to me, it seemed like real adventure. Brother Davis had mentioned the idea to me early in the week, and I had received it with great enthusiasm, feeling that at long last I was getting the opportunity to do some real missionary work.

All that week, when I could manage to squeeze some spare time in between teaching the three R's and applying bandages, I studied the text I would preach from. I knew I could take a short cut, and get by with telling the villagers a Bible Story I had committed to memory, but I hadn't left the United States and traveled to one of the most primitive areas of the world just to "play church." The task that lay before me demanded soul-searching, study, and prayer. I knew it would have to be a simple message, and not some deep theological discourse. Also, it would have to be somewhat shorter than I was accustomed to preaching, as it would have to be interpreted into tribal dialect.

I also made plans for what I'd wear for my inaugural message. I wanted the natives to be impressed with their new missionary lady, so I chose a white dress I'd brought with me, one I'd worn but a few times prior to leaving the States.

About 9:00 Sunday morning we struck out for the village, hoping to arrive in plenty of time to hold an 11:00 A.M. service. The natives were accustomed to eating their morning meal about 10:00. This would give them ample time to finish, and would leave them with no excuse for not attending service.

We had barely entered the dry season, and there was still an ample supply of mudholes in every direction. For the first thirty minutes or so I did a commendable job of avoiding the puddles, but upon approaching a rather rough section of the trail, I lost my balance and plunged headlong into a hole that I just knew the devil had prepared especially for me and my white dress. I could detect that the mission boys accompanying me were doing their best to conceal their amusement, and I guess I would have laughed myself had I been able to view the "tragedy" in retrospect. At that precise moment, however, all I could think of was my beautiful white dress completely covered with gooey mud.

I had two choices: I could forget about the service and return to the mission, or I could continue on, dragging about ten pounds of Liberian mud with each step I took. There was no third option available. My natural instinct was to call it a day, return to Beahjah, and plan the trip for some future time. Suddenly, however, my natural instinct was waylaid by my spirit, and I found myself thinking: "The lives of these people are so uncertain. There could very well be someone in that village who won't be around to hear you preach this time next week." With a sobering thought like that, a muddy dress rapidly lost its importance. I had come to Liberia to deliver the Gospel, not conduct a fashion parade. Just who was I trying to impress anyway—God or the natives?

The villagers were a bit shocked to see their new missionary attired in mud, but after explaining to them through an interpreter exactly what had happened, they seemed to quickly forget the incident and pay close attention to every word of the sermon. Somehow, even in their primitive minds, they were able to recognize and appreciate a spirit that put the "God way" ahead of personal pride.

God certainly blessed our meeting that Sunday, and in the process I was taught an unforgettable lesson in the gentle art of Christian humility.

ELEVEN

The Northern Trek

Nancy could evidently tell that it had been a terribly exhausting and trying experience for me to share my life with her—especially under these circumstances—and she thoughtfully left me to my own musing.

I leaned back and closed my eyes, hoping that I could possibly take a short nap. No sooner had I closed my eyes, however, than a hundred thoughts and questions began racing through my mind—things like, "What will I do to keep myself busy back in the States?" "Where will I live?" "How will I be able to make ends meet?" "Where will I go to church?" "How can I possibly sit back and be an inactive saint after working night and day as a missionary for over 27 years?"

Rose McAllister, a veteran missionary whom I had met in Monrovia some two years earlier while I was processing into the country, had told me that one did not become a "real" full-fledged missionary until he had taken a lengthy trek back into the Bush. Over the past 18 months or so I had made several short trips to the neighboring villages, but as yet I had not attempted a trek.

In the early summer of '45, the Davises and I made a trip to Monrovia for supplies. As usual, we spent several nights in the Assemblies of God missionary home there. During our stay, I became acquainted with Mildred Williams, an Assemblies of God missionary who had been serving for the past two years in the southern part of Liberia. She was preparing to take a trek into the northwestern part of the country in the very near future, and asked if I'd like to accompany her.

In discussing the idea with Brother Davis, he suggested I go, assuring me that this would be an opportunity to get a real feel for the country, and perhaps find a location to establish a mission of my own sometime in the future. With the heavy emphasis placed on the operation of a mission school, doctrinal differences were somewhat overlooked in those early days, and a strong rapport prevailed among most Protestant missionaries.

So, after going back to Beahjah for a few days to gather some needed personal effects, I returned to Monrovia where I joined Mildred in mapping out our planned trek. Our goal was to reach the Kissi Tribe in the northwestern part of Liberia, about a day's walk from the Sierra Leone border. In reaching them, we would pass through the Kpelle Tribe, the Belle Tribe, and the Gbande Tribe.

Neither Mildred nor I was familiar with the northern part of Liberia, so in making plans for the route we would take, we were forced to rely upon a rather crude drawing supplied by one of the older missionaries at the Assemblies of God home. It had been suggested that we clear our proposed trip with the office of the Secretary of Interior, so several days before our planned departure we paid a visit to his office.

Upon learning that we wished to go into Kissi country, the Secretary became quite enthusiastic. "At the present time," he said, "we have no missionaries among the Kissi people." No doubt he was hopeful that upon our arrival we would take steps to establish a permanent station there.

Before leaving his office, he presented us with a letter, bearing his signature and the official government seal, instructing all District Commissioners, tribal chiefs, and village chiefs to fully cooperate with us and offer any possible assistance. "By presenting this letter," we were told, "each village will supply you with a hut and food for the night." The natives who accompanied us, we were assured, would have no trouble in obtaining food and lodging from the villagers.

The following day, which was Friday, was spent packing and making final arrangements for the six-week trek. Since taking enough canned goods for a six-week trip was out of the question, we decided to go by faith, take the Secretary at his word, and plan to live off the land. We did take, of course, an ample supply of coffee, salt, and pepper.

Other items taken included several buckets, some dishes and utensils, a few changes of clothing, bedding, our army cots, mosquito netting, and the two hammock carriers which had been built for us by a native carpenter in Monrovia.

Accompanying Mildred and me would be three mission boys from the Assemblies of God work in Monrovia, two native girls Mildred had brought with her from the mission in the South, and approximately a dozen carriers. We would change carriers each time we entered the territory of a new tribe. Joshua, one of the mission boys, would serve as our guide and liaison with the carriers.

We left promptly at 7:00 Monday morning, taking a flat bed truck up the Firestone Road to Belle Isle, a Lutheran mission station. The Firestone Road had been constructed by the Firestone Company, and connected several of its major rubber plantations with Monrovia. We arrived at Belle Isle in the early afternoon, and spent the night with the missionaries there.

By 7:30 the next morning we were on our way. A half mile or so from the Belle Isle Mission, we came to a river which was a hundred or so feet wide. Several canoe trips were necessary to ferry our group, as well as its paraphernalia, across, but we were soon disappearing into the Bush.

While I had known for some time that we would be taking hammocks with us, it had not really dawned on me until now that human beings would carry them as I was transported in style through the jungle. At first I balked at the idea and flatly refused to ride in the hammock, but at Mildred's insistence I reluctantly gave in and climbed aboard. But how my heart went out to those young men as they struggled over the rough terrain.

The hammocks, which were constructed by stretching canvas over a wooden frame, weighed close to fifty pounds. They were carried by four men, one on each corner, who supported the total weight on their heads. If the hammocks were to be carried for any distance, they would wrap the crown of their heads with banana leaves, thereby providing a cushion.

I guess the reason I felt so badly about using hammock carriers was because I knew the men had no choice in the matter. They were selected by their village chief, and their conscription was backed by Liberian law. After this trek I seldom used hammock carriers, preferring to walk instead. True to the prediction of Commissioner Mooney, this act of compassion would be instrumental in ruining my health, but I had come to Liberia to mend broken lives not break native backs.

We walked, or rather the natives walked, until about noon, averaging perhaps three miles an hour. While we rested at the edge of a village, several of the boys gathered wood for a fire. Within an hour we had eaten our meal and were back on the trail again.

We passed through a second settlement about 3:30, but decided to continue on to the next village before stopping for the night. We soon discovered the first error on our map, as it was after 8:00 when we finally arrived at our destination. According to our calculations, we had covered approximately thirty miles that first day. Joshua, being familiar with the Kpelle dialect, set out to locate the village chief, and within a few minutes we had been provided with a hut, a large cook pot, and some rice and chicken for our evening meal. As we were unpacking our bedding and attempting to establish some semblance of order for our one night stay, the mission girls entered with two buckets of hot water to be used in bathing.

After eating and taking a few minutes to rest, we again sent Joshua in search of the chief, this time to inform him that we wished to have a service that night. The chief was most receptive to the idea, and immediately dispatched a crier to run through the village instructing the natives to assemble at the "town kitchen," the public meeting place in the village.

By the time we arrived, there were perhaps 200 villagers gathered. While few, if any, of them fully comprehended our purpose in holding the service, most of them had at least a rudimentary concept of God, and knew that the missionary had come to do them "good."

Mildred spoke that first night, using Joshua as an interpreter, and sharing with them a simple story of Jesus. Afterwards, I attempted to teach them some easy-to-learn Christian songs, allowing Joshua to translate them into their tribal dialect. Like most Africans, these tribesmen appreciated a song with a lively beat, and I did my best to accommodate them in the songs I selected. Several of the women had brought their sassas, which were hollowed-out gourds with a net of beads attached. They sounded much like Mexican maracas.

By 7:30 the next morning, we had eaten breakfast, the boys had packed the gear, and we were back on the trail. The carriers, who were accustomed to eating but two meals a day, would not eat their morning meal until we stopped to rest at noon. They would not eat again until we had stopped for the night, regardless of what time it was. The natives felt it was very important to go to bed on a full stomach.

I felt like a real "Jungle Jane" that day, as it seemed we encountered almost every animal indigenous to Liberia. Within a span of 10 hours we saw pygmy elephants, pygmy hippopotami, bush cats, and snakes—including the much-feared boa constrictor. Within the next week or so I would add to this list leopards, wild boars, and alligators.

On the second day we were fortunate to arrive at a village about six in the evening. After eating and taking a few minutes to bathe and relax, we once again held ser-

The Northern Trek

vice. We did our best to have a service each night of our trip to the Kissi country. Several times, however, as we got further into the Bush, and the villages got farther apart, we found ourselves still on the trail at 10:00 P.M. On nights like this it was not feasible to have a meeting.

Four more days of treking brought us through Kpelle country and to the edge of the Belle nation. The night was spent at a Kpelle village on the border. After our arrival, the Kpelle chief sent a runner to the nearest Belle village, informing the chief that the missionaries needed a dozen carriers. Our Belle carriers were waiting for us when we awoke the next morning. Before departing, Mildred paid each of the Kpelle carriers $1.75, a quarter for each day of work, and the customary quarter tip.

On several occasions I had heard the Belle Tribe, one of the smaller ones in Liberia, referred to as the "forsaken tribe." It was surrounded on all sides by larger tribes, and had seemingly been forgotten by the Liberian government and the missionaries alike. Try as I may, I can recall but one incident that occurred during our four day walk through Belle country. Perhaps this one event made such an indelible impression upon me that all other happenings were crowded out. The incident to which I refer took place when we stopped to take an afternoon rest at Belle Yella, the tribal headquarters for the Belle.

As we sat in the open town kitchen, one of the village boys went to fetch the chief. Soon, he, joined by the village elders, appeared and seated themselves across from us. Without taking time to introduce himself or even greet us, the village chief asked rather bluntly: "What are you here for?" In answering him, Mildred explained that we were American missionaries on our way to Kissi country, and that we were looking for a place to establish a mission.

Very softly from the back, and almost under his breath, an aged village elder said in broken English: "Someday the Belle people will have their own missionary."

Upon entering Gbande country, the third tribe through which we would pass, we again switched carriers. The Belle boys had witnessed Mildred tipping the Kpelle carriers a quarter, so she had no choice but to continue the fine tradition. We would spend the next five days trekking through Gbande country, and it would be on this part of our trek that we would find the villages to be farther apart.

We had been on the trail for a full ten days now, and I guess that according to Rose McAllister's definition I was fast becoming a veteran missionary. Yet, there was something important missing—the winning of souls to Jesus Christ. In my heart I knew that I could never look into the mirror and see Pauline Gruse, the missionary, until I had been successful in doing this. Bandaging sores and teaching English just didn't seem too eternal.

We spent a total of six days trekking through Gbande country. The actual distance covered was perhaps no greater than that which we had traversed in the four days we spent in Belle country, but as we continued in our northeasterly course, we found the terrain more treacherous and the going much slower. It was about the third day of this leg of our trip that we found it necessary to "flash" our letter from the Secretary of Interior for the first and only time. Prior to this, our reception had been outstanding in every village we passed through or spent the night in.

We had stopped in a Gbande village just before sundown, fearing that if we continued on to the next village we might find ourselves still on the trail at midnight. Most of the villagers were working in the fields upon our arrival. In fact, the only adult we could find, other than an old woman, was the village chief, himself.

Approaching him in the most cordial and courteous way she knew, Mildred asked the chief for the customary hut, cooking pot, and food for the evening meal. As if he had not even heard her, the chief whirled around and started to reenter his hut. Again, and this time with her voice raised an octave or two, Mildred asked him for a hut, cooking pot, and something for our supper. "We have no pots!" he said gruffly, obviously ignoring our other requests.

I was beginning to get more than just a little nervous as Mildred reached into the pocket of her dress and drew out the letter we had been given by the Secretary of Interior.

"Do you mean to tell me that in this entire village there is not an extra cooking pot?" Mildred asked in a demanding tone. The chief didn't comment.

"I have a letter here from the Secretary of Interior in Monrovia," Mildred continued as she waved the piece of paper in his face. "It instructs all village chiefs to cooperate with us by providing a hut, a cooking pot, and some food for our meals. Now, if you refuse to cooperate, I have no choice but to send a boy back to the Commissioner's headquarters, informing him that you have failed to obey the orders of the Secretary. Furthermore, when we return to Monrovia, we will report your name and the name of your village to the Secretary, himself."

The chief didn't say a word, but the look of shock on his face was readily apparent. Disappearing into his hut, he reappeared in no time at all with a large cooking pot. Motioning to a hut across the road from his, he indicated that we would spend the night there. Before we had left, Mildred had also made the chief agree to our holding a service that night. A few minutes later, a small girl appeared at the door of our hut with some rice and chicken for our supper.

As soon as we were alone again, I asked Mildred, "Weren't you afraid to talk to the chief like that?"

"I was shaking in my boots," she confessed, "but one of the first rules for survival among these natives is to stay in command at all times. You'll find that some of these people are steeped in superstition and witchcraft, and at times are nothing more than tools of the devil. You have to stand up to them with the same holy boldness you would use against the devil, himself."

This was just another of the lessons I would put to good use in later years when I established my own mission station.

The final night of our trek through Gbande country was spent at Kolahun, the village where the Commissioner over the Gbande and Kissi tribes made his headquarters. Our accommodations that night, a large mud-brick hut, were a bit more plush than we had enjoyed in previous nights. Later that night, when we were visiting with the Commissioner, he explained that in making the bricks for these huts, cow dung was mixed with the mud. This supposedly served as an exterminator against the many insects so prevalent in Liberia.

Upon learning of our plans to spend some time among the Kissi people, the Commissioner dispatched a runner to the headquarters village for the Kissi, requesting carriers and informing the Paramount Chief that we were coming.

By eight o'clock the next morning we had crossed into Kissi territory. A walk of perhaps four or five more hours had us approaching the headquarters village.

Evidently a lookout had been posted, as when we were still a quarter of a mile or so out, we were met by a delegation numbering at least 200.

From the ceremonial dress worn by many of the people, coupled with the laughter and gaity that prevailed, we could detect that some type of celebration was in progress. We soon learned that we had arrived in the middle of the installation of the new Paramount Chief. He appeared to take special delight in our arriving during his inauguration, no doubt feeling that our presence added some degree of pomp and ceremony to the event.

As we continued our escorted walk into the village, we noticed that many of the villagers, especially the women and children, stared at us with an almost hypnotized look. We were to learn later that most of them had never seen a white person before that day.

Accommodations had already been prepared for us, and we were given one of the largest and nicest huts in the village. A few minutes later, the village chief came calling with his "white thing," a cola nut. Noticing that I didn't immediately begin to eat mine, he reached for it and gave it a big lick to show me it wasn't poisonous.

The next ten days were spent in this village, holding services both morning and night. Between services we talked with the village and tribal elders, trying to glean as much information as possible concerning the Kissi people. There was really no need to walk around the village getting acquainted, as the people were continually coming around our hut, many times just to stare.

One day, as we sat inside eating our noonday meal, it seemed as if the entire village was suddenly crowded outside our door. Soon, they were packed so tightly that little, if any, sunlight could force its way through the door of the hut. All we could see, as we looked out, were several dozen pairs of piercing eyes expertly sizing us up. I had already learned that the Liberian natives were expert character readers, with the unfaltering ability of determining whether or not the concern you manifested was genuine. As the villagers continued to press in, it seemed as if our air supply were being shut off, and I had the sudden fear of being suffocated.

Just then, a little old woman somehow managed to squeeze, push, and shove her way through the throng and to the door of the hut. Bowing almost to the ground, she humbly approached us with a plate bearing four bananas, her gift of welcoming. We thanked her, and she disappeared as quickly as she had entered.

All-in-all the reception from the villagers was quite cordial. However, there was one man, the witch doctor, who didn't seem too delighted with our coming. The witch doctor, or medicine man, of a village was in reality more powerful than the village chief, as he had a tremendous hold on the people through superstition, voodoo, and incantation. While this Kissi witch doctor wasn't familiar with the finer points of the message we were preaching, he understood enough to realize that we were offering the people something powerful enough to break the hold he had on them.

I'll never forget the intense feeling I had the first night we held service in this village. It was as if the Lord had reached down and cut through Satan's binding rope.

Four or five days after our arrival we received a visit from our friend, the witch doctor. He was a very large man, both horizontally and vertically, barely fitting through the door of the hut. Except for the small tassel of hair at the crown, his head was completely shaved.

Attached to the tassel was his "bag of medicine." The bag of medicine usually contained some simple article used by the witch doctor in "playing magic" with the people. He was indeed a sight to behold as he sauntered in and plopped himself down in one corner of the hut.

He couldn't speak a word of English and we were every bit as ignorant of the Kissi language. So, for the next half hour or so, we just stared at each other, no one uttering a single sound. Evidently he wanted to check the two missionaries out for himself. Perhaps he felt he could cast a spell on us and take care of his competition that way. Finally, however, he rose in disgust, let out a grunt, and left.

That night there was a noticeable drop in attendance at the service. The witch doctor had no doubt scared the people away by playing a little magic to convince them they should have nothing to do with the white "God women" and their strange ways. For the next few nights we had our faithful few, mostly women and children, but the turnout was certainly not what we had enjoyed before. Still, the rope had been cut, and I was confident that God, in His own time, would allow the saving message of Christ to be preached in its entirety without fear of remonstration from the village witch doctor.

All too soon it was time to pack our gear and head back to Monrovia. Isaac, one of the mission boys who had accompanied us, agreed to stay in the village for a few weeks before returning to the coast. We already had at least one convert from our efforts, and with Isaac continuing the work for a few weeks longer, we were confident that others would soon follow in making a start for God. The greatest testimony to these natives was seeing one of their own who had been delivered from the fears and superstitions that seemed to bind everyone so tightly.

A few years later I received word that a Swedish Pentecostal couple had gone in among the Kissi people, establishing a permanent mission station in the very village in which we had stayed.

Our return trip to Monrovia was pretty much a reversal of the trek we had made up into Kissi country. We did our best to spend the night in the villages where we had stopped on the way up. In fact, we even spent the night in the village of the uncooperative Gbande chief. This time, however, he was most cordial and accommodating.

The last night of our return trek was spent at Suehn Mission, an outpost sponsored by a Baptist missionary group. It had been almost six weeks since we had seen another white person, and the American meal we had was certainly pleasing to the palate. About noon of the following day we were able to secure truck transportation, and by late evening we were back in Monrovia to catch our breath and purchase supplies for our southern trek.

TWELVE

The Southern Trek

I could smell food being heated in the galley and assumed it was approaching time for the evening meal. It was now 10:00 A.M. New York time (or so I thought), making it 4:00 P.M. Frankfurt time—the time zone that was currently controlling my body. We had been in the air almost five hours now, and in less than three hours I would be landing in New York City—for the very last time.

My assumptions were proven right a few minutes later, as the flight attendants began bringing out trays of food. I still wasn't the least bit hungry, but from force of habit, more than anything else, I lowered my tray table nevertheless.

Upon arriving back in Monrovia, my bone-weary body issued an ultimatum: two weeks to recuperate from the rigorous northern trek, or else. However, Mildred was anxious to go south as soon as possible, and seeing that she was the senior member of our team, her will prevailed—at least somewhat.

The first morning after our return saw me drowsily dragging my exhausted body out of bed to accompany Mildred on a "shopping spree" to purchase the supplies we would need for our southern trek. Two days later we started making the rounds in an attempt to secure transportation down the coast to Greenville, the nearest settlement to Matroe Mission, an intermediate stop on our planned trip into the southern interior.

As it turned out, I did give my body at least a portion of the respite it demanded, as we were unable to find any transportation for a week or so. At that time there was no such thing as a coastal highway connecting the north of Liberia to the south. With our very limited budgets, hiring the services of a bush pilot was out of the question, so our only choice was to wait until we heard of a boat that was going south.

At last we got word of a Lebanese merchant who was planning a run down to River Cess, about two-thirds of the way from Monrovia to Greenville. From there we would be able to continue on by native surf boat.

Since we were reasonably certain we could acquire the services of some mission boys and girls at Matroe, we saw no reason to take any with us from Monrovia. As we boarded the open motor launch that morning, Mildred and I discovered we were the only passengers except for the merchant and his two-crew members.

Aside from the wooden shed covering the engine compartment, the boat was completely open. The launch had not been built with passenger comfort in mind, and there was none. Mildred and I found seats on the slanting roof of the engine compartment, and did our best to keep from sliding off in the constant tossing of the craft. Due to the heavy concentration of reefs that lined the coast of Liberia, it was necessary to travel several miles out to sea.

The going was slow that day, and by mid-afternoon we were still an hour or so out of River Cess. About this time the engine began making some rather unhealthy sputtering sounds, and before long it had conked out completely. The merchant assured us there was nothing to become alarmed about, as this happened often, and they'd have us going in a jiffy. A jiffy and thirty minutes later, however, the three men were still hard at work, and things looked none too promising. All the time the tide was washing us farther and farther out to sea.

We had been helplessly drifting for perhaps two hours when the merchant in River Cess began to worry about our failure to arrive. The owner of the boat had telegraphed River Cess the day before, informing his friend that he was coming. Taking his high-powered binoculars, the River Cess merchant went to a high rock overlooking the coast and began scanning the horizon. Just when he was about to give up hope, he spotted a tiny speck bobbing up and down in the choppy waters of the distant ocean. With the gut feeling that this was his Monrovian friend, he sent a native surf boat out to investigate.

It took our rescuers almost an hour to reach us. By the time we had spotted them, Mildred and I had gotten down to real business in our prayer meeting. The merchant and his crewmen had looked at us rather askance when we began to pray, but by the time we saw help coming we could tell they were silently cheering us on in our efforts to touch God. I remember thinking as I prayed: "How ironic to come as a missionary to the jungles of

I SURRENDER ALL

Liberia, only to drown in the Atlantic Ocean. I could have done this in New York."

After the surf boat finally came into view, it took another twenty minutes for them to reach us. After several moments of discussion between the merchant and the headman on the surf boat, it was decided that the best course of action would be for us to remain aboard the launch and allow the surf boat to tow us back to shore. By rowing against the tide and having to pull our crippled boat, it took almost two hours for the trip back. The sun was just beginning to disappear as we set foot on dry ground for the first time in more than twelve hours. River Cess looked like the closest thing to heaven I had ever seen. This had been a day to remember, and I certainly hoped it was not to be typical of our southern trek.

We spent the night at River Cess, and early the next morning left for Greenville on the same surf boat that had rescued us the night before.

The surf boat, which in reality was nothing more than a mammoth canoe, had been the mainstay of native Liberian coastal transportation for years. It was powered by approximately twenty rowers who propelled the boat with long, sturdy oars. Occasionally, if the wind was brisk enough and prevailed from the right direction, a lone sail would be raised to add to the power supply.

Our accommodations aboard the surf boat were no better than what we had been offered on the motor launch, except that we did have burlap bags filled with yard goods for seats, rather than the unyielding roof of an engine compartment. The trip that day was unusually long and rough, and by the time we reached Greenville, I had a case of seasickness that would have put the Portuguese freighter and spinach soufflé of some two years earlier to shame. It seemed like the world, along with its furnishings, was going around and around and around. I was so sick that I felt I would have had to get better to die.

Seeing my condition, the Lebanese merchant at Greenville was kind enough to offer us a room for the night. The next morning I was feeling somewhat better, so after having breakfast, we made arrangements to hire some local natives to row us and our supplies upstream to Matroe Mission. We arrived at Matroe shortly before noon, and were greeted by Miss Jenkins, the very gracious Open Bible missionary who was working in affiliation with Mildred's group.

Except for an occasional short trek, the next two weeks were spent on the Matroe station, teaching and providing medical care. One of the few trips we did make was to a neighboring village, where we met Reverend Matthews, an aged native pastor who had one of the most extraordinary tales to relate that I had ever heard. I'll do my best to reconstruct it the way it was told to me over thirty years ago:

Reverend Matthews had already been preaching the Gospel for several years when this episode occurred around the turn of the century. To make ends meet, he had left his native village in the southern part of Liberia and gone to Monrovia to "work for money." He had not seen his family for several months. One morning he awoke so homesick that he thought he'd surely die of heartbreak if he couldn't visit his wife and children.

So, with absolutely no money in his pocket, he boarded a native surf boat headed for Greenville. An hour or so out to sea, the headman of the vessel asked the preacher for his fare. Explaining his plight to the captain, the preacher begged and pleaded with him to be allowed to continue on to Greenville, assuring him that he'd pay double on his return to Monrovia. The pleading fell on deaf ears, however, as the captain told the preacher that if the fare was not paid immediately, he'd be thrown overboard. It was impossible, of course, for the preacher to come up with the money, so into the sea he went.

Reverend Matthews was an average swimmer, but certainly not capable of surviving fifteen or twenty miles of choppy sea. According to his own words, he was totally exhausted, and beginning to sink when he was completely enveloped by an overpowering wave. When he came to his senses, he discovered he was riding on the back of a large fish. As if by some supernatural force, the waves were keeping the fish afloat and washing it to shore. This same unexplainable power seemed to also be holding Reverend Matthews to the back of the fish.

The native pastor seemed unsure of the time lapse between being picked up by the fish and landing on the shore. When he arrived, however, there was a large group of natives present to witness what had happened. Upon examining the fish, it was determined that it had been dead for several hours. The only explanation was that God had "prepared a great fish" to deliver Reverend Matthews to shore.

I'll admit that my first reaction was to discount the tale, looking upon it as a bit far-fetched. Then, with almost the next heartbeat, my mind recalled a verse of

Scripture in Jonah: "Now the Lord had prepared a great fish to swallow up Jonah." If God could "prepare a great fish to swallow up Jonah," He could "prepare a great fish to transport Reverend Matthews." So, the prosecution rested, the case was closed, and I believed the account.

Our next stop, as we left Matroe and pushed our way more deeply into the southern hinterland, was Gdeapo (Gid-e-poo), a trek of perhaps six or seven hours. The mission station there was operated by Miss Ramsey, an Assemblies of God missionary working with Mildred's group. Since establishing the mission several years before, Miss Ramsey had run it single-handedly, except for the occasional visits from Reverend Johnson, the Missions Overseer for the southern part of Liberia.

Our arrival seemed to work wonders for Miss Ramsey, brightening her countenance and instantly re-igniting a spark of enthusiasm. We didn't have the heart to leave her right then, so for the next ten days or so Mildred assisted with the school and I did my best to provide some long-overdue nursing care. While we did manage to take a couple of short treks while at Gdeapo, we were back at the mission station by nightfall on both occasions.

The second of these treks, which was taken just three days before our departure from Gdeapo, will forever stand out in my memory. As if it were yesterday, I can still visualize Mildred and me sitting in the public kitchen as a group of the elderly villagers approached us with their gift of mutton and rice. As they humbly and graciously presented their token of friendship, one of the men who could speak broken English, said, "We beg you not go. Please . . . our children need you." It was difficult to look into their pleading eyes and tell them we could not stay, but Mildred felt a definite burden to go farther into the interior, and I certainly did not feel qualified to establish my own mission at this time.

Miss Ramsey was the perfect example of the pioneering spirit adopted by the early women missionaries to Liberia. Prior to the 1950s, the majority of the missionaries to this country (at least the evangelical missionaries) were women. I'm told this was true in other parts of the world also.

Jonathan Swift once said, "Necessity is the mother of invention." This certainly was the case with the mission stations in Liberia that were "manned" by women. During our stay at Gdeapo I was constantly amazed at what Miss Ramsey, with the manual assistance of the natives, had been able to build, invent, and jerry-rig. With this courageous wornan, "where there was a will, there was a way." It was during our stay here that I got many of the ideas I would later employ in the building of my own mission.

Bright and early on a Monday morning, while the sun was still having difficulty peeping over the eastern horizon, we said farewell to Miss Ramsey and began the trek that Mildred felt would be a one-way trip for her. She felt certain that somewhere along the route God would show her the village where she was to establish her mission.

The outer extremity of our planned trip was no more than a four day walk, certainly nothing like the 16 day hike we had made into Kissi country on our northern trek. Possibly Mildred would feel that burning desire on the second or third day. As we wound our way farther into the jungle, I began to hope this would be the case.

About mid-afternoon of our second day out of Gdeapo, we had stopped to rest in a public piazza of a small village, when we were approached by a young native boy who was walking through from a village about five hours farther into the interior. Seeing us, and assuming that any white women this far back into the Bush would have to be missionaries, he came over to satisfy his natural curiosity. When we had assured him we were indeed missionaries, he told us that he was on his way to Matroe, on orders from his village chief, to beg for a missionary for his people.

For a moment or so Mildred said nothing, but I could look right into her head and see the wheels turning and the bells ringing. No, she didn't say a word, but I could read her thoughts as if they were my own.

"There's no need for you to go to Matroe," Mildred told the boy. "She and I are from Matroe and we were already headed for your village. Return and tell your chief to expect the missionaries in his village tomorrow."

After he had left, Mildred asked me what I thought of the idea of knocking off for the day. "It's already almost 4:00," she reasoned. "The nearest village, according to the boys, is another three hour walk. By leaving at 7:00 tomorrow morning, we could get to our village by noon."

I agreed.

The chief of the village where we were resting had already offered us a hut for the night, so one of the boys was dispatched to inform the chief we had decided to take him up on his offer.

After napping for a couple of hours, we had supper, then held our nightly service. I was the preacher for the evening, and felt strongly impressed to speak to them of a Savior who had not only died for their sins, but who had provided for the healing of their bodies as well. In the past I had been a bit reluctant to introduce the subject of "divine healing," as it was difficult for the natives to grasp something as intangible as faith, especially when they knew the missionaries normally carried the basic medical supplies with them.

At the end of my message I asked those wanting healing to step to the front. You can imagine my surprise when almost two dozen filed to the front of the piazza. Once again God had gone beyond the natural instincts of man in honoring His Word.

Shortly after sunup the next morning we were back on the trail for what I felt would be the final leg of our trek into the southern interior. I had watched Mildred throughout the night as she tossed and turned in a desperate attempt to sleep. Yes, I felt almost as strongly as Mildred that this *would* prove to be the village God had selected for her.

While we had brought hammocks with us, we had chosen to walk the first two days of our trip. Today, however, we decided to go ahead and ride the hammocks since we would be on the trail less than half the day and it wouldn't prove too much of a burden on the carriers. An hour or so out, however, I wished we had not made that decision, as we came upon some of the most dense and treacherous jungle I had ever encountered in my stay in Liberia.

The footpath, which was dangerously uncertain to begin with, was made even more hazardous by the creeping vines and broken limbs that dotted the way. The tall grass that lined the sides of the trail rose above the heads of our carriers. In places it seemed to meet at the top, forming a tunnel effect. One could not help but wonder what we would do if we were to encounter a wild animal around the next curve in the trail. We knew they were all around us, and were aware of our every move. We could only hope that we would do nothing to infringe upon their property rights. I could tell from the expression on the faces of the carriers that they weren't too fond of the situation themselves.

We had been trudging through the dense jungle for perhaps three hours when suddenly we came upon a stream that was swollen out of its banks. In dry time the water would have been no deeper than our waists, and wading it would have been a simple matter. During flood time, however, the water would be twice as deep, and getting across would present a stiff challenge. There were the remains of a swinging vine bridge that had once spanned the stream, but time, the raging flood waters, or maybe even someone from the notorious Devil Bush Society, had destroyed it.

For the next few moments Mildred and I put our heads together, doing our best to determine just what to do. Asking the boys to carry us across on the hammocks would be dangerous and inhumane. But, neither of us was anxious to wade across, and swimming the stream was even more out of the question. Finally, the lead carrier, seeing that we were determined to get across somehow, suggested that we ride on the shoulders of the men. He insisted that despite the weight it would be easier for one man to carry us than for four carriers to coordinate their efforts with a hammock in the rapid, totally unpredictable current.

The lead boy went first, checking the depth of the water, and trying to map out the safest path. My carrier went next, closely followed by the boy carrying Mildred. Bringing up the rear of our entourage were the boys carrying the empty hammocks and our supplies. By the time we were halfway across, the water was past the shoulders of the carriers, and it was necessary for them to tilt their heads back to breathe. The crossing couldn't have taken more than three minutes, but it seemed every bit of an hour.

After resting for a few minutes on the opposite bank, we were on our way again. We decided to walk for the remainder of the trip, allowing the boys to carry the empty hammocks. As we continued to weave our way ever-deeper into the interior, I began to wonder just what these native carriers thought of us. Could they detect the love and compassion, or did they look upon us as just another white exploiting them? If only they could see. If only they could understand the intensity of the burden burning within.

Two-and-a-half hours of hard walking brought us to the edge of Seabeahta, the settlement both Mildred and I felt the Lord was leading her to. Just as the village was coming into sight, we were met by a delegation of men from the town. Apparently the boy had made it back to his chief with the message that we were coming.

Relieving the hammock carriers of their burdens, the village men pointed to the hammocks, indicating they wanted us to climb aboard. Then, taking off in a trot, they started for the village. The closer they got, the faster they ran. The men were not experienced carriers, and as the ride got bumpier and bumpier, it became virtually impossible to keep from falling out. Somehow we made it, however.

Entering the village, our carriers ran throughout the town, showing us off and announcing our arrival. When we had made the rounds, we were carried to the public kitchen, where we were formally introduced to the chief and the elders.

The welcome and reception we got was by far one of

the best we had received. We were given one of the nicest and most spacious huts in the village and plenty of chicken and rice for our supper. We were made to wonder who had been evicted from his home to make room for us. We knew enough about the villages to know this was not a motel room reserved for guests. Before leaving, the chief assured us we would have his full cooperation in having a service each night.

After we were alone, Mildred said, "Pauline, this is the place! If there was ever any doubt, it's gone now. This is the place!" I had to admit that I shared Mildred's feelings. It certainly did appear that God had led Mildred to the perfect place for her to build the mission of her dreams.

I stayed with Mildred in Seabeahta for almost two months, helping her make plans for the mission station, and doing what I could to provide the much-needed clinical care. Aside from bandaging cuts and scrapes and helping new mothers take care of their babies, I treated dozens of cases of yaws, an infectious tropical disease that affected so many of the natives. While not a venereal disease, its symptoms were very similar to that of syphilis, and could be effectively treated only with penicillin.

I was anxious for a real move of God among the natives in Seabeahta. I would be leaving for the coast in a matter of weeks, and I did not want to return without seeing a revival erupt. I was deeply troubled by the fact that we had not been making the progress I was sure God intended for us to make. The villagers seemed more interested in appeasing the evil spirits that lurked everywhere than they were in obeying the voice of God, the Spirit that could free them from this bondage of fear and oppression.

Late one night, as I lay exhausted on my cot, reflecting on these things, my mind was directed to a portion of

Scripture found in Acts. Turning there, to refresh my memory and gain fresh inspiration, I read:

> *Many of them also which used curious arts brought their books together, and burned them before all men (Acts 19:19).*

This was the answer to the breakthrough our hearts and souls demanded! We'd build a bonfire and announce a general "ju-ju burning." From the youngest to the oldest, it seemed that every villager had his ju-ju, or special medicine, which he carried with him to please the evil spirits. While it might be nothing more than a rusty piece of metal, or a ten cent coin attached to a piece of string which was worn around the neck, the owner believed it possessed tremendous power both for and over him. It was more than just a good-luck charm, and their unrestrained obedience to the evil spirits gave these ju-jus real satanic power. The village would never know freedom from these evil spirits until the ju-jus had been destroyed.

In discussing the proposal with Mildred the next morning, she was as excited about the idea as I had been. It was decided that for the next three nights we would announce a prayer meeting and ju-ju burning for Friday night. Until then, we would preach in the future tense from the scripture, "Greater is he that is in you, than he that is in the world." Somehow the natives must be taught that they could not have this all-powerful spirit within until they had destroyed their ju-jus and put their total trust in God.

Try as we might, there was nothing in the expressions of the people to indicate whether or not the message of our preaching was getting through. We'd just have to patiently wait and see how many showed up for the Friday night prayer meeting. Friday evening came, and I was almost afraid to stick my head out the door. I guess my faith was somewhat weak right then, as I was fearful that I'd look out and see but a handful gathered around the wood that had been stacked for the bonfire. Finally I could put it off no longer, and I emerged from the hut.

Praise God! Hallelujah! Thank you, Jesus! It looked like the entire village of Seabeahta was gathered and just waiting for the match to be struck. Once again God had done a mighty work in honoring His Word.

Included among the many who brought their ju-jus forward to be burned was the village chief, himself. Later that night, he told us that even in recent months he had eaten "human soup" over his rice.

Even the medicine man came up with his ju-jus, but as we learned later, he kept back his favorite and most potent one. The next week, however, at the close of a service, the medicine man walked to the front and handed me his final ju-ju, a small, black, high-polished gourd. "This has power to kill a man, Ma," he said as he gave it to me.

My first thought was to keep the medicine man's ju-ju as a souvenir. Why, I could already see the effect this, along with the accompanying story, would have on audiences back in the States. As I thought it over, however, I realized that it must be destroyed in the same fashion as the others. How would it look for the missionary to keep the very thing she had instructed the natives to destroy?

I had been in Seabeahta with Mildred for better than two months now, and I felt that it was time for me to return to Beahjah. In my absence, the Davises had left for furlough in the States, and had been relieved by the Petty family. In approximately three months, I, too, would be leaving for furlough, and I was certain there would be a multitude of things to do at Beahjah in assisting the Pettys in getting established and oriented.

I was determined to walk back to the coast, so I left my hammock with Mildred. From Seabeahta I treked to Gdeapo, where I spent a couple of days with Miss Ramsey. From there I walked to Matroe, where I stayed several days with Miss Jenkins. The second day there, I learned that Reverend Johnson, the mission's overseer, was meeting a bush pilot there for a flight into Monrovia. If I waited another day I could hitch a ride with him.

Arriving in Monrovia, I devoted the better part of three days to rest and recuperation at the A. G. home. It was then on to Beahjah to meet the Pettys and start making preparations for my departure.

THIRTEEN

Furlough Away from Home

It was almost 11:00 by my watch—more than two hours since my last little walk—past time to get up and stretch my legs for a few minutes. As I made my way down the aisle, my attention was forcibly drawn to the many sad faces and empty countenances I saw. Here were members of the middle and upper crust of society, with more of this world's goods than any generation before them, yet totally empty and merely living a day-to-day existence. Then, it dawned on me—I probably looked just like them—like life had no meaning and I was merely playing my part in the cruel drama of life.

I had to get hold of myself. I couldn't allow the disappointments of life to ruin my Christian witness. I couldn't quit living just because I was having to retire from the missions field, and as long as I remained a resident of Planet Earth, I had to do all within my power to influence others to Christ. After all, I was retiring as a missionary, not as a Christian.

Still, it was difficult to be happy when your heart was separated from your body by several thousand miles.

March, 1947 finally arrived. At times, during the three-and-a-half year tour, I had honestly wondered if I'd live to see this day, but here it was and it was time for furlough. There had been plenty to do upon returning to Beahjah, but the three months had seemed to drag by so slowly. Was it the confinement of working on the station? Did I actually miss the excitement and danger of treking in the Bush and spending the night in strange villages? Was I overly excited about returning home to see loved ones and share missionary tales?

While with the Pettys, I had received a letter from Wynn T. Stairs, Foreign Missionary Secretary for the United Pentecostal Church, inviting me to apply for license with that organization. The Pettys were sponsored by the United Pentecostal Church, but I had remained with the Church of Jesus Christ, the group I had originally been licensed with. I replied, telling Brother Stairs that I'd give the matter some prayerful consideration and get back with him on my return to the States.

A week before my scheduled departure from Roberts Field, I left Beahjah for the day-and-a-half trek to Arlington, the trading post on the St. Paul River. Arriving in Arlington shortly after noon of the second day, I discovered I had missed my boat and would have to wait until the next morning to catch the "chug-chug" to Monrovia.

Immediately upon arriving in Monrovia, I purchased

my airlines ticket. Then, for the next few days I just loafed at the A.G. missionary home. The day before I was to leave, Charlene Thompson, a newly-arrived Assemblies of God missionary, gave me her almost-new imitation fur coat. "The March weather is still cold back in the States," she told me. "I'm sure I won't be needing this in Liberia, and if I kept it here it would rot before I had a chance to use it again." I felt foolish taking it, as it didn't exactly fit my personality. It certainly didn't fit my frame, seeing that Charlene was a good six inches taller and at least 60 pounds heavier than I. But, I took it nevertheless, and was later grateful that I had.

There were no vehicles available at the home the day I was to leave, so I reluctantly took a taxi the 40 mile trip to Roberts Field. While I had seen a few improvements in Liberia during my stay, none of them had been in the area of domestic transportation. The taxi ride was as bad, if not worse, than the one I had taken on my arrival in Liberia.

My scheduled flight was more than four hours late, and I was beginning to wonder if it would be as difficult to get out of Liberia as it had been to get in some three years earlier. Finally, however, we were air-borne, and I could settle back and try to relax. It was strange—I had the feeling I was *leaving* home, not returning.

The Pan Am DC-6 was my first commercial flight, but a few seconds on board was sufficient to thoroughly convince me that I preferred it to the military plane on which I had flown some three-and-a-half years earlier. Intermediate stops were made at Dakar, Senegal; Lisbon, Portugal; and Ponta Delgada in the Azores. From there it was on to Idlewild in New York City.

Darkness had settled over the city, and a light, cold

rain was falling, as I stepped from the plane and made my way towards the customs area. After clearing, I went straight to the ticket counter, hoping to get an immediate connecting flight to South Bend. "The next flight to South Bend is at 10:30 tomorrow morning," the young ticket agent told me as she looked up from her schedule. She must have detected the look of total bewilderment and desperation upon my face, as she added: "Let me give you the name of a good hotel downtown. Just give it to a taxi driver, he'll know where it is."

Walking to the taxi stand, I couldn't understand why I was feeling so nervous and unsure of myself. Had I been away from civilization so long that I felt like a stranger in my own country? Was this still my own country? The oversized coat I was wearing didn't do anything to restore my self-confidence and composure.

Arriving at my hotel, I saw I had indeed been directed to a "good" hotel. Evidently my "fake fur" had led the ticket agent to believe I was loaded. I felt even more conspicuous as I walked up to the desk of what proved to be one of the best hotels in New York's theatre district. My nerves were almost shattered by the time the bellhop had collected his tip and left me to myself.

I felt on the verge of starvation, but I couldn't bear the thought of going to the dining room and facing the world. Looking at the room service menu, I discovered that my budget would afford nothing but chicken, so chicken is what I ordered. After eating it, however, I sincerely wished I had chosen to starve. If this was what one of the finest hotels in New York City had to offer, I hadn't been so bad off in Liberia after all.

My sixth floor room was getting stuffy, so I opened the window a crack, hoping to invite in some fresh air.

The drizzle of a few hours earlier continued to fall, causing several hundred pairs of headlights to cast a shimmering reflection upon the pavement below. It was well into the morning before restless sleep was able to drown out the honking horns, wailing sirens, and other strange sounds of the city.

I was greeted early the next morning by an overcast sky and the promise of more rain at any moment. Hurriedly dressing, I donned my grotesque fur, grabbed my battered suitcase, and without bothering to eat breakfast, paid my bill, and stepped outside to flag a taxi for the airport. Upon arriving at Idlewild, I had more than two hours before my flight was to leave.

After purchasing my ticket and checking my luggage I found a seat in the waiting room where I could be off to myself. I couldn't understand it. Why had I suddenly become so deathly afraid of people. I had always been a bit shy, but this was bordering on the ridiculous. I felt so conspicuous—like everyone in the airport was staring straight at me. Surely things would change as soon as I landed in South Bend and was met by Doris and the ladies from the church.

Finally! The announcement was made—my flight was ready for boarding. Four uneventful hours later we landed in South Bend, at an airport that had not existed when I left in '43. The rain I thought we had left in New York had followed us to South Bend, and needless to say, this did nothing to help my already-dampened spirits. As the plane slowly taxied up to the passenger terminal, I craned my neck in a desperate attempt to see a familiar face or a waving arm that I recognized. I saw none, but then it was possible that they didn't realize this was my plane that had just landed.

As I deplaned and walked towards the terminal, I wondered if I'd changed that much—how close would I have to get before Doris and the others would recognize me and come running with outstretched arms? I was getting closer and closer, and there was still no sign of anyone. Perhaps only passengers were allowed to leave the terminal. I'd just have to wait until I was inside the building.

I stepped inside, looked all around anxiously, but saw no one that I recognized. What had happened? Perhaps they had been delayed in traffic because of the weather. Sure, that was it! I'd just go over to the baggage claim area, get my suitcase, and wait there. It'd just be a few moments. I waited for thirty minutes . . . an hour . . . still no one had showed up.

"So, you thought your *Friends* would be here to meet you," the devil impishly whispered in my ear. "They don't care about you. Here you've risked your life for the past three years, while they've lived in the lap of luxury, and they don't care enough about you to meet your plane. Some friends, huh?"

It took a moment or so, but I finally rebuked Satan in the name of Jesus, found a nickel, and placed a call to Doris.

"Pauline!" she exclaimed. "We weren't expecting you until tomorrow. Your telegram said the 15th. The ladies from church will sure be disappointed that they missed you, Pauline. Virgil's not home right now, so I have no way to pick you up. Could you grab a taxi and come on out?"

"See!" I tauntingly told the devil as I hung up the phone. "I knew all along that this was just another one of your lies!"

Several days after my arrival in South Bend, I received

a call from Brother Hancock, the Missions Secretary for the Church of Jesus Christ, urgently requesting my presence at the annual convention to be held in three weeks.

The meetings were barely under way when I sensed that something had caused the organization to de-emphasize its missionary activity. From several financial reports that had been read it was evident that I was the sole surviving foreign missionary in the fold. After service, as I shared my feelings with Brother Hancock, he assured me I had read the situation correctly. It had been for this reason, he told me, that he had been so insistent on my attending the convention.

"Do you still feel a call to Liberia?" he asked me. After assuring him that the burden was stronger than ever, he suggested I consider contacting some other Pentecostal organizations for possible support. Upon mentioning that I had been indirectly approached by Brother Stairs of the United Pentecostal Church, Brother Hancock quickly suggested, "Then, by all means get in touch with them—immediately!"

That night, before going to bed, I carefully drafted a letter to Brother Stairs, describing in detail my current predicament, and informing him of my interest in applying for ministerial license, as well as missionary status, with the United Pentecostal Church. Several days after my return to South Bend, I received his reply, asking if I could possibly meet with the Foreign Missionary Board in early May. The meeting would be held in De Ridder, Louisiana. The thing I remember best about this meeting is that E. L. and Nona Freeman, outgoing missionaries to South Africa, met the Board at this time also.

After meeting with the Board and getting its tentative approval, I returned to South Bend and spent a few days with the Klapps. From there I went by bus to Toledo, where I visited with my brother, Leland, for a couple of weeks. Next, I drove down to Lima and stayed with Bob and his new bride for a few days. Bob, who would turn twenty later that year, had become a full-grown man in my absence. There would always be that empty spot in my heart, but I still felt, that all things considered, my decision to allow him to live with his aunt and uncle had been the best for all involved.

Once more returning to South Bend, I made the Klapp home my base of operations, as I found many of the churches in Indiana and Ohio opening their pulpits to me. Seemingly, "Returned Missionary, Pauline Gruse," with all her eerie tales of the West African jungle, was more in demand than "Itinerant Evangelist, Pauline Gruse" had been in previous years.

The 1947 General Conference of the United Pentecostal Church, held in Dallas, Texas, convened in late October. It was during these meetings that I was formally introduced to the organization as an outgoing missionary to Liberia. It was also during this conference that approval was given to my request of delaying my return to Liberia until the latter part of 1948.

While at the conference I was able to arrange quite a number of preaching engagements for the following months. Most of these were in Indiana, Ohio, and the surrounding states. Hopefully, these opportunities would enable me to raise my fare and a good deal of my support before departing for the second tour.

Pentecostals were not bonafide members of the "jet set" in 1948, so I didn't even bother making plans for the next General Conference, to be held in Long Beach, California, a "fur piece" from South Bend.

FOURTEEN

Maheh, Bomi Hills, and Quoy Town

I didn't think it was possible, but I must have been dozing, for the next thing I knew the Captain's voice was on the intercom: "Ladies and gentlemen, it looks like our flight is going to be on time, and possibly even a little ahead of schedule. We should be landing in New York City in less than an hour-and-a-half. The weather in New York City is partly cloudy and mild, with a current temperature of 82."

I looked at my watch. It was 11:30. I felt almost drugged—like I had been in a deep, deep sleep for days. It was several minutes before I could think clearly and get my bearings. I looked out the window at the far-reaching expanse. For as far as I could see, there was nothing—absolutely nothing. Suddenly, I was hit once more by the feeling of terrible loneliness. I must feel, I thought, much like the young serviceman going overseas, leaving everything behind that really matters—not sure if he'll ever return. The only difference was I knew I'd never return. All I would have would be my memories.

It had been an action-packed and fun-filled twenty months, but now my extended furlough was finally drawing to a close. I had enjoyed every minute of it—being with old friends, especially the Klapps, and meeting so many new people as I traveled throughout the Midwest on deputation. I had found it easy to get caught up in the postwar spirit of enthusiasm and optimism that still prevailed in the States, but now the excitement of returning to Liberia seemed to be my strongest emotion. This time, no doubt, I would be establishing my own station, and would finally get to be a real missionary. The first tour had been boot camp, but now I was off to war.

I had just assumed that I would fly out of New York on my return to Liberia, but in discussing the matter with Brother Stairs, he suggested that I travel by boat and depart from New Orleans.

"You've been on the go constantly for the past year or so, Sister Gruse, and I'm quite sure you could use the time to rest, relax, and get your thoughts together. Lord knows you won't get the chance once you've returned to Africa."

At first I rather balked at the idea, as going by boat would delay my arrival in Liberia by at least a month. But the more I thought about his suggestion, the more I liked it. I really could use the rest, and I had enjoyed my cruise aboard the *Maritimos* some five years earlier.

So, early Friday morning, on November 19, 1948, I boarded a bus in South Bend for the 1,000 mile trip to New Orleans. It was late Saturday when I finally arrived.

I had been given the names of several Pentecostal people living in the New Orleans area, but after more than 36 hours of helplessly bouncing around, inhaling nauseating diesel fumes, and eating in greasy spoons, all I wanted was a hotel with a bed, a bath, and a decent restaurant. Upon finding these accommodations, I didn't so much as leave my room, except at mealtime, until early Monday morning.

I was up at the crack of dawn on Monday, and after a light breakfast, caught a taxi to the dock where I was to board the *Del Viento*, a ship registered to the Delta Lines. Normally the *Del Viento* took the most direct route from New Orleans to the coast of West Africa, but for some reason, which was never really clear to me, we made several port calls in South America before heading east across the Atlantic.

Upon boarding, I was immediately shown to my cabin. Unlike the *Maritimos*, the *Del Viento* was not terribly overcrowded, and I was able to enjoy the privacy of my own room. It was small, yet comfortable, and would afford me ample opportunity to relax, meditate, daydream, make plans, and catch up on my long-overdue sleep and correspondence.

At lunch, the second day out to sea, I met the Dix family, who were Missionary Alliance missionaries returning for their second tour in the Belgian Congo. Upon learning that I was traveling alone, they graciously invited me to join them, whenever I wished, in shipboard activities, and to accompany them ashore on our various stops in South America.

Several nights later, Mr. Dix entertained a number of the passengers with a slide presentation from their previous tour of duty. Of special interest were the shots taken of natives who were "butchering" an elephant they had just killed. I had to admit, however, that it was bordering on the grotesque to see the men crawling around inside the huge animal they had just slit open. I was certainly thankful that I had allowed my stomach a few hours to digest supper before viewing the slide presentation.

Of our South American port calls, the two I remember best are Fortaleza and Recife, both in Brazil. Our stop in Recife was the last before heading east out to sea. On more than one occasion, in the smaller ports, it was not possible for the *Del Viento* to enter the harbor, as it had not been dredged deeply enough to handle large ocean liners. In cases like this, we would drop anchor several hundred yards out to sea, then go ashore by motor launch.

One afternoon, at a port somewhere between Fortaleza and Recife, Mrs. Dix barely missed serious injury as she was boarding the motor launch to go into town. Just as she was stepping onto the smaller craft, a wave pushed it against the ship, pinning her foot between the two boats. At first no one thought much about the incident, as nothing appeared broken, and Mrs. Dix insisted there was no pain. By the time we had arrived at shore, however, the foot had swollen to gigantic proportions, and it was impossible for her to walk on it. Locating a policeman, we got directions to the nearest doctor. Fortunately, examination proved the injury to be just a bad bruise, but our tour of the town had to be cancelled.

Finally, after almost 33 days aboard the *Del Viento*, we arrived at Dakar, the seaport capital of Senegal. Several hours later, we were once again at sea. Our next stop would be Monrovia, the capital of Liberia.

Upon nearing Monrovia, I was somewhat surprised to

discover that we would not be able to actually enter the harbor. For some time there had been talk of deepening the port to allow the huge ore boats to enter, and I had just assumed that these improvements had been made during my two-year absence. So, as I had done on several occasions in South America, I found myself boarding a small motor launch for the final few hundred yards.

It was late Friday afternoon, December 24th, when I arrived in Monrovia. All government offices had closed at noon for the Christmas holidays, and would not reopen until Monday morning. So, upon claiming the luggage I had carried with me, I caught a taxi and went to the Assemblies of God home to spend Christmas and wait to clear into the country the following week.

I suffered a severe case of mixed emotions that weekend—I missed being with family and friends for Christmas, I dreaded the governmental red tape that I knew I would encounter on Monday, and I was anxious to get settled and begin functioning as a missionary.

The long, lonesome weekend was finally over, and to my pleasant surprise, clearing into the country wasn't nearly as difficult as I had feared it would be. Did I know my way around better, were they easier on veteran missionaries, or had they streamlined procedures somewhat with the ending of the war? To be honest, I didn't really care what their reason was. I was just happy to get everything approved, processed, and stamped, so I could be on my way and about the Lord's business.

In the final meeting with the Missions Board, several weeks before my departure, I was informed that I would be initially assigned to Maheh Mission Station, rather than return to Beahjah where I had spent much of my first tour. I would be working with Georgia Regenhardt, a first-term missionary from Mississippi, who had replaced the Haney family in the summer of 1947. I was assured that after a year or so full consideration would be given to my desire to launch out and establish my own station.

Sister Regenhardt, who had served as an instructor at Pentecostal Bible Institute prior to coming to Liberia, was about my age, give or take a year. We found that we had much in common and instantly established a warm and lasting friendship.

One of the first things I noticed upon arriving at Maheh was the increased emphasis being placed on the spreading of the Gospel to the surrounding villages. There had always been efforts made to reach the natives with the message of Christ, but heretofore it had sadly taken a back seat to the operation of the mission school—the taking in of orphans, the teaching of the three R's, and the bandaging of cuts and scrapes.

I, like all the missionaries before me, had been terribly disappointed and disillusioned upon learning that the preaching of the Gospel was something you did in your spare time, but I had been repeatedly assured that there was little, if anything, that could be done about it. The main reason the Liberian government was so gracious in allowing us to work in their country, I was told, was the educational and medical services we could offer.

Priorities were quickly changed, at least in the ranks of the United Pentecostal Church, with the election of Wynn T. Stairs as Foreign Missions Secretary. One of his first communiques to the missionaries in Liberia "instructed" them to *immediately* begin de-emphasizing the mission school concept, freeing them to evangelize the outlying villages. With the increased efforts towards preaching the Word came a gradual cooling between the

Maheh, Bomi Hills, and Quoy Town

Pentecostals and other Protestant missionaries.

Shortly after her arrival, Georgia had been joined at Maheh by Gladys Robinson, a rookie missionary from Tennessee. Gladys, who had "preacher's blood," wasted no time in obeying Brother Stairs' directive, and immediately began treking to the neighboring villages to hold meetings. In recent weeks, however, her activities had been confined to Bomi Hills, a mining town about five hours from Maheh. Soon after her arrival in Liberia, Gladys had passed through Bomi Hills enroute to another village. As she walked through the town, the Spirit of the Lord suddenly came over her, strongly impressing her that she would soon return to this site to establish a work.

The mines in Bomi Hills, which were extremely rich in iron ore, had not been worked in years. In the early 1900s a German concern had operated the mines for awhile, but for some unexplained reason had suddenly discontinued their efforts. Then, in the mid '40s a long term agreement had been reached between the Liberian government and the Liberian Mining Company to reopen the mines.

With the reviving of the mining operations, there was an immediate influx of almost 3,000 native workers to the Bomi Hills area. The workers represented tribes from every part of Liberia. What a tremendous opportunity to spread the Gospel to even the most remote parts of the nation.

Approaching the Paramount Chief of the Gola Tribe, Gladys and Georgia were successful in obtaining a parcel of ground right outside the main gate to the mining area—the perfect location to open a work. For a few dollars they were able to secure a deed to the property from the office of the Secretary of the Interior. Of course, the land would revert back to the Gola people in the event the mission work was discontinued.

The situation was just too perfect to be mere coincidence, so Gladys and Georgia gladly accepted it as the will of the Lord—a confirmation of the feeling Gladys had experienced the first time she walked through the village. The Missions Department, upon being notified of the opportunity, agreed wholeheartedly with their decision.

So, in September of 1948 Gladys packed her bags and set out for Bomi Hills, leaving Georgia to run the Maheh station alone. For years the natives had traveled to Bomi Hills to worship *Genii*, one of their primary gods. Gladys knew she would have her work cut out for her, trying to introduce the One True Living God to these tribesmen, but there was no doubt about it—she was in the will of God and He was preparing to do a great work in Bomi Hills. There would no doubt be struggle and sacrifice, but failure was unknown in the center of God's will.

The first few days at Maheh were spent unpacking, rearranging, cleaning, and doing my dead-level best to somehow make my hut at least partially livable. I also used this time to reorient myself to living in the West African Bush. Within a week, however, providence and Georgia had dragged me into the full swing of things, and the States seemed like a million miles and at least a hundred years away.

Although we were under direct orders to spend more time preaching and less time on the station, we could not abandon the mission altogether. Liberian governmental regulations required that we maintain a regular school year, offering classes through grade six. In addition, we were expected to provide basic health care to the villagers. Failure to comply to the satisfaction of the education and health officials, would mean the loss of our visas. Thus, for us at least, the next few months continued to mean teaching, nursing, and hoping, planning, and praying for a better day—one when we would be able to devote more time to evangelizing the neighboring villages.

The next four months at Maheh were typically missionary—long days and short nights, along with the mountains, valleys, sacrifices and frustrations that were a part of the job.

About once a month Georgia or I would make the trip to Monrovia to check the mail and pick up what supplies our $50.00 monthly allotment would allow. Usually there would be at least one letter awaiting us, from someone back in the States, informing us that at a certain time on such-and-such day the Lord had burdened them to pray for us. Invariably, in retracing the past three or four weeks, we would discover that at that particular time one or both of us had been going through a severe trial.

Only an unmarried, West African female missionary could possibly understand the tremendous encouragement letters like this would bring. There was sure to be another struggle just around the next curve, but we could always be assured that right that moment, somewhere back in the States, there was some dear saint of God allowing himself to be used of God in intercessory prayer. What a joy it was to be able to meet these people when we returned for furlough.

Two services were held each day at Maheh. The children living on the mission were required to attend, and we could always count on several faithfuls from the village. Georgia and I would take turns in leading the services. In addition to preaching and teaching, my primary duty consisted of providing nursing care. Occasionally I would assist Jeanette, our native teacher, with the classes. Georgia's main job was the maintenance, upkeep, and remodeling of the mission.

On most weekends one of us would make the five hour walk to Bomi Hills to be in Sunday service with Gladys and do our best to lend her some moral support. In March, Georgia and I began to detect that Gladys was under a tremendous amount of stress. She was trying to do too much in too short a time. On several occasions we tried to mention it to her in a subtle way, but she would just brush it off, assuring us that she was fine and that there was absolutely no cause for our concern.

For some time now it had been a practice for our missions, in cooperation with a Black Pentecostal group from the States, to take turns hosting a three-day fellowship meeting. Bomi Hills had been selected as the site for the meeting in May. As the time drew near, however, Gladys realized and readily admitted that she was in no condition to handle the arrangements by herself. So, it was decided that I would go to Bomi Hills a week or so early and assist her in getting things ready. From the moment I arrived, I sensed that Gladys was on the verge of a nervous breakdown, and needed complete relief rather than assistance.

The next week or so was devoted to much fasting, prayer, and Bible study, not to mention the hours and hours of just plain old hard work.

We were just entering the rainy season, but Friday morning dawned with the promise of a day filled with warm sunshine and gentle breezes. Surely the Lord was already smiling His approval upon our efforts. The first service was scheduled for 2:00 that afternoon. This would give the villagers ample time to finish their noon meal and afford the missionaries and natives traveling from other towns plenty of time to make the trip.

As the morning continued to wear on, however, I became increasingly restless and fearful. Except for Gladys, Georgia, me, and the local villagers, the only ones present were a few natives who had drifted in from nearby settlements. What if no one showed up?

One o'clock came, and still no one had arrived. Georgia could detect the look of disappointment and despair on my face, and gently, yet sternly, reminded me, "Where two or three are gathered in my name, there am I in the midst of them." With a sermon like that, what else could we do but go ahead and start the meeting?

About 3:30, just as Georgia was getting up to preach, our first visitors arrived. Brother and Sister Richardson, along with Sister Martin, were Black Pentecostal missionaries from the States. For some time now they had been working at Gudage Mission, a station about eight hours from Bomi Hills. A resounding "Hallelujah" went forth as they walked into the thatched roof church. Georgia was more than happy to relinquish the pulpit long enough for the three missionaries to leave their testimonies.

The rain we had hoped would not come for at least three days was falling in torrents by time for the evening service. The thatched roof was amazingly waterproof, but there were no walls to hold out the driving rain. The weather, however, was no match for the outpouring of the Spirit of God. The first night there were 31 in the altar, and before the meetings had ended, nine had been filled with the Holy Spirit.

As the services continued the following day, several other missionaries arrived. None, however, had the impact of Pearl Holmes, who arrived late in the afternoon of the third day. Sister Holmes, who labored at Zoradee Mission with her husband, Aaron, had already devoted more than 50 years of her life to the country of Liberia. Since she was Black, herself, Sister Holmes possessed a unique rapport with the natives.

The few days I spent with Gladys convinced me more than ever that we should not leave her alone at Bomi Hills. She had to have some help, and it was only reasonable that I be the one to stay behind. I originally intended to stay six or eight weeks, but it would be almost eight months before I would feel the liberty to return to Maheh.

For the first two or three months I assumed complete responsibility for the operation of the Bomi Hills Mission. This included oversight of the school, routine health care, the conducting of all services, and feeble attempts at providing maintenance for the grounds. I had somehow been successful in convincing Gladys that it was best for all concerned if she restrict herself to complete rest. Her recovery would come much sooner this way.

About half way into the first week it became exceedingly apparent why Gladys had not been able to stand under the pressure. How could any one person ever keep up with all that was expected? By the grace of God, and no other way, I somehow made it and was able to keep my sanity in the process. By mid-summer Gladys was well on her way to recovery and capable of reassuming some of the responsibilities around the mission.

As my workload was lightened somewhat, I was able to take an occasional trek to some of the nearby villages. Without a doubt, our visits to Buleswah were the highlight of my stay at Bomi Hills. For some time now the village elders had begged us to hold services, but Gladys' condition had prevented our doing so.

At the conclusion of our first service, a young man came running forward and immediately began to pour his heart out to God. It had been but a simple message about the love of God, but deep conviction had gripped the heart of this young man. Within moments he was speaking fluently in an unknown language. As he continued to speak in tongues, a strange look swept across the face of the chief's son-in-law, who was standing nearby. Walking over to the man, I asked the reason for his sudden startled look.

"That . . . that young boy over there is speaking in a tribal dialect that is unknown in this area—one which I'm sure he does not know."

"Are you sure?" I grilled him.

"Yes," he assured me. "It's spoken by a small tribe in another part of our nation. I learned it several years ago when I was in the Liberian army. I'm certain the boy has never had the opportunity to learn the language. As far as I know, I'm the only one in this region who knows the dialect. How is this possible?" he continued.

Needless to say, this was all the invitation I needed to further instruct the chief's son-in-law on the subject of speaking in tongues.

An hour or so later, after those praying at the altar had finished, I was approached by a middle-aged looking man, who introduced himself as the blacksmith from a neighboring village. For the next few minutes he was to tell me a story that would wrench my heart like a vise and would shock me into the realization of just how late we were in spreading the Gospel, and that we didn't have a second to spare or waste. I will tell the story in my own words, as his command of English was poor at best.

Ma, about 15 years ago I had a dream, or a vision,

one night. In my dream or vision I was taken to a place where there were many people. Everyone there seemed in awful torment, and their screams were so loud and terrifying that I had to stop my ears to block the sound. The heat that came from the place was so intense that even from a great distance it was impossible to stand it for more than a few seconds.

Next, I was taken to a place that was so beautiful, peaceful, and serene that words could never describe it. After standing in awe for a moment or so, I begged to remain there, but was told that this was quite impossible at the present time. I then asked what I must do to return to this place. I was told that I must begin praying to the One True God, placing my complete trust in Him instead of the black magic of the witch doctor. And, I would have to quit lying and stealing, and return all the items that I had stolen to their rightful owner.

The next morning when I awoke, my dream was just as real as the night before. That day I began praying to this God. I didn't know who He was, or where He lived, but I was convinced that He was the only hope I had. As I continued to pray to this God, I became impressed that I should tell my entire village about this God so that they, too, could pray to Him. Some listened and followed my advice, but most dismissed it as "just a dream."

For 15 years I continued praying to this unknown God, still not knowing who He was or where He lived, but hoping that someday someone would be able to tell me about Him. When I heard you talking about your God tonight, I knew He was the One I had been praying to. Thank you so much for coming.

Several weeks later we returned to Buleswah. This time the daughter of the chief received a marvelous baptism of the Holy Spirit, and the chief, himself, was visibly shaken by the power of God. Before we left for Bomi Hills, the village elders made us promise to return in the near future to assist them in constructing a church house. They made us further promise that once the building was finished, we would continue holding services in their village. They were willing to forsake their native mode of religion for the "God way," but only with the assurance that the white man would stay behind to explain his God to them.

I returned to Maheh in late January of 1950, to discover all sorts of late-breaking news. I hadn't been in contact with Georgia for almost a month, and it seemed as if everything had happened in that period of time.

There was to be a missions conference at Maheh the middle of next month, and Brother Stairs, the Foreign Missions Secretary, was planning to attend. A brand new pickup, purchased especially for Maheh Mission, was on its way. And, Georgia was scheduled to leave on furlough in just a few short weeks.

"I'm sure Brother Stairs will be able to tell us who my replacement will be," Georgia assured me.

As the time for the conference drew near, there was a certain air of excitement and expectancy that ruled. This would mark the first time that anyone from the headquarters office had visited Liberia. Soon after his arrival, Brother Stairs informed me that I was to be Georgia's replacement at Meheh, and that at the present time there was no one available to assist me. I was certainly grateful to God for the training I had just received at Bomi Hills.

I tried my very best to appear brave and completely self-assured. I wasn't the least bit worried about being at

Maheh by myself—I could handle it. But secretly, deep down inside, where it really counts, I was more than just a little apprehensive. In fact, when I had time to think about it, I was downright scared to death. Running the Bomi Hills Mission, with its 20 or 30 students, had been almost more than I could do. And, even though I had done all the work, it had just been for a few months, and I at least had Gladys around to encourage me and offer good, sound advice.

Maheh would be different. There were almost 50 students here, and it would be at least a year before anyone could come to assist me. There would be no one around to boost my morale when I sorely needed it. I was beginning to feel really discouraged, and quite sorry for myself, until the Lord spoke to me one night in prayer. By the time the conversation had ended, the Lord had successfully convinced me that it had been Him, and not Gladys, that had seen me through in Bomi Hills.

After several weeks I began to see that things weren't really as bad as I had envisioned. The school was larger, but there were two teachers available to assist me. So, for the most part, I was able to restrict my activities to nursing, conducting the services, and building and remodeling around the mission station.

The major construction project of the year was the building of a new church on the grounds. The old one had become sadly dilapidated from several years of severe Liberian weather. The fact that we had outgrown the building had been made even more apparent at the recent missions conference, when many had been forced to stand outside to listen to Brother Stairs preach.

While Brother Stairs was in Maheh, he had told us to expect delivery of our new truck sometime in early

March. However, it was not until the middle of April that we received word of its arrival. Reverend Falconer, the Missionary Superintendent of the National Baptist Church, had assisted us in getting the truck classified "For Religious Purposes Only," and we were able to avoid paying any duty.

The day we were to pick it up, Gladys walked in from Bomi Hills, and we caught a ride into Monrovia together. It had been years since I had driven, and I had never been behind the wheel of a truck, so Gladys had agreed to accompany me and drive us back to Maheh. Momo, one of the older boys on the mission, was learning to drive, and could soon serve as our chauffeur.

It was just a stripped-down, 3/4 ton Chevy pickup, but it looked and drove like a Rolls Royce to us. The lack of roads in Liberia would force us to continue walking almost everywhere we went, but the few times we could ride would go a long way in making our lives much more livable.

As we neared the mission, we were immediately surrounded by several dozen boys and girls, running around the truck and forcing Gladys to slow down to almost a crawl to avoid running over them. Our repeated warnings to them fell upon deaf ears. Most of them had seen a truck or a car before, but to have one at their very own mission station was still another matter.

After supper, Gladys suggested that we go for a little spin and perhaps give me a driving lesson. We had just entered the rainy season, and this was not the best time to teach "Drivers Ed," but dry time wouldn't come for another six months or so, and life couldn't come to a standstill over a mere 100 inches of rain.

We had driven for a mile or so, when Gladys slid the truck to a stop, shifted into neutral, and said rather matter-of-factly, "It's your turn now, Pauline."

Reluctantly I slid behind the wheel and waited until she had walked around and gotten in on the passenger side. Holding my breath, I pushed in the clutch just like she told me to, and shifted to the position she indicated. Then, with the neck-breaking, herky-jerky motion of someone not accustomed to synchronizing the accelerator and clutch, we began lurching, bouncing, and sliding down the muddy road.

After a few hundred feet the ride became relatively smooth, and I was beginning to feel quite proud of myself. Suddenly I caught wind of Gladys saying something to me—actually shouting would be more appropriate.

"Pauline . . . shift to second! Pauline . . . shift to second! Pauline . . . you're gonna blow the engine into a million pieces . . . shift to second!"

What was I to do? Where was second?

About that time, I somehow remembered where second was, but just as I shifted, the truck began to slide sideways. Gladys grabbed for the wheel, but it was too late. We had run into an embankment. We were okay, but the truck had a dent on the front fender. Right then and there Gladys and I decided to postpone my driving lessons until the dry season came some six months later. Maybe the rapture would come before then, and she'd never have to teach me.

The Lord wouldn't come for awhile, but that was my last attempt at driving . . . forever.

As was the case in Bomi Hills, we held two services each day at Maheh. I had been in charge of the mission for almost two months now, but not one single person had been saved. Sure, I had driven a lot of nails and cut quite a few boards. Sure, I had bandaged dozens of cuts and scrapes and assisted in a birth or two. Sure, I had witnessed the children improving on a daily basis in their ability to read, write, and work math problems. But I had not come to Liberia for these reasons. God had not stubbornly followed me through a life of heartbreak, failure, and loneliness for this.

Where had I failed? Where had I missed the will of God? What was I doing wrong? Where was the fruit of my labors?

I prayed, and I prayed, and I prayed, but still there was no one. It was as if the Lord wasn't even aware of who I was, where I was, or what I was attempting to accomplish for Him. He wasn't listening to a word I had to say, and He didn't have the time to talk to me.

As the days wore on, and my apparent failure continued, I began to sense a cloud of intense satanic oppression slowly, but completely, enveloping me. Only those who have labored among the demon powers of the West African bush can imagine the evil spirits that were lurking about. It was as if I were being literally crushed by a devilish force from without. I was nearing the point of hysteria, and felt compelled to run into the bush as fast as my legs would carry me, screaming to the top of my lungs.

Early one evening, when the duties of the day had finally been completed, and I was busily straightening my hut, I heard a voice speaking to me.

"They're out to get you!"

"They're out to get you!" the voice repeated.

The voice didn't identify itself or tell who "They" were, but I recognized it as the voice of God, and I knew that "They" were the demon spirits that ran so wild and free throughout Liberia.

"They're out to get you!" the voice repeated again, "but don't panic!"

I SURRENDER ALL

Don't panic! I had the strange feeling that if I allowed my instincts to control my actions, and ran into the bush screaming like every cell in my body had this craving inner desire to do, I would be defeated. Not panicking seemed to be the divine key to survival.

I tried to do just as God had instructed, and began getting ready for bed. As I lay there, staring at the thatched roof, I began to sense that someone was walking around my hut. As I continued to stare above me, I began to actually hear the footsteps as they incessantly marched around at an almost maddening cadence. Around and around and around they went, with an ever-quickening pace. Around and around, saying nothing, but with the determined gait of a bloodthirsty army.

They were out to get me alright, but the voice of God had plainly told me that my only refuge was to not panic. I began to call upon the Lord, trying all the time to remain as calm as possible. Suddenly, I became aware of singing in the distance. I could barely hear it for the noise of the marching feet, but I assumed the boys on the mission were having a prayer meeting. As the singing grew louder, however, I determined that it was coming from above my hut, and not from the boys hut. The more I listened, the closer the voices seemed to come. The closer they came, the louder they got, and the more they drowned out the sound of the marching feet.

I continued to listen, and could tell that it was a song of victory they were singing. I couldn't understand any of the song except the word "Hallelujah," which was in every verse. Finally, it was as if the heavenly choir was inside my room, hovering just a foot or so above my bed. At that moment, the sound of the marching feet disappeared, and instantly the feeling of hysteria and oppression left. A moment later, the choir began to ascend, and the voices grew gradually more faint until I could hear them no more. In a minute or so I was asleep.

I awoke the next morning, completely rested, and with a sense of total victory and liberation. We had met the enemy head on, and he had been defeated. I hadn't been told this in so many words, but I was convinced that a revival was just around the corner.

The next Sunday night, about half way through the service, the doors of heaven suddenly burst open and there was a rushing flood of God's spirit and presence. That night three received the Baptism of the Holy Spirit. The revival continued for a month, and before it was over, seventeen had received the Holy Spirit.

The following month, I took a weekend trip to the neighboring villages of Bolah and Boughbai. On this trip, two were saved and a total of twelve were baptized. It was becoming increasingly evident that the Lord knew exactly what He was doing at all times, and had poured out His spirit at just the right moment.

For the next few months things remained rather routine around the mission station—whatever that means. For the time being at least, there were no more demons marching around my hut, and there was a steady flow of new souls into the Kingdom. Towards the end of the summer, however, there was a tragedy that gripped the heart of everyone on the mission, and threatened to launch a vicious attack upon our faith.

Paul, Silas, and Peter, three of the older teenage boys on the mission, had gone on an evangelistic trip to one of the neighboring villages. Peter had been quite ill upon their return, but we had just put him to bed, assuming it was nothing serious. By morning, however, the condition had worsened, and I began to recognize the symptoms as that of yellow jaundice.

For several days a prayer vigil was maintained on the mission, and everyone fully expected God to heal Peter's body. With each passing day, however, his condition worsened. I decided that we'd better send Peter to the hospital in Monrovia, so I had Paul, Silas, and several of the other boys put him on a stretcher and take him to the main road. If they waited long enough they could catch a ride from one of the mining trucks going into town.

It was almost a day-and-a-half before they got him to the hospital. Several days after his arrival, Peter died. It was difficult trying to explain to those on the mission, especially the boys who had taken Peter into Monrovia, why God had allowed him to die. Then, the spirit of the Lord came upon me and gave me the wisdom to explain to them that occasionally God selects a special person and does more through his death than the person could have done in an entire lifetime.

In 1951, shortly after the first of the year, Otis and Nancy Petty were transferred from Beahjah to Bomi Hills, where they relieved Gladys for a long-overdue furlough. Shortly thereafter, Georgia returned from furlough and reassumed the operation of the Maheh Mission. She was accompanied on her flight by Brother Stairs who had come for our second missions conference which was to be held once again at Maheh. I had assumed that I would return to Bomi Hills after the conference to take care of the school while Brother Petty devoted his attention to an extensive building program.

In discussing the proposal with Brother Stairs, however, he had different ideas. In his opinion, it was time that I strike out on my own. In discussing the matter further, it was agreed that the most likely site was the village of Quoy Town, located about halfway between Bomi Hills and Monrovia. While Quoy Town was almost exclusively Moslem, there had been good response to meetings Brother Petty had held there in recent weeks, and it was felt that a full time missionary could achieve great success there.

Brother Petty and Brother Stairs could easily detect the doubts I had about going into a Moslem stronghold, but Brother Petty assured me that the natives in Quoy Town were not devout Moslems. "Most of them are more devoted to their black magic and witchcraft than they are to the Moslem religion," he said. "Your biggest battle will be against tribal religion, and not the Moslem faith," he continued.

Establishing my own mission had been my dream since the day I first set foot on Liberian soil—at least I had successfully convinced myself that it was my dream. However, as the time drew near for my dreams to become reality, I wasn't quite sure if this was what I wanted or not—at least not right at that moment.

I knew in my heart that there was no choice—that there were entirely too many unreached villages to afford us the luxury of three missionaries on one station, but I was still unsure of my ability to start from scratch. When would I ever learn that God was much more interested in my willingness than in my abilities?

I returned to Bomi Hills and worked for two or three months, all the time trying to muster the courage to make the big break. Finally, however, I accepted the fact that it was now or never. So, a few days later, Brother Petty and I made a trip to Quoy Town to meet the chief and village elders and make arrangements for my move there.

The villagers were very enthusiastic about the possibility of having their very own missionary, and went so far as to offer me the use of the village town house as my hut. Other than the chief's hut, this was the nicest in the village. It was agreed that after I had been in the village for awhile I could select a site for the mission. Until then, I could use the town kitchen for services and school.

I was tremendously encouraged by the initial response we had received, and it was with a great deal of excitement that I returned to Bomi Hills to pack my things for the move to Quoy Town. Perhaps things wouldn't be as difficult as I had anticipated. And, with the nice hut I had been provided, along with the kerosene refrigerator Brother Stairs had promised me, living conditions would be the best I had had since coming to Liberia.

For the first few weeks, there was a tremendous response to the services, with perhaps as many as 80 or 100 people in attendance at most meetings. Perhaps the most enthusiastic was the village elder, the chief's father, who said, "Ma, I like this *God palaver*."

After a month or so, however, the Moslem leaders saw that there was more to my being there than just a school and medical services. Almost overnight there was a drastic drop in the number attending the services. Before long there was hardly anyone except some old ladies, a few children, and the village elder. The night the village elder failed to show up was sufficient to convince me that it was going to be a long uphill struggle making any headway in this village.

For the next two months I continued to hold daily services for the few that came. By the end of the two months, however, there were just two or three small children that attended on a regular basis. I could see that I was fighting a losing battle on every hand. The village leaders had been primarily interested in education and medical treatment, and had accepted the services as the price that they must pay for what they wanted. In the following weeks, however, the leaders began fighting me even in the area of education, insisting that they be allowed to choose the students that attended the school, rather than permitting all to attend as prescribed by Liberian law.

The straw that broke the camel's back was the day one of the village women came "calling," demanding that I immediately vacate the town house. "You have no business living in the nicest house in town!" she screamed.

A few days later, when Brother Petty drove over to see how I was faring, I told him that I was ready to leave—that I had done all I could do, and felt the Lord wanted me to labor somewhere else. After discussing the matter further, Brother Petty agreed with my decision, and arrangements were made to move my things back to Bomi Hills.

More than 20 years later, elders from Quoy Town would beg Larry Blake, missionary in Monrovia, to please send them a missionary. "We made a terrible mistake when we ran Ma Gruse off," they lamented.

It was late in the evening when we finally arrived back at Bomi Hills with my belongings. I was dead tired from the strain of the situation and the long hours spent in moving, but felt that I must write Brother Stairs a letter before going to bed, explaining to him my decision to leave Quoy Town. Then, with bated breath, I waited almost four weeks for his reply, fearful of what his response would be.

When his answer finally did come, I quickly saw that my worry had been for naught. He told me that he respected my decision, and suggested that our timing had perhaps been off. He went on to state, however, that I should not allow my roots to grow too deeply in Bomi Hills, as he still desired that I strike out on my own as soon as possible.

During the next few months, as I attempted to prepare myself mentally for the inevitable move, the devil did all within his power to discourage me—to convince me that my next attempt at establishing a mission would prove no better than Quoy Town. It was during this time that God allowed three rather frightening things to happen to me as a means of proving that He was still on the throne, that I was in His will, and that as long as I stayed in His will nothing was going to defeat me or harm me. The first of these incidents took place shortly after my return to Bomi Hills.

Betsy was a good ole hen—faithfully performing her duty each morning. She was an only chicken, and I depended upon her for my daily breakfast. Occasionally she would decide to take her time, and I'd be forced to patiently wait until she'd laid her egg. Lately, I'd been thinking how nice it would be to have two eggs for breakfast, and maybe even some chicken to mix with my rice. With this in mind, I began sacrificing for the future by skipping my egg every so often.

One night, just after dark, I decided to go out to the kitchen and count the eggs I'd saved, to see if I had enough for Betsy to start setting. The moon was almost full, and I knew my way around the compound, so I didn't feel it was necessary to use the flashlight I was carrying. I found the bottle-shaped basket containing the eggs next to the cook stove, where I always kept it.

Just as I started to reach my hand into the mouth of the basket, a voice beside me said, "Don't stick your hand in there!"

"I must be imagining things," I thought, and once more began to reach into the basket.

"Don't stick your hand in there!" the voice repeated.

After the second warning, I decided I'd better listen to the voice. Flipping on my flashlight, I aimed it into the basket. For a moment I froze at the sight of the large poisonous snake, body coiled, tongue sticking out, and ready to strike. I could tell he had just swallowed his first egg.

After standing paralyzed for a few moments, a deep-settled peace seemed to come over me, and I calmly did an about-face and slowly left the kitchen. The next morning I cautiously reentered the kitchen, fully expecting to find an empty egg basket. Much to my surprise, however, it appeared the snake had not treated himself to a second egg and had left the kitchen shortly after I had.

The second incident occurred several weeks later, and also involved a snake.

It was mid-afternoon, in the heat of the day, and I had retired to my hut to rest for a few minutes. I was asleep in my chair in the corner of the front room, when I was suddenly awakened by the screams of Viola, one of the girls who assisted us on the mission.

"Ma, don't move! There's a big snake right under your chair. Don't move . . . I'll go get one of the boys to help."

I had no trouble obeying her, as I couldn't have moved if I wanted to. Finally, I was able to slowly lift my legs off the floor and onto the chair. My feet had been no more than six inches from the snake. Just as I had completed the maneuver, James entered the room. Lifting the deadly snake with a large stick, he carried him outside and killed him.

The snake had meant no harm, having come in to get out of the sun, but the incident had been enough to once again convince me of just how terribly vulnerable I was, but that nothing could harm me as long as I remained in the protective, loving embrace of God.

The third incident occurred a month or so later, and while it didn't involve a snake, it did involve an animal every bit as dangerous—a leopard.

For several days now, Brother Petty and several of the boys on the mission had been finding evidence of leopards prowling around the mission compound at night—evidently in search of chickens.

One night, actually in the wee hours of the morning, I was awakened by a horrible sound on my roof. At first I thought it was pelting rain, but as I regained my senses, I realized there was something alive up there—a man or a large animal. The palm leaf roof had proven to be quite rain proof, but I was sure it was not man or animal proof. Any moment now, whoever it was would fall through. The sound continued for a few more seconds, then whatever it was slid off the roof. Something told me it was one of our leopard prowlers.

The next morning I told Brother Petty about the incident. He was nice enough about it, but I could detect that he was a little hesitant to believe my story. In a few moments, however, he returned rather sheepishly.

"You were right, Sister Gruse. We spotted leopard tracks all around your hut. You're fortunate that thing didn't fall through the roof."

Later that day he returned and gave me a rifle for my protection. I seriously doubt that it would have done much good, however, seeing as how I didn't know the first thing about firing a gun, and was ashamed to ask him for instructions. But, for some reason I just didn't feel I would ever need to use it anyway.

FIFTEEN

Fassama Mission

I had planned to spend some time reading the Scriptures during this flight, and it suddenly dawned on me that we would be landing shortly, and I had not even opened my Bible. I reached into my purse for the small edition that I carried with me on trips, and opened to the New Testament. I had leafed through just a few pages when my eyes fell on Matthew 6, which contains what is commonly referred to as the "Lord's Prayer."

I began to read, "Thy kingdom come. Thy will be done in earth, as it is in heaven." Was I really living this prayer in my life? It was one thing to read it, but still another to really be willing to allow God to have His will in your life—no matter what.

"God help me," I prayed, "to arrive at a place of complete submission to You and those You have placed over me before I meet that Board next week."

Yes, God had done more than enough in the past few months to convince the *average* person that He was in full control and very much on the throne. But then, I was not your average person. I was a thick-headed Dutchman, and God seemingly had to keep reminding me—over and over and over.

The burden flatly refused to leave, no matter what, and I was forced to accept the fact that for some unexplained reason God wanted me, Pauline Gruse, to be a missionary somewhere in Liberia. Now, it was quite evident that there wasn't room for me at Bomi Hills, or for that matter, at any of the established mission stations. Putting these two facts together left me with no choice—I had to go out and establish my own mission. I was beginning to wonder if God was reading Brother Stairs' mail.

I could readily accept the fact that I had no choice, yet the apparent failure at Quoy Town continued to haunt me from time to time. Just when I would think that I had conquered all my mental blocks and had overcome all my phobias, the memories of Quoy Town would come to call, and the devil would once again do his fiendish best to deceive me into thinking that this would be the story in everything I attempted. It would be a number of years before I would learn enough of God to view Quoy Town in the proper perspective—to accept my apparent failure as having been in the will of God.

In the early part of 1952, I received a letter from Brother Stairs, assuring me that he was still counting on my establishing a new mission in the very near future. He then went on to inform me that Geneva Bailey, a newly-appointed missionary, would be accompanying Gladys on her return to the field in early April. Jean, as we came to know her, had been appointed by the missions board for the express purpose of assisting me in the establishment of a new mission. This being the case, Brother Stairs continued, it would be best for me to remain at Bomi Hills until her arrival.

I had met Jean some four years earlier, while visiting Tulsa on my furlough. She had been a student, as well as the cook, at the Bible College at the time. She was almost 15 years younger than I, and had never been married. Despite the difference in our ages, I was confident that we would be able to establish an outstanding rapport and form a tremendously successful missionary team.

Just knowing that someone would be joining me on this venture into the unknown proved to be the spark of enthusiasm that re-ignited my daydreaming and planning. Still, as in the past, there would come those moments of doubt, and I would fight more battles with myself before we would actually strike out on our own.

I had been in Liberia almost two years before taking my first long trek, but Jean had barely had a chance to catch her breath and unpack her bags before I began bombarding her with ideas and proposals concerning our upcoming trip into the interior. In looking back on the situation, I guess I should have allowed her a little more time to recover from the initial culture shock, but she seemed to survive despite my lack of wisdom and patience.

We had tons and tons of ideas, some that might work, and many more that didn't stand a chance, but neither of us had any definite plans—other than we wanted to go to a tribe that had never had a missionary. Since we would be accompanied on the trek by several of the boys and girls from the Bomi Hills Mission, it would be necessary to delay our departure until their semester break in the middle of July. Those few that chose to remain with us could attend classes at the mission we established, and the rest could easily return to Bomi Hills in time for the next semester.

The enthusiasm that had been generated by Brother Stairs' letter was only intensified by Jean's arrival. The excitement continued to grow each day, as I witnessed lifelong dreams slowly, yet surely, materializing into reality. At first, Jean, too, approached our planned trip with eagerness—with the zeal of a raw recruit. But, as May rolled into June, and June approached July, it gradually dawned on both of us that we were no longer playing games—that this one was for real.

The conditions at Bomi Hills might seem rather crude at times, but this was the very center of culture and civilization when compared to the dark, unknown recesses of the jungle where we might eventually find ourselves. What was presently just a dot on a crude, hand-drawn map, could very possibly be our home for many years in the future—perhaps the place where we would die. We would be attempting to build a Church in a savage, uncivilized area, among a people who most likely had never even heard the name "Jesus." Men who were so steeped in superstition and ruled by evil spirits that only a miracle could begin to free them. Something told me that Quoy Town could be child's play compared to what we were about to face.

It was about this time that I began experiencing severe abdominal pains. At first I dismissed them as simply a result of nervous tension—something that would pass in a few days. But, when the pain persisted, and began to grow more intense with each passing day, I decided the condition warranted medical attention. After a thorough examination, the doctor in Bomi Hills suggested I make arrangements to enter the hospital in Monrovia.

"I really can't say for sure what the cause of your problem is," he told me. "I strongly suspect it might be kidney stones, but I do not have the equipment for further testing, and would not wish to do the surgery unless I was certain."

From my courses in nurses training I had to agree with him that the symptoms did point toward kidney stones, but I agreed with him wholeheartedly in his decision to not operate until he was certain.

Arriving at the hospital in Monrovia, I was subjected to every test they had available, yet nothing organically wrong could be found. In between tests, and at night, the Lord started talking to me—getting down to real specifics. I was reminded of the story of Jonah, and how he had run from the call of God upon his life—simply because he was afraid. Suddenly I recognized my hospital bed as a "great fish" the Lord had prepared for me. When I realized the purpose for my illness, the Lord was able to talk to me further.

As the tests continued to come back negative, the pain began to subside, completely disappearing within a week. I was well, I was no longer afraid, and I was rip-roaring and ready to go.

I returned to Bomi Hills to find Jean bedfast with a serious case of malaria. She had begun feeling badly the day I left for Monrovia. For several days she had tried her best to ignore the chills and high fever that seemed to come about the same time each day, but by the fourth day her strength was gone and she was forced to admit that she was critically ill.

Evidently the Lord had "prepared two great fish" while He was at it, as the first thing Jean told me as I entered her room was, "The Lord's been talking to me, Pauline, and I'm ready to go. The only problem is that I don't have the strength to get out of this bed, let alone go traipsing with you through the jungle."

For several days I tried to coax Jean into at least trying to get out of bed—even if it was to take just a few steps. "That's the only way you'll ever regain your strength," I assured her. Finally, after three days of "gentle urging," she gave in. "I guess it's now or never," she said, as she desperately struggled to plant one foot on the floor.

It was just a few faltering steps at first, but within a few days she had regained enough strength to walk around the missions compound. Amazingly enough, a week later Jean was feeling strong enough to go with me into Monrovia to buy the supplies we would need for our trek.

There was plenty to do upon returning to Bomi Hills with the supplies. We would be leaving in just two days. Forty-eight hours to repack all the supplies into boxes light enough for the men to carry them over the rough terrain, select what we would put into the cardboard suitcases we had bought in Monrovia, and comb the area for 20 carriers willing to embark on a long trek in the worst part of the rainy season.

After spending the better part of the next day in search of carriers, we were still one man short. The next morning, I remained behind to do some packing, and Jean once more set out, determined to not return until she had found another carrier. Around noon, she returned with her mission accomplished. The next morning, however, her recruit had not showed up by the time we were ready to leave.

We had a major decision on our hands. What would we eliminate? We had not packed luxuries or extras—everything we had was a basic necessity. Finally, after mulling over the situation for almost 30 minutes, we decided that our only choice was to leave a box of foodstuffs behind. This would mean depending more upon the hospitality of the villagers, but this was our only choice. The other items we carried could not be obtained from the natives.

We left Bomi Hills, following a small mountain in a northeasterly direction—in search of a people that had never had a missionary. About four hours out, we crossed the Maheh River in dugout canoes. Shortly thereafter it began to rain as it does only in the African tropics. I honestly couldn't imagine it having rained any harder during the Flood.

The rain continued to fall the remainder of the day, soaking us and everything we carried. It wasn't feasible to carry an umbrella as we walked, as the treacherously slippery trails required that both hands be free at all times. It was too hot and humid to even think of wearing a raincoat. So, we had no choice but to expose ourselves to the torrential downpour and try to focus our attention on something else—like the people we were taking the Gospel to.

After sloshing and slipping and sliding for more than six hours, we approached a small village and decided to call it a day. Our clothes were soaked, as well as everything we had with us. Not even our cots had escaped the constantly pouring rain. Thinking that I might find some dry clothes in my suitcase, I found that it was not only soaked, but falling apart.

The next morning, bright and early, we ate a hurried

breakfast, packed our still-damp gear, and were on the trail again. It wasn't raining as we left, but the clouds covering the sky threatened to open at any moment.

After walking for an hour or so, I noticed that Jean was limping rather badly. Walking up beside her, I asked if she'd turned her ankle. "No," she answered rather embarrassed, "I think I'm developing blisters. But don't worry—it's nothing serious."

I'd warned Jean that sandals were not the proper footwear for trekking, but she had insisted that they were the most comfortable shoes she had, and she was confident she would encounter no problems. By the time we had arrived at the village where we would spend the night, however, both feet were covered with blisters and it was all Jean could do to walk.

The hut we were given by the village chief would have experienced great difficulty in obtaining a AAA rating. The door was ill-fitting and did little if anything to keep the driving rain where it rightfully belonged. Perhaps its only function was to allow the rat population the freedom to come and go as it wished. The village was evidently very poor, as it appeared quite an effort for the chief to scrounge up enough food for our supper. Finally, however, he did appear with two eggs and a little bit of chicken and rice.

The next morning the condition of Jean's feet was even worse. It was obvious that there was no way possible for her to continue. Our plans had been to walk all the way, so we had brought no hammocks. After discussing the situation from every conceivable angle, it was decided that I would walk on to Bopolu and arrange for carriers to return for Jean. In explaining our plight to the village chief, he agreed to find better housing for Jean until the carriers could return for her.

Arriving at Bopolu, I spent the night at the Bopolu Bible Mission, a station operated by a Black Baptist group from the States. At that time there was a couple and two single women running the mission. The next morning I walked over to the Commissioners Headquarters located near the mission. Commissioner Mooney, who was over the Belle tribes, the Kpelle tribes, and two Gbande tribes, seemed genuinely concerned when I told him about Jean, and promised to dispatch carriers immediately to bring her to Bopolu.

With the first order of business out of the way, he began to question me closely about our purpose in coming to his territory. After learning of our desire to work among a people that had never had a missionary, he said, "If you want to really make a name for yourself, go among the Belle people."

The only name I was interested in proclaiming was that of "Jesus," but the moment Commissioner Mooney said what he did, my mind shot back to a scene some seven years earlier, a scene in which an aged village elder had said, "Someday the Belle people will have their own missionary."

That was it—that was where the Lord wanted us. I decided right then and there to take Commissioner Mooney up on his suggestion, but not for the reason he had proposed.

Upon finishing our conversation, Commissioner Mooney left to round up two teams of carriers and a hammock. He returned in a few minutes, assuring me that everything had been taken care of, and that Jean would be in Bopolu the following day. Normally, one four man team would have been sufficient for such a short trip, but I had informed Mr. Mooney that Jean was a rather large woman, weighing in excess of 200 pounds, so he thought it wise to dispatch a relief team.

I had determined to leave the following morning, with a message for Jean to wait at the Bopolu Mission until she had heard further from me. Upon learning of my plans, however, Mr. Mooney strongly suggested that I postpone my departure for a day.

"I promise you the carriers will have your friend back by late tomorrow. Perhaps her feet will have healed enough for her to travel with you. If not, you will have missed but one day."

Sure enough, just as Mr. Mooney had promised, Jean arrived just after dark the following day. It was evident after one quick look that Jean was in no condition to travel—not even by hammock. In fact, it would most likely be a week or so before she would be ready to continue.

Jean was most receptive to the idea of going into the Belle country. In sharing with her the incident of the village elder I had met on my first trip into Belle country, she said she was beginning to feel like Paul answering the "Macedonian Call."

In discussing the matter further, it was decided that I would leave the next morning to do some advance scouting. Once I had located an attractive site, I would send the boys back to Bopolu to fetch Jean so that she could join me in an appraisal of the situation.

The rain was already falling in heavy sheets as we departed the next morning. Our immediate goal was the village of Belle Yella, tribal headquarters for the Belle. On several occasions, in later years, I would make this trip in one day, but considering the heavy loads the boys would be carrying over the slippery trails, I thought it best to plan on a two day trek.

Early on the second day, we met Peter, a young Belle man on his way to the coast in search of employment. Upon learning that I was a missionary on my way to Belle country, he proudly showed me a book he was carrying. The book, which concerned missionary activity in Liberia, had been given to him by a missionary at the Lutheran mission he had attended in another part of Liberia.

Thumbing through the book, my attention was drawn to an account of Lutheran missionaries who had passed through Belle country years earlier. Their assessment was that there was "no material" among the Belle people. For some strange reason this statement only intensified my desire to build a stronghold for the Lord among these people.

I said goodbye to Peter, and we prepared to leave. But after I had taken just a few steps, I heard him calling: "Stop, Ma, I'm going back with you!" Peter did return with us, and served for many years as my main interpreter to the Belle people.

It was 11:00 P.M. of the second day when we finally arrived in Belle Yella. The rain had been pouring for two straight days, and the trails had been much worse than we had anticipated. As we entered the village, there was no moon shining through, and the night was pitch black as only an African night can be. Even the carriers seemed a bit frightened as we walked into this unknown town.

We stopped at the first hut we came to, and asked permission to come in out of the rain. The occupants of the hut were quite surprised, to say the least, to see a white woman in their village, especially at 11:00 at night, and in the middle of a rain storm. It was understandable that they were quite reluctant to let us in. But, thanks to Peter, they were convinced that we would do them no harm, and consented to allow us to share their hut. After we had been there a few moments, one of the older boys left in search of the village chief.

A few minutes later, the chief of another Belle village arrived. Chief Weedor was the chief of Fassama, and like all the other village chiefs, he maintained a home and several wives in Belle Yella. An important part of being a Belle chief was to attend tribal meetings, engage in palaver, and attempt to butter up the Paramount Chief who lived in Belle Yella.

Chief Weedor emerged from the black night, carrying a lantern, and wearing a rubber raincoat that he had no doubt obtained while serving in the Liberian army. Walking straight toward me, he stopped just inches from my face, and began staring with those dark, piercing eyes that seemed to be looking straight through me. After what seemed like an eternity, he finally broke the silence:

"What did you come here for?"

"I'm a missionary," I explained nervously, "And I've come here to find a place among the Belle people to build a mission."

There was silence once again for several moments, as I sucked in my breath, wondering what his next move would be.

"Ma, I'm so glad you've come. We need you to help us."

A moment or so later, he sent one of the village boys to locate a hut where I and the girls could spend the night. Early the next morning, he reappeared with a chicken and a cane jar of rice for our breakfast.

I thanked Chief Weedor for the food, then turned to enter the hut.

"Ma, what village are you going to?"

"Well," I answered after a brief pause, "I . . . I guess I'll just stay here in Belle Yella . . . where most of the people are."

"You don't want to stay here, Ma," he answered. "Belle Yella is the only Belle village this side of the mountain. Besides, there is already a government school here. We really need you in Fassama, Ma. Fassama is a much larger village."

Now this put things in a totally different light. Commissioner Mooney had said nothing of a school in Belle Yella. But then, I hadn't told him of my plans to settle there, and he hadn't suggested that I do so.

Chief Weedor went on to say that in a few days he would be returning to Fassama, and that he would be greatly pleased if we would accompany him.

"It's just a six hour walk, Ma. Go with us and you'll see that Fassama is the town where you want to build your mission. We need you much more than any of the other villages, and in Fassama you'll be closer to the other villages."

Well, I certainly had nothing to lose in going with him, and since Belle Yella didn't appear a likely choice, I decided to take Chief Weedor up on his offer. The next day I dispatched a runner to Bopolu to inform Jean of my decision, asking her to remain there until she had received further word from me.

The driving rain was coming down in torrents as we left for Fassama several days later. At times it was as if it were raining sideways. After walking for approximately two hours, we came upon a mountain range which Chief Weedor said we must cross. Somehow, in informing me that it would be a six-hour trek, he had failed to mention that four hours of the trip would be devoted to crossing this mountain.

"Fassama is just on the other side," he said.

We climbed and we climbed and we climbed, finally reaching a height of almost 2,000 feet. The already-narrow pebble-covered path was made even more treacherous by the constantly falling rain which caused the path to feel as if it were covered by a myriad of well-greased ball bearings. As we neared the top, the path seemed almost vertical, and it became necessary to hold onto roots and small bushes and crawl on hands and knees. The path was so steep that I was afraid to look ahead, for fear that I would become dizzy, lose my balance, and fall backward. This would be the first of many such trips that I would make over the years as I traveled in and out of Belle country. The only alternative was by plane, and it would be some time before we would enjoy this luxury.

I'd be a hypocrite to try to convince you that the devil didn't have his moments during this four-hour climb and descension. There were several times when my feet would slip and I was sure that I was about to go tumbling down the mountainside. I had never been one to want to climb a mountain simply because "it was there," and I'd have to be a mountain goat to take the Gospel to Liberia. Would I ever get a chance to establish a mission, or would I meet my death on the side of some lonely mountain?

The devil began to speak—"If you're really in the will of God, why is it that you must go through so many hardships?"

As we got higher and higher, and the pathway became even more perilous, Satan's arguments began to make sense. But then, my mind went back to Calvary, and the cruel price Jesus had so willingly paid—so that those people on the other side of the mountain could be saved. I recalled a verse of Scripture where Paul, a missionary who had suffered much more than I was suffering, had said:

> *We are troubled on every side, yet not distressed, we are perplexed, but not in despair; Persecuted, but not forsaken; cast down, but not destroyed.*

Finally, we were safely on the other side, and still in one piece—at least physically. In less than an hour, we would be in Fassama. At this point, Chief Weedor sent a runner ahead to inform the village elders that he was coming, and that he was bringing a missionary with him.

A mile or so before we reached Fassama the rains let up—for a few minutes at least. Still, I was soaked to the bone and in the mood for nothing but some dry clothes and privacy when we arrived. Chief Weedor had other plans, however, as he marched me straight to the town kitchen, a large oval building, where we were met by the village elders and quarter chiefs who spent several minutes in closely scrutinizing me and grunting in response to a speech the chief was making regarding my arrival and purpose in being there. As the session continued, a sizable crowd of villagers began to congregate outside the kitchen.

I was too tired and frightened at the time to notice the complete absence of girls and young women in the village—at least those between the ages of eight and twenty. I would later learn that the girls Devil Bush was in progress, and that for some time now the girls had been in the bush undergoing rigorous and extensive training.

Finally, my hearing was over, everyone seemed at least reasonably satisfied, and I was ushered to the building that would serve as my home for the next few days—until Jean arrived. It was a terribly small, typically round thatched-roof hut, with a three-foot high door that offered some privacy but certainly nothing in the way of protection. There was barely enough room for my soaked army cot and an open cook fire in the center of the room.

But, it was a place to sleep, it was dry in spots, and it did offer a certain degree of privacy. As I started unpacking a few things, I managed to breathe a sigh of relief, and once more began feeling that warm, soothing, satisfying glow of being in the will of God. It was strange, but I suddenly had the sensation of finally coming home.

I awoke early the next morning refreshed—realizing that for the first time in many nights I had enjoyed a good nights sleep. After breakfast, I quickly drafted a letter to Jean, informing her of my arrival in Fassama, and briefly sharing my feelings about the place with her. I went on to describe the difficulty in crossing the mountains, and suggested that she not attempt to join me until she was able to make the trip on foot. At that time, I honestly didn't feel it was possible for hammock carriers to cross the mountains, especially with a woman Jean's size. I later learned, however, that Commissioner Mooney, who weighed well in excess of 200 pounds himself, often crossed the mountains with carriers. But even then it seemed so terribly inhumane to ask them to do so.

After sealing the letter, and telling Chief Weedor of my plans, I sent two of the older boys back to Bopolu with the letter. About a week later, in the middle of the afternoon, Jean came walking into the village with the boys. From the paleness of her countenance and the frightened look in her eyes, I could tell that my brief description had not adequately prepared her for the crossing of the mountain.

But, in later months, she, like I, would become a veteran mountain goat, and it would be just part of a days work in the life of a missionary.

An hour or so after Jean's arrival, Chief Weedor escorted us to a larger hut in another part of the village. This would remain our home for the next four months—until we began work on the mission.

A day or so later, just as we were finishing breakfast, Chief Weedor, along with several of the village elders, came to call. After trading small talk for a few moments, they informed us that they had come to show us a site which would be ideal for the mission we were planning. The location was across the creek from the village and had, in fact, been the site of the village prior to World War II. It appeared to be a much better spot than the present one, and it remained a puzzle to us why the move had ever been made.

Returning to the hut, Jean and I held a business meeting—discussing at length the pros and cons of settling at Fassama. I assured her that from past experience I was certain that we could never expect to receive a warmer reception—no matter where we went. However, the concern that seemed to be foremost on our minds was the mountains. We'd have to cross them every time we went to the coast to get the mail, visit the other stations, or buy supplies.

Yet, neither of us could escape the intense feeling that God had specifically called us to the Belle people. The only place to locate on the other side of the mountains was Belle Yella, and there was already a government school there. And, even if we did choose to settle in Belie Yella, we would have to cross the mountains to reach the other 15 Belle villages. What was most important—souls or supplies? Once this decision was quickly reached, it was firmly decided that Fassama would become our base of operations and the site for our school.

With this decision made, it was now necessary for one of us to return to Bomi Hills to contact Brother Stairs regarding our plans and await his approval to proceed. Actually, the trip would be a multi-purpose one. Several of the older students who had accompanied us to Fassama had to return to Monrovia to begin the second semester of school. And, if we were going to settle here, it would be necessary to bring in additional supplies.

It was evident that Jean was in no condition to make the five-day trek to Bomi Hills. She had not really been ready for the three-day walk from Bopolu, and the trip had only served to prolong, and perhaps even worsen, the condition of her feet.

Needless to say, Jean wasn't exactly elated over the idea of staying behind. Chances were that I'd be gone for the better part of a month, and she'd be all alone—no closer than a hundred miles to anyone she knew. For a woman who had been on the field just four short months, she was being asked to endure a lot. And while she did show some apprehension, I must admit that she proved to be a very courageous woman.

I felt as though I hadn't slept a wink the night before, yet I still beat the roosters up that morning. I had gone to bed with the mountains on my mind. I had tossed and turned all night long with the mountains on my mind. I had risen the following morning with the mountains on my mind. I was scared to death at the mere thought of crossing the mountains again, but unless I wanted to follow the theory of Columbus and get to Bomi Hills by going around the world, this was the only route.

The early morning sky was surprisingly clear as we said good-bye to Jean and disappeared into the jungle. The sun had barely peeked over the horizon, and before it would have time to raise itself much more, clouds would begin to fill the sky, and once more the rain would start to fall.

The procession consisted of three older boys who were returning to Monrovia for secondary school, three younger children who were going back to the mission school in Bomi Hills, and Viola, a young native woman who planned to stay with us in Fassama and work in the school—all led by an apprehensive 49 year old American missionary from a small town in Indiana.

Chief Weedor had suggested that I take carriers with me from Fassama—to bring back the supplies I would be purchasing in Monrovia. This way, he argued, I could avoid the risk of arriving in Bomi Hills and discovering that I couldn't employ enough carriers for the trip back. But, to pay 20 men for the five day trip down to Bomi Hills would be an additional $25.00 expense—$25.00 that we didn't have.

It was mid-August and in the middle of the heaviest part of the rainy season. By the time we had arrived at the base of the mountains, it had once again started to rain.

Crossing the mountains was just like I had remembered it and feared it would be—every bit as steep, every bit as slippery, every bit as exhausting, and every bit as scary. At last, however, we had huffed and puffed and slipped and sloshed our way up to the top and down the other side. The worst part was over. The trek would be a snap from here on out—or so I thought.

For the next day-and-a-half the only discomfort we had to contend with was the constantly-falling rain that kept us and everything with us thoroughly soaked. The third day, however, our lot changed drastically. As we approached the Po River, we could see that it had overflowed its banks by more than a hundred yards. It was impossible to see where it stopped on the other side. What had once been a gently flowing river about 150 feet wide, and perhaps ten feet deep, was now a raging, rushing force, with seemingly no boundaries and an unknown depth.

The only way to cross it was by means of a "monkey bridge," a rather crude bridge constructed of vines woven tightly together, and suspended between trees on either side of the river. With its hammock-like effect, it would bounce and sway from side to side whenever someone crossed it.

The natives, who are naturally sure-footed, would literally run across the bridge, without even bothering to hold on to the makeshift handrail. Finally, after everyone else had crossed, I mustered up enough courage to crawl over—much to the delight of the boys and girls who had accompanied me. I actually thought I would get seasick from all the motion, and was deathly afraid to look down, for fear that I would plunge into the mad, swirling stream below.

When I reached the other side, I discovered that our problems had just begun. The trail was completely covered by water, and it was impossible to tell which way it ran. To further complicate the matter, there was a small river feeding the Po at this point, and there was the distinct possibility of following it instead of the trail. I could feel the spirit of fear coming over me, and was honestly beginning to wonder if this was the end. Suddenly, with no time to spare, the Spirit of God impressed me with the word "Trust." Not even a complete sentence—just the word "Trust."

The feeling was so strong and certain that I felt I had no choice but to step out by faith—and "Trust." *Hoping* that we were following the path, we began to slowly wade. The water was getting deeper with each step, and soon it was up to my neck. It was necessary to tilt my head back to breathe, and the younger children had to be hoisted onto the shoulders of the three older boys. I kept repeating over and over—Trust . . . Trust . . . Trust.

Just when it seemed that all hope was lost, a little native man appeared out of nowhere. "Ma," he said, "I've come to lead you across so you won't lose your way." Once we were safely across, he disappeared before we had a chance to thank him. Angels, I'm told, come in all shapes, sizes, and colors.

The next day or so we didn't have any major rivers to cross, and things remained relatively calm. But, towards noon of the fifth day we neared the Maheh River to discover that it, too, had swollen out of its banks. At first there appeared absolutely no way to get across, but in walking up the river a few hundred yards, one of the boys came upon a raft which was tied to a cable which had been stretched across the river. The raft, which was made of four logs, fastened by pegs and vines, was barely large enough for two people.

I was scared out of my wits to think of what would happen if we were in the middle of the river when the raft capsized or the cable broke, but we had come too far to turn back now, and we'd just have to trust that God had chosen this as our means of transportation.

In discussing the matter with the boys, it was decided that the safest, and possibly the only, way to cross with the raft was to loop the tie rope over the cable. Then, by sliding the rope along the cable, the raft could be slowly guided to the other side.

I selected Kenney, the strongest of the boys, and told the rest that we would make the maiden voyage. If we made it, then Kenney could ferry the others across. Stepping onto the raft, I sat in the middle and held on for dear life. Kenney stood up and slowly slid the rope along the cable. We were being tossed about like a toy boat, but everything seemed to be going according to plan until we reached the halfway point. Suddenly, with no warning, the rope snapped, and down the stream we raced.

I wanted to scream with everything in me. We were doomed. God had gotten me out of a lot of fixes, but I was a goner this time. At that moment the voice of God spoke to me audibly, over the rush of the river:

"Don't scream! The boys and girls are looking to you for strength. Don't scream! just remain calm."

About that time, Kenney kicked off his battered tennis shoes and jumped into the raging waters. I wouldn't have believed it was possible had I not seen it with my own eyes, but Kenney began swimming and pushing the raft towards the shore. After 15 or 20 minutes of battling the waters, we reached our destination, and an exhausted Kenney fell to the ground.

After making sure he was alright, I yelled across to Viola and the rest of the boys and girls and told them it was too risky to attempt to cross. I instructed them to go back to an abandoned hut we had passed a little earlier and wait until we could go to the nearest village and send help.

After giving Kenney a few more minutes to catch his breath, we struck out for a village which was about an hour's walk. This was evidently to be the day of miracles, as the first one we met upon entering the village was

Viola's brother, who just "happened" to be visiting some friends. He immediately volunteered to return for Viola and the others.

Choosing not to use the raft, Viola's brother persuaded the two older boys to swim across the river. He would then carry the others over, including Viola, one at a time, by allowing them to cling to his back as he swam. Less than four hours after he had left, he returned to the village with six frightened, but otherwise perfectly sound boys and girls.

My original plans had called for us to arrive in Bomi Hills late on the fifth day, but after our ordeal with the raft, I decided we would spend the night in the village where we had waited for Viola's brother, and continue the next day. We were less than three hours from Bomi Hills, and could reach it by mid-morning if we left at a reasonable time.

We arrived in Bomi Hills shortly after 10:00 the next morning, to find things pretty much as we had left them. The Pettys and Gladys were hard at work, getting things organized for the next semester which would begin in a few days. After lunch, I retired to my hut, where I spent the next 30 minutes carefully wording a letter to Brother Stairs, informing him of our burden to work among the Belle people, and explaining why Jean and I felt that Fassama was the only logical place to establish our mission and base of operations.

The next morning I went into Monrovia with the Pettys to mail my letter, check our mail, and begin purchasing the supplies I would be taking back. It would be two weeks before I could expect to receive a reply from Brother Stairs, but by faith I was going to start purchasing supplies. I almost felt like I was sinning—riding into

Monrovia in a truck, instead of walking.

The next few days were put to good use—resting, reading my Bible, answering letters, enjoying the company of fellow missionaries, talking with the mission children, and worrying about Jean up there in Fassama all by herself. I wondered how her feet were doing, and whether she had been able to begin holding services.

One morning, after we had been in Bomi Hills about a week, Viola approached me with some rather startling and unexpected news.

"Ma, I'm sorry, but I won't be going back to Fassama with you. I am to be married in a few weeks to a boy that my sister introduced me to several months ago. He asked me to marry him before we left to go to Fassama, but I told him no. He asked me again yesterday, and I told him yes."

Well, needless to say, this came as quite a shock. We had really counted on Viola's helping us in the school, and after questioning her about her fiancé, I was not in favor of their marriage. He had been baptized, but as yet was not Spirit-filled. I had seen too many unhappy marriages originally founded upon one partner's promise to continue seeking for the baptism of the Holy Spirit. But, Viola was old enough to make up her own mind, and it was evident that she had done just that.

The next week I decided to pull out all the stops and allow my faith to take another step ahead. I began rounding up carriers. I refused to be discouraged by our difficulty of a few weeks before. Swollen rivers, monkey bridges, and runaway rafts had taught me that God was in this thing, and I was going to find twenty men who were willing to help me in the work of God!

It was surprisingly easy—even easier than I had had

faith for. But, invariably, the first question they would ask after showing interest in the job was, "Ma, are you going to pay us or the chief?" I later discovered that it was common for an unscrupulous chief to assure an unsuspecting missionary that he should be paid for the carriers' services, and that he would in turn see that his men got their money. The chief would then give each man perhaps ten per cent of what he had earned and keep the rest for himself.

I had been in Bomi Hills for two-and-a-half weeks when the letter finally arrived. I was certainly shaking for someone who knew what the answer would be. I carefully opened it, almost afraid to begin reading the words. "Praise the Lord!" Brother Stairs agreed wholeheartedly with our decision, and assured me that the folks back home would be expecting to hear glowing reports of revival from Fassama Mission. "Fassama Mission"—that certainly had a good ring to it.

Well, we had the go ahead, so it was time to be leaving. The next day was spent packing the supplies and notifying the carriers that we'd depart early the next morning. As I packed, I silently prayed that the rivers would be down. I realized that the mountains would be just as tall and every bit as steep, but for some reason crossing them seemed like child's play after the experiences we'd had with the raging rivers.

The return trip to Fassama was practically uneventful when compared to our trek down of a few weeks earlier. The rains had slackened considerably, allowing the flood waters to recede, and we encountered little or no difficulty in crossing the rivers.

It was early September when I returned to Fassama. I had been gone almost five weeks. I found Jean in good spirits, excited about the work in Fassama, and thrilled that Brother Stairs had given us his blessing. In my absence, she had wasted no time in initiating nightly services in the village palaver kitchen.

The blisters on her feet appeared to be completely healed, and she assured me that she was ready, willing, and able to make a trek to Bomi Hills to bring back the rest of the supplies we would need. Upon her return we would begin making some definite plans toward building our mission station on the site Chief Weedor and the village elders had suggested. We both agreed that since Viola would not be assisting us, it would be better to delay opening the school until we had moved to the new site.

One afternoon, several days after Jean had left for Bomi Hills, I heard a terrible commotion that sounded as if it was coming from down near the creek. Stepping out of my hut to investigate, I was told that the Medicine Man was down there "playing his medicine." He had been paid $6.00, quite a sum for that part of Liberia in 1952, to "play his medicine" for a woman who had suffered for weeks from insomnia—being constantly tormented by the serpent and the banana plant. The natives believed that the banana plant had human qualities and traits.

I started to run down to the creek to get a better view of the bizarre spectacle, but was quickly restrained by a village elder who stood nearby.

"Ma, you can't go down there!"

From the insistent tone of his voice, I knew it would do no good to argue, or for that matter, even ask why. Still, I was determined to see what was going on. Spotting a large crate several feet from my hut, I ran over and climbed on top of it. Straining my eyes, I could see at least a dozen men, stooping over until their heads almost touched the ground, and forming a snake-like chain that slithered along the creek bed like a serpent in search of its prey. As they squirmed and wriggled, a woman ran beside them, dousing the men with water.

Leaving the creek bed, they wormed their way into the village and toward me. The two young girls that stood beside me suddenly ran screaming into the hut.

"Come in, Ma! Come in, Ma!" they begged. "They'll tear your cloth!"

"They won't tear my cloth. They won't hurt me," I assured the girls confidently.

By now the Medicine Man and his assistants were within 50 feet of me, and creeping ever closer. My self-confidence was beginning to wane. I could now see the glassy stare of their eyes and tell that they were under the control of an evil spirit—that they were seeing something the natural eye could not perceive. Stopping just inches from my feet, they began going through a series of weird contortions—grunting, growling, and groaning—as if they had caught the serpent and were doing battle with him.

My knees were literally knocking together, and I wanted to scream and run into the hut, but I didn't dare move or show any outward signs of emotion. Something told me that the entire village was watching me—watching to see if the God of the White missionary was as powerful as the medicine of the Medicine Man.

Under my breath, I said, I plead the blood of Jesus! I plead the blood of Jesus! I plead the blood of Jesus!"

Just then, there was a gentle breeze of peace that swept over me. The men acted as if the serpent had gotten away, and off they wriggled in pursuit.

A week or so later, right in the middle of the evening service, the "Devil" came to town. Word quickly spread, and within minutes everyone had retreated to the safety of his own hut. No one was allowed to look upon the Devil when he came into a village. The natives commonly believed that except for whatever ceremonial ornamentation he might be wearing, the Devil entered a village completely naked.

No one would admit, and few knew who the Devil was. Only those few within the tribe who had the responsibility of choosing the Devil knew his true identity. The Devil, or the leader of the Devil Bush, was the most powerful man in the tribe when he chose to become active—even more powerful than the village chiefs and the Paramount Chief.

I had often heard of the Poro Society, or the Devil Bush, as the natives refer to it, but it was not until I had come to Fassama that I actually saw it in operation. The Liberian government had been quite successful in controlling it in the coastal regions, but in the more remote areas the Devil Bush was still a very real and powerful force.

Every Belle boy and girl, upon reaching the age of ten or so, would be required to leave his village and spend a period of time in the bush. He would not be allowed to return to his village or family until the Bush "broke." Years ago, the Bush had lasted eight to ten years. Recently, however, it had been shortened to four years. In the future, it would bow to government pressure and hold the Bush sessions only between school semesters.

It was during the Bush that the boys and girls learned the trades that would sustain them for the remainder of their lives. However, most of the time was devoted to indoctrinating the young people into the secret ways of the Devil Bush. When the Bush broke, there was an initiation ritual in which each boy and girl received an injection of "medicine." The injection would cause large welts to rise along the spine, "marking" them for life as members of the Devil Bush.

Towards the middle of December, Commissioner Mooney paid a surprise visit to Fassama to see how Jean and I were faring. While he was there, arrangements were made to begin construction of the mission station the first of the year. Mr. Mooney insisted that Chief Weedor have his men build the church and our house—under our supervision, of course. As it turned out, the Belle men didn't prove overly industrious at times, and on one occasion it was necessary for the Commissioner to dispatch a soldier to Fassama to "encourage" the men to work a little harder.

The church was actually a multi-purpose building. The back part served as a carpenter shop and tool shed, while the front was our sanctuary and classroom. The building was open-ended and had half-walls on the side. And, as you would expect, the floors were dirt and the roof was thatched.

Our house was really just a four-room hut, constructed of mud and bamboo. It, too, featured a thatched roof and a dirt floor. But, at least it didn't carry a 30 year mortgage. For the next couple of years it served as a home for Jean and me, along with the first mission girls we had. Seventeen years later, when I was finally "forced" to leave Liberia, the hut was still standing, despite the wind and the rain and the bugabugs.

Our first furniture consisted of two army cots, some shipping crates, and a wood cook stove brought over the mountains on the backs of the carriers. Later, with the help of some of the mission boys, we built two beds, complete with bamboo and palm leaf mattresses.

When time permitted, we planned to start construction on a house for the boys, as well as a cook kitchen separate from our house. Once this was accomplished, we would begin thinking about a more suitable house for Jean and me. We could then turn the hut over to the girls.

Our first mission children, other than those we had brought from Bomi Hills, were three of Chief Weedor's sons. In the next few months we gained an additional seven boys and five girls. Actually, some of these students were in their late teens, and graduates of the Devil Bush. But, since they were unmarried, and just beginning their education, we normally referred to them as our "boys and girls."

There were many things to teach the students in addition to the Bible related subjects and the Three R's. In their training, however, we were careful to do nothing which would in any way disrupt the native economy or way of life—nothing which would allow the boys and girls to become dependent on "luxuries" which would not be available to them in later life.

Tribal mores dictated that the men do the cooking, so this became the procedure on the mission station. In later years we installed a pump on the mission water well, yet we continued to insist that the girls carry the water from the creek. Once they were married and moved into the village, they would not have access to a well with a pump.

There was perhaps one area in which we deviated from this practice in the matter of personal grooming and hygiene. Regardless of local custom and tradition, their bodies were the temple of God, and deserved the very best of protection and maintenance. This would be one habit they could continue to follow, wherever they went. And, hopefully, they would teach the importance of health care and personal grooming to those they came into contact with.

It was a rigid rule on the mission that everyone must work for everything he got—including his personal Bible. It was genuinely felt that this would cause the young people to be more appreciative and protective of what they had. Without a doubt, our greatest joy was to see one of these young men, a former member of the Devil Bush, take his Bible and trek to a neighboring village where he would boldly proclaim the saving message of Jesus Christ.

SIXTEEN

Oh, No—Not Another Furlough!

For several minutes I had been staring blankly into space—seeing really nothing I guess. Then I saw it—what I had dreaded from the moment I boarded—the "Fasten Your Seatbelt" sign. A few moments later the voice of the Captain could be heard over the din of the cabin: "This is Captain Brinkley speaking—we are beginning our approach to Kennedy, and will be landing in approximately 15 minutes. Please observe that I have illuminated the 'Fasten Your Seatbelt' sign."

In early February of 1953 we sent a team of carriers down to the coast for additional supplies. Upon their return, some three weeks later, they brought a letter from the Missions Department which stated that I should plan on taking my furlough no later than mid-April.

It had been better than four-and-a-half years since I had set foot on Liberian soil for the second time, but in all honesty I had spent precious little time daydreaming about life back in the States. True, there were those weak moments, when I had second thoughts about the will of God and Pauline Gruse, but for the most part I was *totally* involved in the work of a missionary.

Things were starting to fall into place here at Fassama, and I had the satisfying feeling that I was finally exactly where God wanted me, doing precisely what He wanted me to do for the remainder of my life. I fully expected to die and be buried on the Fassama Mission Station.

Still, there were some people back in the States that I dearly missed—like Bob, my son, who was almost 26 now, Leland, my brother, and the Klapps, my special friends who had always been there with open arms when there was seemingly no one else who cared.

And, I was fully aware of the necessity of maintaining contact with the people back home—sharing with them the results of their faithful prayers, their days of fasting, and their unselfish financial support.

Tentative plans called for me to leave Fassama around the first of April and depart for New York about two weeks later. This would allow me a week to rest and prepare for the rigors and pressures of furlough. Several days before I was scheduled to leave, word was received from Brother Petty that E. L. Freeman, missionary to South Africa, would be coming through Liberia on his way back to the States, and that in all likelihood he would want to visit Fassama. Brother Petty suggested that I remain at the station until his visit.

Brother Stairs had asked Brother Freeman to take a swing through the Gold Coast (now Ghana) and Nigeria on his way back to the States. In the past few months correspondence had been received from a native who claimed he had received the Holy Spirit, was baptized in Jesus name, and was doing missionary work in these two countries. Follow-up letters had requested financial assistance, and the Missions Department was anxious to learn the legitimacy of these requests. Upon locating the man, however, Brother Freeman discovered that he had been jailed—not for preaching the Gospel, but for common theft.

I remembered having met the Freemans in De Ridder Louisiana in 1948 when we were both meeting the Missions Board for appointment. Strange as it may seem, the Missions Department had asked Brother Freeman to take a furlough by himself, leaving his wife, Nona, and their children behind to look after the work.

After finding our "would-be" preacher in jail, and shedding tears for the lost souls of those two nations, Brother Freeman had taken a flight to Monrovia. While there, he had met Robert Mason, a young Assemblies of God missionary who had a small four-passenger plane. Arrangements were made for Robert to fly Brother Freeman to Gumbata, a Lutheran missions outpost near Belle Yella. From there he made the day-and-a-half trek over the mountains to Fassama. Before parting company, Robert agreed to meet Brother Freeman at the air strip at 10:00 A.M. six days later.

The moment he arrived, it was evident that Brother Freeman was no veteran treker. His feet were covered with blisters—from stem to stern. Two days later, there was little, if any, improvement, and it was obvious that walking was out of the question for Brother Freeman. We both detested the idea of using hammock carriers, but we were on a tight schedule, and there appeared to be no alternative.

It was slow going, and terribly strenuous for the carriers, but by late evening we had arrived at Gumbata. The next morning we walked the three miles to the air strip. Several of the carriers continued on to Bomi Hills with my luggage. Fifteen or twenty minutes after we arrived at the clearing, we spotted a speck in the sky. A few moments later the plane had landed, and we were ready to depart for Monrovia. Brother Freeman would leave directly for New York, and I would continue on to Bomi Hills to await my luggage.

I reluctantly crawled into the back of the plane, next to the baggage Brother Freeman and I had brought with us. He and Robert occupied the front seats. I had taken a similar flight some six years earlier, but the only thing I could recall about it was that I had been scared to death the whole time. I tried not to let it show, but I was scared to death this time also. As Robert revved up the engine, and the aircraft began to shiver and shake in anticipation of taking off, the three-and-a-half days trek through the jungle suddenly didn't seem so bad after all.

The plane began to move down the runway, slowly gathering speed. We were getting closer and closer to the 100 foot trees at the end of the clearing and we were still just a few feet off the ground. I closed my eyes and held my breath, knowing for certain that this was the end of the line. For several moments I remained in this lifeless state, as I listened to the groan of the engine. When I dared open my eyes, I was surprised to see that we were several hundred feet above the jungle.

For a moment Robert was silent. Then he said: "Whew, I didn't think we were gonna make it! That runway is just too short for this much weight. That's the last time I'm gonna try that!"

Oh, No—Not Another Furlough

Upon discovering that there had been real reason for my concern, I vowed to myself that I'd never again fly aboard a small aircraft. In later years, however, as the trails became longer, and the mountains got higher, I was glad that I had only made the vow to myself and could break it.

In less than an hour we were landing on the beach just outside Monrovia. I said goodbye to Brother Freeman and watched as he hailed a taxi and left for Roberts Field. I then grabbed my lone bag and caught a ride into Monrovia. It was almost noon when I reached the A. G. home, where I would spend the next night or so. After a hasty lunch, I walked downtown to the offices of the Department of Internal Affairs, where I began filling out the mountain of paper work necessary for departing the country. Surprisingly, in less than three hours I had satisfied all the requirements and was free to go. If I hurried, I could still make it to the Pan American offices to purchase the ticket for my flight to New York.

It would be several days before the carriers arrived in Bomi Hills with the rest of my things, and I could use the few extra days rest, so I booked passage for a flight ten days later. No one back in the States knew exactly when to expect me anyway.

The following morning the Pettys drove down from Bomi Hills and took me back to the mission station. Three days later the carriers arrived with my trunks. The next week or so was spent doing virtually nothing. I hadn't realized just how exhausted I was until I was able to stop long enough to think about it.

Early Monday morning, April 13, I awoke and prepared for the trip to Roberts Field. My flight aboard the Pan Am DC-6 was scheduled to depart at 11:30. Who knew, it might even leave on time this flight.

Saying goodbye to the Pettys, and promising to write, I climbed the stairs and settled into my seat. Within minutes the prop engines were roaring, and we were speeding down the runway. As we lifted off, I had a feeling similar to that of six years earlier—only more intense—that I was leaving on a trip, not going home. The landing gear had not even been retracted, and already my heart was yearning for the Belle people—my people.

Our route was exactly as it had been on my first return flight—Dakar, Senegal; Lisbon, Portugal; Ponta Delgada in the Azores; and then on to Idlewild. This time, however, when I landed in New York, I didn't get to spend the night in a hotel, as I was able to get a connecting flight within a couple of hours. But, it was just as well—I wasn't exactly in the mood for a chicken dinner anyway.

The first stop was Cleveland, to see my brother, Leland, who had moved from Toledo during my second term. After a few days with him, it was on to Lima, Ohio to see Bob and Rosemary. I was a grandma now, with Nanette almost three, and Steve nearly one. After spending a week or so with them, I traveled to South Bend to visit with Doris and Virgil Klapp.

For the next few months I made the Klapps' home my base of operations, as I traveled throughout Illinois, Indiana, Ohio, and even Canada.

General Conference was held in St. Louis that year, in the middle of September. At the conference I met the Missions Board and received a reappointment. During the annual missions service an appeal was made and my fare to Liberia was raised. It was also during this conference that Valda Russell, a native of Jamaica, was appointed to go to Liberia to assist in the work at Bomi Hills. Gladys

Robinson had been forced to return to the States several weeks earlier with a condition that was later diagnosed as advanced cancer.

In the early part of November I received word that Gladys was in very unstable condition and not expected to live more than a few days. Taking time out of my busy schedule, I traveled to Tennessee to spend some time with her. It was after I arrived back in Liberia that I learned Gladys had died on December 10th.

I'd been on furlough just a little more than seven months, but already my heart was burning to return home. I had enjoyed seeing Leland again, but the situation had been a strain for both of us, and I had to accept the fact that time, distance, and different priorities had done much to erase the closeness we had once enjoyed. The week with Bob and his family had been a sheer delight, but he was a grown man now, and my "kids" back at Fassama needed me. And, while everyone, especially the Klapps, had treated me like a queen, my heart dictated that it was time to quit sharing plans and get down to work.

Response and pledges of support had been outstanding both in my travels and at General Conference, so Brother Stairs quickly agreed to the request to cut my furlough short. If I left in early December, I could join Valda Russell in New Orleans and sail aboard the Delta Lines.

SEVENTEEN

Dedicated to LaVerne

For several minutes now I had been able to sense that we were descending. I had watched out the window as the plane cut through the thin, wispy clouds. Soon, we had broken through the ceiling, and there was the "Big City" below us. I thought of the many refugees that had seen a sight quite similar to this for the first time, and the hopes and dreams for the future that must have filled their hearts.

Strange, but at that moment I would have traded that scene, and a thousand more like it, for just one glimpse of Fassama, as it suddenly appeared out of the jungle. I detested, if you really want to know the truth, flying in those little matchbox missionary planes, but right then I would have swapped that 707 for one without giving it a second thought.

The sun was just beginning to disappear over the western horizon when we finally pulled into the bus station in downtown New Orleans. After claiming my baggage, I took a taxi the few short blocks to the hotel where I had arranged to meet Valda. She had already checked in when I arrived, so after freshening up a bit, we had dinner together in the hotel restaurant. Returning to Valda's room, we sat up until the wee hours of the morning, as I did my best to answer the multitude of questions she had about missionary life, Liberia, and Bomi Hills in particular. I had never met Hubert and Dorothy Parks, the couple who had replaced the Pettys at Bomi Hills, so she'd just have to wait and meet them and form her own opinion.

It seemed like I had just dozed off when I was awakened by the clanging of the alarm, announcing that it was time to get up and on our way to the wharf where we would board the Delta Lines ship. We were glad, upon arriving, to discover that this sailing would not include a side trip to South America, but that we would go straight from New Orleans to Dakar, and then on to Monrovia.

Christmas that year was spent somewhere in the middle of the Atlantic. I had been given a brightly wrapped package just before I left, with explicit orders: "Do not open 'til Christmas!" So, with a dinner on board that included all the trimmings, the company of Valda, and the gift, I had all the ingredients for a happy and complete Christmas. Next year promised to be even better—I'd be home in Fassama for Christmas.

Twenty-two days after lifting anchor in New Orleans, we sailed into the harbor of Monrovia. In my absence, the government had dredged the port to allow the large ore boats to enter. I was certainly relieved to learn that we would not have to travel the final few hundred yards in an open motor launch. It was January 4, 1954 when my feet touched Liberian soil for the third time.

After clearing customs, Valda and I began craning our necks in a desperate attempt to spot someone who might resemble a Pentecostal missionary—someone who might have come to the ship to meet us. When we had just about given up hope, we heard someone say behind us:

"Praise the Lord, ladies! We're Brother and Sister Parks. You two must be Sister Gruse and Sister Russell."

After a few moments of small talk, they assisted us with our bags, and we followed them to the missions pickup. Plans called for us to spend the night in Bomi Hills, then return to Monrovia the next morning to process through the Department of Internal Affairs, as well as the Department of Education. After clearing the government offices, I would devote a couple of days to buying supplies. We would most likely stay two or three nights in the A.G. home.

Returning to Bomi Hills, I spent a day recruiting enough carriers to take all our supplies back to Fassama. In addition to Jean's extensive shopping list, there were two beds and a kerosene ice box, luxuries we had heretofore not enjoyed.

I was a fifty year old grandma now, but there was still just one way to get to Fassama—by foot—five days of walking through jungle and over mountains. I was certainly blessed that it was "dry time." At least the rivers would be in their banks.

The trek almost did me in. It was hard to believe that eight short months could make such a vast difference. Had the "soft" life of furlough ruined me for trekking? As I came walking into the village, with every muscle and bone in my body racked with pain, I determined that we must build an airstrip. I just didn't see how I could walk in too many more times.

I SURRENDER ALL

I arrived in Fassama to find that Jean had been busy as a beaver in my absence. When I had left in April, we had barely begun the foundation for our permanent home, but upon my return, the house was almost complete. There was some finish work to be done, and Jean had forgotten how I wanted the bath, but for the most part it was complete, and ready to be lived in.

We had built the home with the idea of a family replacing us someday in the distant future—if the Lord tarried. It was a large house, with eight full-sized rooms and a screened-in veranda. It was constructed of mud, supported by poles that were approximately ten inches in diameter. It had a zinc roof, which we had imported from Canada, and a dirt floor, which we covered with native rattan rugs.

Jean had handled all the mission duties in my absence—the school teaching, the preaching and Bible teaching, the nursing, the building, and the farming. Upon my return, she began concentrating on farming and teaching school, and I devoted most of my time to being a contractor and nurse—a likely combination. We divided the preaching and Bible teaching duties.

After putting the finishing touches on our house, I launched into the construction of a separate building for the school. Since opening the mission station, the church building had doubled as a classroom.

There had been a steady stream of adults, teenagers, and children being baptized and receiving the Holy Spirit while I was on furlough, and the revival continued after my return. In the more than 17 years that I would labor at Fassama I would see practically every boy or girl that came to live on the mission station receive the Holy Spirit.

After I had been back a month or so, Jean and I decided that the time had come for us to launch out and have services in the neighboring villages. After all, we had been called to the Belle people, not just the Fassamites. Our first outreach services were conducted in Gonjdeah, a village about two hours from Fassama. From the very start, the village chief, an elderly man, showed extreme interest. About the sixth week, however, he failed to show up for service. At first, we didn't think much about it, assuming he was either ill or had been forced to attend to some official duty. When he was still missing the following week, however, we began to be concerned. The next morning, in discussing the matter with Chief Weedor, we learned that the old chief had been found dead—mysteriously poisoned. It was never determined what the motive was, but we had our strong suspicions.

In early January of 1955, we received a letter from Brother Stairs, informing us of some personnel changes that would be taking place in the near future. Jack and Sandra Langham, recently-appointed missionaries, would soon be arriving to relieve the Parks at Bomi Hills. Dorothy Parks had become quite ill, necessitating a return to the States after a little more than a year on the field.

Also arriving in a few weeks would be LaVerne Collins, a first-term missionary who would be relieving Jean at Fassama so that she could leave for furlough. It was requested that Jean depart immediately for Bomi Hills, to assist VaIda until the Langhams arrived. Upon their arrival, Jean would be free to leave for the States.

Within a couple of weeks, Jean was packed and on the trail. She arrived at Bomi Hills five-and-a-half days later, just in time to ride into Monrovia and meet LaVerne. Before returning to Bomi Hills, Jean assisted LaVerne in processing into the country. The next Monday, LaVerne began an eight-week teacher orientation course sponsored by the Liberian Department of Education. This was a requirement that had recently been enacted.

LaVerne arrived in Fassama in mid-March—just in time for the beginning of the new semester. She was the first passenger to land on the new makeshift runway we had constructed several miles from the mission. Upon her arrival, LaVerne pretty well took over the duties that had been relegated to Jean—that of teaching in the school and overseeing the farming operation of the mission. Like Jean, she shared the preaching and Bible teaching responsibilities with me.

LaVerne, who was single, was approximately ten years younger than I. In addition to graduating from Apostolic College, she had attended two universities in Arkansas. Prior to receiving her appointment to Liberia, she had taught in the public school system for a number of years.

For the first few months after LaVerne's arrival, things were quite hectic on the mission, and we really didn't have the opportunity to trek to any of the other Belle villages for services. We did plan, however, to take a long trek as soon as the semester break arrived. At night, when we would have a few spare moments, we would discuss our upcoming trip, and I could see LaVerne's eyes light with excitement at the thought of traveling back into the jungle. At times, it seemed that life on the mission station was just a little too tame for her.

Plans called for us to depart about the 20th of July, soon after the current semester had ended. As the date approached, however, I began to notice that LaVerne was looking increasingly pale and gaunt. On several occasions I asked her if she was feeling okay, but each time she assured me that she had never felt better in her life. Finally, on the 18th of July, just two days before we were scheduled to leave, LaVerne got to the point that she could no longer pretend or ignore, and had to admit that she was ill and would have to go to bed. Even then, however, she insisted that it was just a virus or something, and that in a day or two she would be fully recovered and able to accompany me on the trek as planned. I knew LaVerne's condition was more serious than she let on, but I pretended to agree with her nevertheless, not telling her that I had dropped all plans for our trek.

At first I assumed that LaVerne had contracted malaria. She had not been faithful in taking her pills, so this was a distinct possibility. But after a few days I began suspecting that her condition was something more involved.

For the first few days LaVerne complained of a serious headache, as well as a general throbbing that seemed to cover her entire body. In addition, she ran an extremely high fever most of the time. Towards the end of the first week her headache seemed to subside somewhat, but she began to repeat over and over, "Oh, I feel so sick. I can't exactly put my finger on it, but I feel so sick all over."

During the first week LaVerne remained in bed most of the time. The few times she did attempt to walk, she could manage no more than a stiff shuffle. Entering the second week she was completely bedfast and was getting noticeably lower with each passing day.

LaVerne maintained a strong appetite well into the second week of her illness, yet she continued to lose strength. Perhaps this could be explained in part by the fact that she was finding it impossible to sleep for more than a few minutes at a stretch.

Several times each day during the second week I had

the older boys and girls on the mission join me in LaVerne's room for an old-fashioned prayer meeting. Each time we felt the presence of the Lord in a real and unmistakable way, but we could seemingly not feel that calm assurance that God was going to heal her body.

About the middle of the week I asked LaVerne if she wanted me to send some of the boys to Bomi Hills to inform Brother Langham of her condition. He could arrange for a plane to fly in and pick her up. Her answer was a firm "No!"

Sunday, July 31, some of the girls helped me lift LaVerne into a chair so I could change her bed linens. When we laid her back in bed, she sank down into the pillow, closed her eyes, and began breathing rather heavily. My first thoughts were that she had finally managed to fall asleep. A few moments later, however, her breathing became quite irregular and she began making rasping noises in her throat.

I was afraid to give her a drink for fear that she would choke, so I began moistening her lips with a damp cloth. Finally, after an hour or so, she opened her eyes to a tight squint, and tried to speak. After several attempts, she gave up, but continued to stare at me and follow me across the room each time I rose to dampen the cloth.

I continued to sit at her bedside throughout the night, wiping her fevered brow, moistening her parched lips, and frantically praying to God that somehow, in His infinite love, mercy, and wisdom, He had burdened some dear saint back in the States to pray for the urgent need at Fassama Mission Station. I wondered if Doris and Virgil Klapp, or perhaps someone back in Tulsa might be on their knees at that very hour, crying out to God in intercessory prayer.

By 8:00 Monday morning it was evident that it was just a matter of time—that unless LaVerne had medical attention, or the Lord directly intervened into the affairs of men, she would soon be dead. I asked her, hoping that she could understand what I was saying, if she wanted me to send Sammy to Belle Yella to get the government medical officer. There was no response, but I thought I could detect in her eyes that the answer was "yes," so I sent him. Going against LaVerne's earlier wishes, I dispatched one of the other boys to Bomi Hills, with instructions to "get there as fast as you can—Sister Collins is dying!"

About an hour after the runners left, there was a sudden stiffening in LaVerne's neck. I knew that death was knocking at the door and that only the Lord, Himself, could keep it from opening. With my hand on her forehead, and my eyes lifted toward heaven, she drew her final gasping breath, then passed into eternity, barely seven months after her arrival in Liberia.

For a few moments I stood frozen, my mind refusing to function, and my eyes staring into blank infinity. Slowly I turned and walked from the room and into the yard. Several of the boys were milling around the door, and in response to their inquiring eyes, I whispered softly, "Yes . . . she's dead . . . Sister Collins has passed away."

I'd been through a lot in my 51 years—an awful lot—but the next three days would easily prove to be the most difficult of my life. There would be times when I would honestly wonder if I could keep from losing my mind. In fact, for weeks afterwards I would suffer from the ordeal. Actually, to tell the truth, I would never fully recover from the incident.

I had told the runner to hurry, but it would be at least three days before he would arrive in Bomi Hills. Then, it would take at least another day for Brother Langham to arrange for a bush pilot to fly him in. There were no facilities in Fassama for embalming the body, and the extreme heat and humidity would hasten the decaying process. Still I had hopes of delaying the funeral until Brother Langham could arrive.

The first order of business was to arrange for a coffin. Chief Weedor sent one of the village carpenters over, and within a few hours he had built a crude pine box. With the help of one of the boys, the coffin was carried over and placed on the veranda. Finding some material we had been saving for draperies, I lined the coffin as best I could.

Next, I gave LaVerne a sponge bath, dressed her in her favorite outfit, and did my best to fix her hair the way she wore it. Then, upon locating her dentures, I went through the gruesome and macabre ordeal of prying open her mouth while I put them into place. I was visibly shaking, my head was spinning, and I felt as though I was in a trance as I walked out the door to get a breath of fresh air.

I called across the yard and got several of the boys to assist me in placing LaVerne into the pine coffin. There was nothing to do now but sit by the coffin and wait—wait for Brother Langham to arrive so we could have LaVerne's funeral.

The runner had made record time, arriving in Bomi Hills late Wednesday evening. It was impossible to charter a plane at that hour of the day, so Brother Langham had no choice but to wait until early the next morning. Up at the crack of dawn, he drove to the air field and made arrangements for a flight to Fassama. The pilot agreed to wait for a couple of hours while Brother Langham drove into Monrovia to send a telegram to the States, notifying the Missions Department of LaVerne's condition. Feeling he'd have no need for his rifle in Monrovia, Brother Langham had left it with the pilot. But, for some unknown reason, shortly after Brother Langham left for Monrovia, the pilot took off for Fassama, carrying the rifle with him.

I was sitting on the veranda, by LaVerne's coffin, when one of the boys came running up with news that the plane was landing. Looking in the direction, of the mountains, I could see a tiny silhouette descending in the sky. Rushing to the landing strip, I fully expected to find Brother Langham, and possibly Sister Langham, stepping out of the plane. I was stunned to find just the pilot.

"Where are the missionaries?" I asked him. Shrugging his shoulders, he handed me the rifle.

"Where are the missionaries?" I demanded. Again he shrugged his shoulders.

"That'll be a hundred dollars," he stated rather matter-of-factly, as if he had just done a tremendous service to mankind.

"A hundred dollars for what?" I managed to stammer.

"For the delivery of this rifle. It's the standard fee for a trip up here—regardless of what we carry."

Any other time I would have refused his ridiculous demands, but this was not any other time—I was on the brink of insanity or a nervous breakdown or perhaps both. So, I told him to wait while I went back to the mission to get the money.

After paying him, I returned to the house stunned, confused, perplexed, and in a state of shock. Coherent thoughts refused to come, and I had absolutely no idea what to do next. Moses, bless his heart, maintained his composure, and came to the rescue.

"Ma, we can't wait for the missionaries. We're gonna

have to bury Sister Collins right away. She's swelling so much, Ma, that she'll soon burst."

Following Moses' advice, we moved LaVerne to the church, where she lay in state for a couple of hours. After giving the children and the town's people an opportunity to view the body, we conducted a short and simple ceremony, then laid LaVerne to rest near the mission station.

Early the next morning, Jack and Sandra Langham arrived. Plans called for Brother Langham to stay about a week, and for Sister Langham to remain with me for as long as I needed her. During the week that Brother Langham was at Fassama, a revival broke loose and 13 were baptized.

Sandra Langham stayed for two weeks after her husband left. I'll never be able to describe the strength and comfort she provided during those first difficult days. However, there were some aspects of the tragedy that time alone would erase, and still others that would always remain a part of me.

For several months after LaVerne's death I would awaken in the middle of the night, feeling that I was choking, and hearing eerie sounds that I was certain were coming from the direction of the veranda. And, I would never be able to forget the experience of trying to insert LaVerne's dentures. From that moment on I would have a phobia about sleeping with my partial bridge in.

There were many, many, many shortages at Fassama. In fact, about the only things we had plenty of were shortages and grass. Grass! There was grass everywhere—long, thick, stubborn blades of grass that seemed to delight in growing a foot or more overnight. Each week the boys would spend hours upon hours with their crude sickles, doing their best to keep the mission grounds from reverting back into a jungle. Almost from the time we had arrived, Jean and I had discussed the need for a power mower. It had to be a power mower. A push mower would be no better than the sickles—maybe even worse.

While Jean was in Bomi Hills, assisting Valda until the Langhams could arrive, she ordered a Lawn-Boy power mower for Fassama. It finally arrived by plane in early October of 1955, just as the rainy season was drawing to a close. Along with the mower, the pilot brought enough gasoline and oil to last us for a month.

Jean had a slight working knowledge of the mechanics of a mower, but a lot of good that would do us with her in the States and us in West Africa. I was totally ignorant of both the inner and outer workings of the contraption, and the boys on the mission had never seen one in their lives. But, by putting our heads together and reading over the instructions a half-dozen times or more, we managed to identify and mount the handle, locate and fill the gas tank, and attach the starter rope. The directions also described the method of depressing the metal clip onto the spark plug in order to stop the engine.

I allowed the boys to start the mower, then I took over and cut a strip close to the house. As I mowed, the children from the mission, along with a dozen or so boys and girls from the village, followed closely behind, laughing and screaming, and rolling and turning somersaults in the freshly cut grass.

It was almost nightfall, and time for service, when I got to the end of my row. I told the boys we'd shut the mower off, and that I'd let them mow the entire grounds in the morning. The instructions had suggested stepping on the clip to kill the engine, but I wasn't about to do this. I still

I SURRENDER ALL

remembered well the time I had been shocked by a washing machine, and I was terrified of this happening again.

So, I directed one of the boys to find a large stick which we could use to press the clip against the spark plug. In a few moments David returned with what was more of a pole than a stick. I don't know if it was the pole, the clip, or a joint effort, but I do know that the clip snapped in two before it ever touched the spark plug.

"What are we gonna do now?" I exclaimed in dismay. Finally, after racking my brains and scratching my head, I decided that we really had no choice. The only solution was to have the boys cut grass until the mower ran out of gas. At first they were having the time of their lives, as they fought over whose turn it was next. After an hour or so, however, the game had turned into work, and they were more than ready to quit. The only problem was that the tank wasn't empty yet. They had been mowing almost two hours when the engine drew its last breath.

From then on, whenever it was time to mow the grounds, we would fill the tank to capacity, and the boys would mow until their tongues were dragging the ground. Not one time did any of us think of only partially filling the tank so that the mower would run out of gas more quickly.

One morning, while I was in the house doing some chores, I suddenly realized that the lawn mower was no longer running. Robert hadn't been mowing more than a few minutes, so he couldn't be out of gas. My heart sank as I thought, "Oh, no, Robert has done something to break the mower!"

In a few moments Robert came running up to the house, grinning from ear to ear and just bubbling with excitement.

"Ma, Ma, guess what!"

"Robert," I asked him sternly, "Have you broken our lawn mower?"

"No, Ma," he answered out of breath. "I've got sense for it."

"You've got what for it?"

"Sense for it. I've got sense for it, Ma."

"How do you have sense for it, Robert?" I asked him.

"I learned, Ma, that if you push the mower into the tall grass it will stop."

Well, from that moment on we had an improved method for turning the mower off when we were tired of mowing. No more mowing until we had run out of gas. I suspected that this new procedure wasn't exactly prolonging the life of the mower, but what else could we do?

Several months later I mentioned our predicament to a pilot who had brought in our supplies. Reaching for his tool bag, he followed us back to the mission. After having the boys start the engine, he pulled a plastic handled screw driver from the tool bag, which he used for shorting out the spark plug.

"Always be certain," he warned, "to use a screw driver with a well insulated handle."

In the ensuing months I learned a lot about that mower, including how to tear it down and completely overhaul it. Believe it or not, it always worked like brand-new after I had reassembled it. Despite the fact that the mower was not designed for heavy jungle grass, the old Lawn-Boy gave us uninterrupted service for many years.

On February 11, 1956 Jean returned to Liberia for her second term. Five days later, after successfully clearing the government offices and buying supplies, she set down on our makeshift airstrip. This would prove one of the final landings here, as the pilots were becoming increasingly vocal and belligerent about the dangers of landing on the clearing.

With her Jean brought several cases of powdered milk and canned goods. We would continue to live off the land as much as possible—taking advantage of the avocados, bananas, cherries, grapefruit, lemons, limes, mango plums, oranges, pineapples, and plantains that grew right there on the mission station. Still, there were times when these delicacies were not in season, and a balanced diet, which was a necessity in the tropics, did require more than fresh fruit.

Also included in Jean's baggage was a 1,200 watt generator which we would use to supply power for our new home. Several months later we would receive a 3,000 watt unit which would be used for the larger church building we were planning to build.

Shortly after Jean's return I became seriously ill with what I determined to be an intestinal infection. Several days of pain and agony, coupled with memories of LaVerne's sudden death, were enough to convince me that I needed to see a doctor. That way, I reasoned, when God healed me I'd have a doctor's opinion of what I had been healed of.

It would take three days for a runner to reach Bomi Hills to charter a flight to come in and pick me up. Upon his arrival, chances would be slim that a pilot could be convinced to land here. With this in mind, I decided to allow the boys to carry me down in a hammock. It was still dry time, so perhaps the trip wouldn't be too difficult- once we had crossed the mountains.

Shortly after arriving in Bomi Hills the doctor confirmed my preliminary prognosis. I indeed had an intestinal infection. It was two full weeks before I had regained enough strength to even think about returning to Fassama. Brother Langham was easily successful in convincing me that I was in no condition to walk in. On the other hand, I flatly refused to have the boys carry me back in. This left but one mode of travel—by air.

After an hour or so of "Yankee palaver" Brother Langham persuaded the pilot to lay aside common sense and agree to fly me in. Upon landing, however, and almost flipping the plane end over end, the pilot convinced me beyond a shadow of a doubt that this would indeed be the last time he, or for that matter, any pilot, landed at the Fassama "Airport." It was now evident that unless Jean and I wished to return to taking five-and-a-half day walks to the coast, we'd better waste no time in constructing an adequate landing strip—one which would be pleasing to even the most discriminating bush pilot.

Around the first of April Jean and I began holding weekly services in the village of Belle Barbima, about an hour-and-a-half walk from Fassama. From the very start there was tremendous enthusiasm among the villagers, with several being baptized in Jesus name and filled with the Holy Spirit. For about two months we took turns going to Belle Barbima for the Sunday service. After that, we began sending Moses, James, Joseph, and some of the other older boys.

It was about this time that I performed my first wedding ceremony among the natives, To the best of my knowledge this was the first Christian marriage in this part of the Belle country—for at least as far back as anyone could recall. Actually, it was a double wedding, with James marrying Mary, and Joseph marrying Helen. All four of these young people had been living on the mission station for several years. Both young men had come to us for marital counselling. As part of our advice we had encouraged them to follow the native tradition of providing a dowry to the parents of the young lady. Tribal custom taught that a girl was not properly married until the dowry, however small, was paid.

The first part of December that same year we received word from the Foreign Missions Department that a miracle had just been performed—a decision had been made to purchase an airplane for the work in Liberia. The pilot would be William Cupples, newly-appointed missionary to Liberia. He, along with his wife, Frances, and their daughter, Ruth Ann, were due to arrive shortly after the first of the year.

Upon receiving this glorious news, Jean and I intensified our efforts towards building a first class landing strip near the mission. It took eight long, backbreaking months, cutting down trees, digging up stumps, and removing bugabug mounds, but when we were finally through, we had a 50 by 2,000 foot runway that many of the bush pilots reported to be the finest country landing strip in all of Liberia.

In January of 1957 Jean's right arm became infected from a shot she had received, and it proved necessary for her to go down to Bomi Hills for several weeks. While she was gone, Brother Langham came up to Fassama to assist me in the work. During his stay, he took a quick trip over to Belle Yella, feeling that perhaps now was the time to establish a work there.

Jean returned to Fassama about the first of February, and we immediately resumed work on our new church building. A week or so later we received our new 3,000 watt generator. The next few days found Jean and me playing the part of electricians. My job was to crawl over the rafters, stapling the wire every foot or so, and splicing the connections. Jean, who readily admitted she was not up to playing the part of a monkey, accepted the responsibility of installing the light sockets, the plugs, and the switches. Amazingly enough, when we had finished and cranked up the generator, everything worked, and there were neither sparks nor smoke.

The building was finally complete, and we stood back, rightfully proud of the 25 by 60-foot structure that we had built—built by ourselves, without the able assistance of any men.

Two months later, in May of 1957, the Cupples came to Fassama for a two week revival, While they were there, the girls Devil Bush broke, and Chief Weedor brought the hundred or so girls over to the mission in all their ceremonial regalia. One of the girls in that group was Kubah, destined to become the Soo, or the head woman in the Devil Bush. Later, however, she would give it all up to become a Christian.

In October of 1957, acting on the advice of Brother Langham, the Cupples family moved to Belle Yella to begin a work. The missions plane would be based in Belle Yella, but would continue to be available to all the missionaries.

A missionary conference was held at Bomi Hills in April of 1958. During the conference Brother Stairs informed us that I would be leaving for furlough in early spring of next year. The Cupples, who had met with extreme opposition in Belle Yella, would soon move to Fassama to be my relief. They would more than likely remain after my return, as Brother Stairs felt that the opportunities at Fassama could easily justify three missionaries. By now it was evident that Fassama was the mission station of the future—at least the near future.

Upon their arrival, Brother Cupples immediately began construction of their home. They had come several years too early to inherit the one Jean and I had built. Brother Cupples' primary duty those first few months was to evangelize the neighboring Belle villages. Jean still had the school as her main responsibility, and I devoted much of my time to the operation of the clinic.

The month of January, 1959 was a very special month for me. First of all, on the 7th of the month little Eddie Cupples was born in the Liberian Mining Company Hospital at Bomi Hills. Then, a week or so later, I received a precious and heartwarming letter from my son, Bob. In the letter he assured me that he fully understood my decision of some 25 years earlier. It had been best for all concerned that he be raised by his Aunt Bertha. He went on to tell me that he was proud of the work I was doing in Liberia, and that he and his family were looking forward to seeing me in the near future.

In my life I have received many cherished gifts from some dear and notable people, but I must honestly say that none are as priceless as the letter I received from Bob. I guess that next to God, Himself, Bob's approval meant more to me than that of anyone else. We had both made a tremendous sacrifice so that I might bring the Gospel to Liberia, and just knowing that my son stood behind my efforts meant all the world to me.

EIGHTEEN

Furlough Number Three

I could feel the thud of the wheels as they made initial contact with the runway. This was quickly followed by the reversing of the huge jet engines. Within moments the voice of the flight attendant could be heard: "Welcome to New York City, ladies and gentlemen. We will be deplaning shortly. Please remain in your seats, with your seatbelts fastened, until the aircraft has come to a complete stop. If you will be staying in New York, please have a nice stay. If you will be making connections, our personnel at the Pan American courtesy counter will be delighted to assist you. It is now 1:50 local time. On behalf of the entire crew, it has been a pleasure serving you. Thank you for flying Pan American.

It was on Monday morning, March 2, 1959, after a five year term in Liberia, that I left Fassama in preparation for my third furlough. The only trekking I had to do this time was the distance from my front door to the landing strip near the mission. In less than an hour Brother Cupples had safely deposited me at Bomi Hills, where I spent the remainder of the day and much of the night visiting with the Langhams and Valda. Early the following morning Brother Langham drove me into Monrovia in the missions pickup.

The next three days were spent clearing the government offices, buying my airlines ticket, and picking up a few curios for some special friends back in the States. The nights were spent in an attempt to relax at the A.G. home.

I was up before the first peek of sunlight Friday morning, trying to rearrange my luggage to make room for the gifts I had purchased. Finally seeing that it was just no use, I was faced with the choice of what to leave behind. With these lofty decisions made, I joined the staff of the home for breakfast. After eating and joining in morning devotion, I said goodbye to my hosts and caught a taxi for Roberts Field.

Upon arriving and checking with the Pan Am desk, I discovered that my flight had been delayed two hours. So, with almost four hours to kill, I sought out a secluded spot in the corner of the waiting room—a place where I could make good use of this free time. Taking my Bible from the tote bag I was carrying, I began to read, trusting the Lord to lay some thoughts on my heart—some thoughts that could be developed into messages for the folks back "home." I had a burning desire for God to anoint and use my ministry during this furlough. I was not the least bit interested in going from church to church telling "stories" and displaying artifacts.

I had surely become lost in the Word of God, as before I knew what had happened my flight was announced over the public address system. Jumping up, I stuffed the Bible and note pad into my tote bag, and began rummaging through my purse, frantically trying to locate the plane ticket.

As I walked through the gate and onto the ramp towards the plane, I had that same strange feeling—the feeling that I was leaving home, not returning. Yes, as strange as it might seem, after more than five years of jungle living I was reluctant to leave. With each passing year I was becoming more and more burdened for these people. With each passing year they were becoming more and more my people. It was as if the Lord were telling me that it was for these people that I had been born, that it was for these people that He had spared and directed my life, and that without these people there would be no justification for my existence.

The first few weeks of my furlough were pretty much a carbon copy of the one six years earlier. From New York I flew to Cleveland to spend a few days with my brother, Leland. Then the following weekend Bob and Rosemary drove up from Lima and I returned home with them for a week or so. This visit, without a doubt, proved to be the highlight of my furlough. From Lima I took a bus to South Bend to visit with Doris and Virgil Klapp and establish my base of operations for the next twelve months.

After spending several weeks with my special friends, resting up and occasionally ministering in some of the local churches, it was time to begin my rigorous and demanding deputational tour. This time most of the services were scheduled for the Illinois-Indiana area. Tremendous growth within the ranks of the United Pentecostal Church had made it possible to limit my travels to these two states.

I SURRENDER ALL

In late September there was a week or so break in my itinerary to attend General Conference in St. Louis. While there, I met with the Foreign Missions Board and was reappointed. On Sunday night at 6:00 I was the nervous, stage frightened main speaker for the annual Youth Service. After Conference it was back to the grind as a "Missionary on Furlough." As before, I confined my activities primarily to the assemblies in Illinois and Indiana. I took a few days off at Christmas to be with the Klapps in South Bend. After the first of the year I was at it again, with plans of staying on the road until the latter part of February. In the early part of March I would depart for New York where I would board a flight for West Africa.

Everything went according to schedule until I reached New York. I had accepted the kind invitation of T. J. and Lorine Miller to spend a couple of days in their home and minister in the Manhattan church. After service the first night, we returned home and were preparing to eat a snack when I began experiencing severe pains in my lower back. At first I dismissed them as the result of tension and being on the go too much. I excused myself for the night and assured the Millers that a good nights sleep would do the trick. Over the next few hours, however, the pain grew steadily worse until it had reached agonizing proportions—surpassing even the pangs of childbirth. By four o'clock that morning I was positive that I had at least one large kidney stone.

It was all I could do to keep from screaming to the top of my lungs, but for the next three or four hours I bit my tongue and remained silent—at least enough to keep from waking the Millers. About 7:30 Lorine came in to check on me. One quick look and she could tell that I was in extreme pain. A few moments later, sensing that something was wrong, Brother Miller came to the door and joined his wife in insisting that I allow them to take me to the nearby emergency room.

It's strange, and I suppose I'll never be able to really explain it, but there have been times in my life when I have felt definitely led to take my physical need straight to the Lord, completely forgetting that there was ever any such thing as medicine or a doctor. At other times, however, I have not experienced this leading of the Spirit, and have felt at perfect liberty to see a physician or take medication. Well, this just so happened to be one of those "faith times," and I had no choice but to refuse Brother and Sister Miller's request.

"I don't want to go to the hospital, Brother Miller. I feel that if we'll just trust God, He'll heal me. There's no doubt in my mind—God wants to heal me!"

Well, what could he say? How could a pastor that preached divine healing argue with my case? So, with the two of them kneeling by my bedside, we had us a prayer meeting. The pain was still there—full strength—when we had finished, but I had the calm assurance that at any moment it would begin to subside. In a few moments it did begin to diminish, and within an hour or so I had drifted off to sleep. It was about mid-afternoon when I awoke. The pain was still there, but it was much, much less than it had been at its height.

I ate a light meal, then rested for a few hours as I read my Bible. By 8:00 the pain had become only a dull throb and I was ready to turn in for the night. When I awoke the next morning the pain was completely gone—just a soreness to remind me of the ordeal and testify to the fact that God was a prayer-answering, healing, kidney stone-dissolving God.

I was claiming complete healing, and didn't feel that I needed any additional time to recuperate, but I let the Millers talk me into it anyway. The next day Brother Miller received a call from Brother Stairs, informing him that he and Brother Morgan, the General Superintendent of the United Pentecostal Church, would be coming through New York in a few days on their way to West Africa. Upon learning that I was still in New York, he suggested that I wait and travel with them.

It was approximately a week later when we left for Africa. Due to some mechanical problems with the aircraft our flight was more than ten hours late in departing. After intermediate stops in Lisbon, Portugal and Freetown, Sierre Leone, it was on to Roberts Field, where we were met by an anxious and terribly worried Brother Langham.

After claiming our baggage and clearing through customs we drove to Bomi Hills for the night. The next morning Brother Langham took me into Monrovia to process through the government offices. Three days later he flew me to Fassama to begin my fourth term.

NINETEEN

Raised from the Dead

"1:50? That can't be right!" I thought to myself half aloud.

"Nancy, the stewardess just said it was 1:50. That can't be right . . . can it? I've got 12:50, and I'm positive I set my watch correctly back in Frankfurt."

"Did you allow for daylight saving time?" she asked me rather amused.

"Daylight saving time?" I'd forgotten about daylight saving time—the time when Americans take the longest days of the year and add another hour. There was probably a lot more about America that I had forgotten.

"Oh, God," I said before I could catch myself, "I don't belong here!"

It was with a great deal of anticipation and enthusiasm that I reassumed my duties at Fassama. The opportunities there excited me. How rewarding to spend another four or five years reaching new souls with the

Gospel, not to mention being instrumental in the spiritual growth of those who had already made a commitment. Fassama was now our largest work in Liberia, and there would never be an idle moment. Still, I couldn't wait to get unpacked, roll up my sleeves, and get back to work.

Upon my return the division of duties was primarily as it had been in the past. As senior missionary, I was still in charge of the work. Jean's main responsibility continued to be the running of the school, and as before, I oversaw the operation of the clinic. We would still divide the preaching and Bible teaching duties.

In July of the preceding year it had become necessary for the Cupples to return to the States in order for Frances to have surgery. There had been no replacement available, so after their departure it had proven necessary for Jean to run the mission single-handedly for almost eight months.

With the Cupples leaving, Brother Langham had become the pilot, and the plane was once more based in Bomi Hills. There were two scheduled flights to Fassama each month, and if an emergency arose Jean could always reach Brother Langham with the ham radio Brother Cupples had left her.

Several days after my arrival in Fassama, Brother Langham flew Brother Stairs and Brother Morgan up to look the situation over. While they were there Brother Morgan preached a three night revival in which 15 were baptized in Jesus name. One of these 15 was Kubah, the teenage girl who had been selected as the next Soo of the Devil Bush. It was only a week or so after being baptized that Kubah received the Holy Spirit.

As would be expected, the leaders of the Devil Bush were incensed with the thought that one of their own, especially the one they had groomed to be the next Soo, would forsake them in favor of going the "God way."

One morning, as Kubah was on her way to the mission, several men from the Bush grabbed her and dragged her to the village palaver kitchen. As a crowd started gathering, the men began tearing her clothes off and taunting her. When they had become bored of this, they proceeded to carry her to the creek where they planned to beat her.

Up until that point Kubah had not resisted. Knowing the evil spirit by which these men were directed, she felt it best to remain silent. But, if they became carried away in their beating they could kill her. Finally, in desperation, she warned them that if they harmed her the missionary would find out. This was the magic word. The men knew me well enough to know that I'd waste no time in informing Commissioner Mooney, and that he, in turn, would take immediate steps to disband the Devil Bush. He had threatened to do this several times in the past.

Upon learning of the treatment Kubah had received, I insisted that she not spend another day in the village. It was only a few weeks after she moved onto the mission that I began to detect a certain sparkle in the eyes of Yapallo whenever Kubah was near.

Several months later a tragedy visited Bomi Hills which left us all grief-stricken and in a near state of shock. It was a typical Liberian June morning, and Sandra Langham had gone into the village to do some shopping in the Mining Company store. When she had left, Sharon, their twelve year old, had been in her room reading a book. Jackie, their older son, had been in the yard playing with Sam, one of the native boys.

She had been gone several minutes when Jackie and

Sam decided to go inside and rest for a few minutes. When they entered the living room, Sam spotted a .22 rifle leaning up in the corner, and picked it up to examine it. Suddenly he was pointing it at Jackie.

"Put that thing down!" Jackie demanded.

He was preparing to do as instructed, when Sharon emerged from her room to see what all the commotion was about. Having no idea that the weapon was loaded, Sam swung the barrel around and pointed it straight at Sharon, simultaneously pulling the trigger. With a sickening crack the weapon discharged, the bullet striking her in the heart and killing her instantly.

The Langhams refused to press charges, knowing that the boy had not known the rifle was loaded. The Liberian government, however, did force him to spend a short time in jail. Sam practically lost his mind in the aftermath, and months later had not fully recovered. Naturally the Langhams were literally beside themselves over the accident, as well as the circumstances. Valda, who had become very attached to Sharon, and who is by nature a highly emotional person, took it as hard as Sandra Langham, herself.

In the latter part of August, 1960, after four-and-a-half years on the field, Jean returned to the States for a well-deserved furlough. About a month after her arrival she attended the General Conference being held in Dallas, Texas. While there, she met with the Foreign Missions Board and received appointment for her third term. In the ensuing months, however, she began to feel that it was not the will of God for her to return. For weeks she toiled with the decision, then reluctantly gave in to the voice of God.

From August of 1960 until March of the following year I was the only missionary at Fassama. The task would have been absolutely impossible had it not been for the fine young men who had received their training on the mission and were now proving to be a tremendous asset to its operation. Several of the boys like Moses, James, Joseph, Peter, and Yapallo could be depended upon completely. Then, of course, there was Teacher Konah, the man from the Gola tribe who had come to us several years earlier. Without his assistance in the school I would have surely lost my mind.

It was in the early part of the fall of 1960 that those special glances between Yapallo and Kubah blossomed into a beautiful romance. It wasn't long until I was asked to perform still another marriage ceremony.

Chief Weedor had not minded his three younger sons becoming Christians. In fact, he had "given" them to us as our first mission children. But Yapallo was different. The chief had plans for Yapallo. He was the oldest son and the one Chief Weedor had chosen as his successor. He had not been sent to the mission and his decision to go the "God way" had been entirely his own.

For years Chief Weedor had been an ardent supporter of our efforts, coming to our defense on more than one occasion. The moment Yapallo began attending services, however, this enthusiastic attitude began to cool. Several weeks later, when Yapallo was baptized and filled with the Spirit, the chief's attitude became downright belligerent. Still, he maintained a hope that one day his son would "come to his senses" and realize how much he was throwing away—things like his father's 15 wife harem.

Yapallo's marriage to Kubah, however, seemed to convince Chief Weedor that he had lost his son forever. With this acknowledgment, concern suddenly turned to hatred, and the chief began doing everything imaginable to harm, and even kill his son.

Yapallo became deeply grieved over the hateful attitude of his father and sought every possible avenue to bridge the gap that had developed. His mother, one of Chief Weeclor's older wives that had been discarded, suggested that Yapallo call on his father and present a "white thing." Several days later Yapallo did just that, taking a piece of country cloth with him. Upon his return several hours later, Yapallo's countenance betrayed the fact that his mission had been a failure.

Shortly after his return Yapallo began experiencing abdominal pains. By nightfall the pain had reached an excruciating level, and Yapallo was certain that he was going to die. He had been the epitome of good health when he left to visit his father, so we could only surmise that the old chief had poisoned him. Calling in some of the boys we laid hands on Yapallo and anointed him in the name of Jesus. Within minutes he had drifted into a deep sleep. The next morning he awoke with no trace of sickness.

Chief Weedor had been foiled in his first attempt, but he was not about to give in that easily. Several months later there was another attempt on Yapallo's life—this time by members of the notorious and bloodthirsty Heart Society, a kindred group to the Devil Bush.

Knowing the feelings and attitude of Chief Weedor, we had recently begun locking the doors of all the mission buildings at night. This night, however, one of the smaller boys had forgotten to lock the door after he came in. Shortly after midnight, after everyone had retired, three men stole into the room where Yapallo and Kubah were asleep. Just as they were preparing to spring on Yapallo, Kubah awoke. The men fled into the night, their mission aborted. We never learned who they were, but we knew who was behind their efforts.

At that point I felt it better to send Yapallo and Kubah to Bomi Hills for awhile. Chief Weedor's wild and insane attempts on his son's life were proving detrimental to the spiritual well-being of the entire mission. The couple could be active in the work in Bomi Hills, and Yapallo could most likely find employment with the mine.

As time went on, Chief Weedor seemed to lose all touch with reality, directing his vengeance toward the people of the village as well as the mission. Evidently he tried once too often to poison someone, as charges were brought against him before the Commissioner. Chief Weedor was found guilty and was sentenced to prison for one year. Upon his return, he tried desperately to regain his position as village chief, but was unsuccessful.

Finally, in early March of 1961, the Cupples arrived in Liberia to begin their second term. A week or so after their return they flew into Fassama. I would continue to oversee the operation of the mission, as well as devote many hours each day to the running of the clinic. Teacher Konah could pretty well handle the operation of the school, freeing Brother Cupples to handle the building projects and do evangelistic work in the neighboring villages.

It was in the early part of December, well into the dry season, and a most unlikely time for what was about to transpire. Early Monday morning I had begun to hear the beating of the drums in the village. All day long the steady, monotonous thumping could be heard. At first I thought little of it—just a few of the natives having a party—drinking a little too much cane gin—doing a little dancing. By nightfall, however, the drums could still be heard, and they continued throughout the night. Early the following morning there was still that same steady beat—reverberating through the air in an annoying sort of way. At breakfast I asked Moses what the drums meant.

"Oh, Ma, they're playing medicine," was his answer.

All day Tuesday and once again into the night the drumbeat persisted. The sound continued through Wednesday and Wednesday night and into Thursday. By now it was getting on my nerves, and I caught myself becoming edgy and short-tempered with the students. The drums had now been beating, without respite, for more than 72 hours.

Noon Thursday arrived, and classes were dismissed for the day. After lunch, as usual, the afternoon would be devoted to the various chores around the compound. I went to the door of the veranda with my whistle, and was preparing to signal the students to report for work detail. Peering outside, I spotted several large, black rain clouds that had suddenly appeared from nowhere, and were now hovering ominously over the mission. The next moment I began hearing the thunder rumbling in the distance. Almost simultaneously the rain began to fall in torrential sheets.

The atmosphere was literally charged with confusion and it seemed my eardrums would surely burst from the deafening noise that was coming from parts unknown. Suddenly, without the least warning, a bolt of lightning struck the cola tree by the corner of the veranda. After striking the tree, the bolt jumped several feet and hit me squarely in the face.

Immediately I felt the sensation of my face shriveling. The sensation then began to spread rapidly, soon reaching the outer-most extremities of my body. My grip gave way, and my legs would no longer support me. As I fell helplessly to the floor, I looked into the sky and saw a bright ball of light—brighter than the noonday sun—so bright that it would have blinded the eyes of a mortal.

"Jesus, I'm your child," I softly whispered. "if this is the day, and this is the way, then I'm ready to go."

I was dead!

The boys knew it was time for work, and that even if I had postponed it until the rain let up, I would normally have informed them. After a few moments, James volunteered to dodge the lightning that still danced around the compound and run to my house to see if anything was wrong.

Pushing open the screen door of the veranda, he quickly spotted my crumpled body lying in a heap, my eyes rolled back and my face contorted.

I was dead!

Again braving the elements, James dashed as fast as his legs would propel him over to the Cupples' house. Before James had a chance to catch his breath, Brother Cupples could sense that an emergency existed over at my house. Running out the door, with his wife close on his heels, he followed James through the driving rain across the compound. By now several of the other mission boys had detected that something was terribly wrong over at Ma Gruse's house.

Brother Cupples' first words, upon arriving and observing my twisted, lifeless body, were, "She's dead . . . Sister Gruse has been struck by lightning and she's dead."

I was dead!

I was basking in the glory, peace, and rest that can only be found in unhindered communion with God. I was suspended somewhere between heaven and earth, and

I SURRENDER ALL

vividly remember looking down and seeing my body. "That temple of clay *used* to *be* my body," I thought to myself.

For several minutes longer I remained suspended somewhere between heaven and earth—closer to heaven I suspect. Then, I felt compelled to look directly overhead. When I did, I saw what appeared to be a huge bellows descending from heaven, heading straight for what used to be my body. It was a glistening, pure white—much whiter than anything I had ever seen on earth. Upon touching the body, it began to breathe life into it, and I could feel myself being slowly drawn back to the spot where the body lay. As I neared the spot where it lay, I cried out:

"No, Lord! Please don't make me return. I don't want to go back. I've just finished laying down all my burdens and cares and I'm thoroughly enjoying living here in paradise. Why . . . why must I return?"

"Because," I was told, "your work here on earth is not yet done."

I was back in my body now—semi-conscious, but still completely paralyzed. I suddenly became aware of Brother Cupples and the mission boys standing over me and praying with all the strength and faith they could muster. I could distinctly hear Brother Cupples screaming, "Pray! Pray! Pray!"

Suddenly I felt a hot flame of fire entering my body—exactly where the lightning had struck. Slowly, but surely, it began to burn its way down the left side of my body. Reaching my foot, it made an exit and reentered at my right foot. Then, at the same deliberate pace it began to slowly climb up the right side of my body.

The moment the flame reached my face, I became

fully conscious and regained complete mobility. I was extremely cold and weak, but very much alive. The natives were astounded and at a total loss for words. All the Cupples could manage to say was, "Hallelujah, Praise God, Thank You, Jesus!"

The next day we learned that an elderly man in the village had been saying all Thursday morning, "The missionaries are going to see something today." The best we could figure out, the devil, using some of his choice lieutenants, had fully intended to have the lightning strike and kill one of us in an attempt to bring discouragement to the entire mission. God, however, had taken these evil intentions, turned them inside-out, and used them as a means of renewing and increasing our courage.

For the next few months things were relatively calm around the mission—just the normal amount of emergencies and catastrophes and skull-scratching decisions. The peace and tranquility was broken in March of 1962, however, when I fractured my wrist while doing some work on a building we were constructing in the village of Fassama.

For some time now I had been working on this special project—trying to prove to the people that I was interested in the welfare of the village as well as the affairs of the mission. I had finished the job with the exception of installing the window frames and applying the mud dabbing. It would be necessary to set the window frames first so that we could dab around them. And, unless we got on the ball and completed the job, the termites would go to work and destroy our many hours of labor.

Early one morning, as I was sitting at my desk on the veranda, I determined that today was the day. We must install the window frames today. I'd just have to force

I SURRENDER ALL

myself to take the day off and finish the job. Calling for Robert, the mission boy who had helped me in times past, I announced that we would be spending the day in the village.

I was still seated at the desk, making mental notes of the material and tools we'd need, when the voice of God spoke to me: "if you go to the village, you'll break a bone." Trying my best to ignore the voice and pretend it was just my imagination, I continued with my planning. Again the voice of God spoke to me this time more sternly—"You are going to break a bone if you go!"

Arriving in the village, Robert and I immediately began building the frames with the 2 X 4's we had brought. Finally, about noon, we were ready to install the first one. Our strategy called for Robert to climb onto the cross beam and drive nails into the top of the frame, while I remained on the ground and drove nails into the bottom.

Fearing that Robert, as he so frequently did, would strike a nail off center and send it flying through the air, I decided to step back while he did his part. I was confident that the frame was wedged tightly enough so that he would not need any assistance while he nailed. Well, wouldn't you know it? The frame was not wedged tightly enough, and the first blow from Robert's hammer sent it tumbling down—striking me in the forehead, breaking my glasses, and bloodying my eye. The impact of the failing frame knocked me off balance, and in an attempt to break the fall, I landed on my wrist. The sickening snap, accompanied by the terrible pain, was sufficient to convince me that I had indeed fractured my wrist.

Immediately several of the boys in the village ran to get Brother Cupples. Within minutes he had arrived and agreed with my prognosis. After they had assisted me back to the mission, Frances Cupples helped me get cleaned up and into a fresh dress. I was then flown to the Lutheran hospital in Zor Zor, where my wrist was X-rayed and the broken bone set. In the process of healing, however, the set slipped and the bone grew back crooked. Several years later, while visiting a doctor in the States, I was told that the set should have never been attempted without the placement of a pin.

When, oh when, would I ever learn. Here I was pushing 60, and seemingly still not able to recognize, distinguish, and be obedient to the voice of God at the most critical times. Oh well, perhaps I wouldn't be the only one in heaven with scratched knees, cut hands, and the broken bones of stubbornness. I had to admit that we were indeed blessed to be serving a God who was so merciful and compassionate to such a slow-to-understand people.

One morning, in the early summer of 1962, I awoke with a strange thought on my mind—an extremely strange thought. At first I found it impossible to believe—that this thought could be coming from my brain. Yet, the harder I tried, the more the thought refused to leave—the thought that I should consider retiring from the mission field upon completion of my present term in the spring of 1963.

I would never be able to fully explain, at least to my satisfaction, why this thought had come into being. Certainly nothing had happened to ease my burden, my health was still reasonably good for a woman my age, and nothing had happened to discourage me or hurt my feelings. So, it must just be the will of God changing for my life.

The more I thought about it, the more sense it made. Brother Cupples was doing a tremendous job at Fassama, and was well qualified to assume charge of the mission.

The Foreign Missions Board would encounter no difficulty in finding a replacement to assist the Cupples. Yes, this was the will of God.

A week or so after the birth of this thought, my mind was completely made up, and I sent a letter off to Brother Oscar Vouga, the recently-appointed Director of Foreign Missions, informing him of my decision. Several weeks later, I received his reply, stating that it was with deep regret that he had accepted my notice of resignation, but that he fully understood my decision. He went on to assure me that the United Pentecostal Church would always be grateful for the almost 20 years I had devoted to the nation of Liberia.

At the 1962 General Conference Else Lund was appointed as missionary to Liberia. She would be my replacement in Fassama, and was scheduled to arrive in Liberia in early April of the following year.

In December of 1962 a week-long missionary conference was held at Fassama. Three services were held each day, with an average adult attendance ot at least 100. In addition to the missionaries, there were natives from the Belle, Gola, Gbande, and Kissi tribes. During the course of these meetings, six were baptized and five received the Holy Spirit.

A few weeks later I was the dedicatory speaker for the new church building in Bomi Hills. The title of my message was, "The Purpose of this Building."

TWENTY

Rediscovering the Will of God

I said goodbye to Nancy and Jennifer, and wished them well in their new assignment in California. "Have a good time at Grandma's," I told Jennifer. I continued to remain seated until almost everyone on the plane had filed out. Then, very slowly, I got up, checked my seat to make certain I had everything, and began walking towards the front. I stopped at the storage area by the door, got my tote bag, then said goodbye to the stewardess and began the long walk down the ramp and to the baggage claim area.

I tried to forget that this would be the last time I'd claim my baggage and clear through customs, but what I was really trying to forget was that I'd never return to Liberia. They hadn't really told me in so many words, but I knew it just the same.

It was a soggy, wind-swept Monday morning in early

I SURRENDER ALL

May of 1963. Just enough sunlight had managed to filter its way through the clouds to announce to the world below that night was officially over and a new day had begun. For several hours I had lain awake, listening intently to the rain that pelted the roof over my head, slowly coming to the realization that this would be my last morning at Fassama—the very last ever.

It was becoming increasingly more difficult to accept the decision I had made—the decision not to return to Liberia after my furlough. Else Lund had arrived to take my place now, and with Brother Cupples' able leadership the operation of the mission would continue uninterrupted. I was certain that I would not be missed. Perhaps this was what hurt me the most.

Maybe I really was feeling sorry for myself—at least a little bit. I really didn't know. Suddenly, however, it fully dawned on me that I was sobbing—that great big tears were coursing their way down my cheeks, drenching the front of my gown. I had to get hold of myself. In less than two hours I would be facing the people from the mission, and they must not see anything but a smile on my face.

The entire mission, and many from the village, were at the airstrip to see me off. I tried as best I could, but after a few minutes it was utterly impossible to stop the tears that insisted on streaming from my eyes. There were more tears and the waving of hands as I stepped aboard the plane and took my seat. Within a few moments I could feel the wheels of the aircraft gathering speed as we moved towards the far end of the runway. Almost before I knew it we were airborne and the clearing that was Fassama had blended itself into the dense jungle below.

Why? Why had I made this decision to leave Fassama forever? I really couldn't explain it—not even to myself. If

I was really and truly in the will of God, then why was I having such a difficult time accepting it? Oh well, perhaps I was just refusing to be sensitive to His will—placing my own happiness above the master-plan of God.

It was about 10:00 in the morning when we arrived in Bomi Hills. Plans called for me to spend the night there, then drive into Monrovia the next morning. My brief stay at Bomi Hills was one of the most difficult days of my life trying desperately to control and hide my true emotions. Inner desires dictated that I cry like a baby and unburden myself completely, yet circumstances demanded that I put on a front, be slightly hypocritical, and pretend that I was happy as a lark to be finally returning to my beloved homeland.

No—I in no way wanted to retire from the field, yet for some strange and unexplainable reason I felt a compelling force to do exactly that.

My return flight was identical to previous trips. Upon arriving in New York I was able to make quick connections to Cleveland, where I spent several days visiting with Leland. From there I flew to South Bend for a week or so with the Klapps. While there, the matter of employment was brought up. To be perfectly honest, I really hadn't given much thought to the subject of supporting myself once I had returned to the States. It had been a full 20 years since I had had this worry. But, as before, Doris and Virgil came to the rescue and offered me a job working in the rest home they owned in Argus, Indiana.

For the next few months I devoted many long, hard hours to working in that rest home. There was no church in Argus, so I began attending services in Liberty, Indiana. Occasionally I would be invited to minister in one of the local churches, but for the most part ex-missionaries didn't seem to be in as much demand as active ones.

I was comfortable, with all the necessities of life. I knew that as long as the Klapps owned the nursing home I would have a place to work, a roof over my head, clothes on my back, and food on my table. Yes, I had reasonably good health, loyal friends, a good church to attend, and very little pressure. Yet, I was miserable—absolutely miserable.

I was merely functioning and existing—not living. I was miserable. Had God brought me back into my body so that I could work in a nursing home in Argus, Indiana? There was nothing wrong with emptying bedpans, changing sheets, pushing wheelchairs, and serving meals, but was this the unfinished task He had been referring to that day when He overruled my desires and forced me to return?

Still, there had been that feeling—that very real and intense feeling—that feeling that I had served my time, and that there were now others, much younger than I, who were ready, willing, and able to perform the task much better than I could now do it. Sure, I still had the burden, but "common sense" told me that I was over the hill, past my prime, and eligible to begin resting on my laurels. After all, I was almost 60, and I had devoted 20 years to the field.

In mid-October of 1963 I took a few days off work to attend the General Conference in Memphis, Tennessee. After my arrival, I was asked by Brother Vouga to take part in the Foreign Missions service. Ena Hylton, a native of Jamaica, was appointed to Liberia during this conference. She would be going to Bomi Hills to replace Valda, who was due to leave for furlough shortly.

After conference I returned to Argus and once more

busied myself with the work of the nursing home. There was much to be done for these elderly and invalid people, and one could easily get a burden for the work here. Yet, for some unknown reason I could not feel comfortable with what I was doing. I had that constant gnawing of my conscience—that somehow and somewhere I had missed the will of God for my life—that it *had not* been the voice and will of God that had directed my path away from Liberia.

In March of 1964 I attended a missions conference held in Bloomington, Indiana. I really couldn't understand why I felt so compelled to attend, but somehow I knew I must go. It was sometime in the course of the first service that I became gripped by a burden as strong as any I had ever experienced. It suddenly dawned on me that I was as much out of the will of God as I had ever been—that I should be in Liberia right that very minute—not sitting there in a pew in Bloomington.

I honestly can remember nothing of the remainder of the evening—just that I sat in a trance, crushed by the vice-like grip of conviction. The moment the service was over I made a beeline for Paul Box, the Foreign Missions Secretary.

"Brother Box, I'm afraid I've made a terrible mistake in not returning to Liberia. My burden is there, and nowhere else, and without a doubt that is where God wants me right this very minute. I'm fully convinced that I'll never find peace in my soul until I return. What can I do? How can I go about getting reappointed? How soon can I return?"

"Well, Sister Gruse," he answered when I finally gave him the opportunity to reply, "You'll have to meet with the Missions Board and apply for reappointment. I'm afraid they won't be meeting until General Conference this fall. Why don't you let me send you an application. Between now and October you can do some real praying and soul-searching."

I returned to Argus to resume my duties in the nursing home. In the early part of the summer I received a letter from M. D. Padfield, President of Pentecostal Bible Institute in Tupelo, Mississippi, asking if I would be interested in coming to the Bible college as an instructor. Georgia Regenhardt, an old cohort from Liberia was teaching in the school at the time and had informed Brother Padfield that I was not currently involved in the full-time ministry.

Decisions . . . decisions . . . decisions. Just when I thought I had sorted through all the alternatives and made up my mind here came another decision. After careful prayer, I answered Brother Padfield, informing him that I fully intended to return to Liberia within a few months and that it would not be fair to him and the school to begin something I could not finish.

A week or so later I received his reply, asking me to at least come for the fall semester. Much could be accomplished in one semester, he assured me. I would have a unique twofold ministry—teaching, as well as passing my burden for missions on to others.

Conference was held in San Antonio, Texas that year. I arrived two days early to meet with the Missions Board. They really put me through it, closely scrutinizing both applicant and application. Finally, however, after they were sure it was a genuine burden and not just nostalgia, they said the magic words. There was one stipulation—I would be returning to Bomi Hills, not Fassama.

To be very honest, Fassama had been my first choice,

but I didn't hesitate to accept their appointment and conditions. The important thing was that I'd be returning to Liberia to work among my people—the people of small stature that God had told me about almost 50 years earlier.

At that same conference Valda Russell was reappointed for another term, and Samuel and Joyce Latta were appointed for their first term in Liberia. As in times past, I was given short notice that I was to be one of the speakers for the Foreign Missions service.

TWENTY-ONE

The End???

Not fully aware of what I was even doing, I walked down the corridor to the baggage claim area. After finding my suitcases, I put them on the conveyor belt and got in line for customs inspection. I had purchased just a few inexpensive items in Germany, so it had not been necessary for me to fill out a declaration form. For the next few minutes I was completely lost in thought as the line slowly inched forward towards the customs inspector. I was caught by surprise by the "You're next!" Evidently I looked like the honest, grandmother type, as the agent scarcely examined my luggage. He gave me the nod, and it was all over. I was officially back in the United States.

It was 2:00 P.M. on March 2, 1965 when the Astro-jet departed South Bend for New York's Kennedy Airport. The terribly uneventful flight took just under 55 minutes. Checking with the girl at the Pan American desk, I

I SURRENDER ALL

discovered that my 8:00 P.M. flight was still scheduled to leave on time. My, my, my—how tame and boring and totally predictable the life of a missionary was fast becoming. Where were the days of delayed and cancelled flights, missed connections, two-day bus rides, nights in stuffy hotels, and meals in greasy spoons? It was getting to the point that the only adventure and excitement left was the winning of souls. But, this was more than sufficient, and I was thankful that this was one aspect of missionary life that only the coming of the Lord could erase.

Six hours and 45 minutes after lifting off from Kennedy we were landing in Dakar, Senegal. After an hour's stopover we were once again airborne. It was now after 4:00 A.M. South Bend time, and I had been awake almost 24 hours. By all rights I should have been more than ready to at least catch a catnap, but the excitement and apprehension of returning to Liberia after an almost two year absence would not allow sleep to come.

Reclining the seat back slightly, I laid my head back and closed my weary eyes. I could hear the humming of the engines and the clatter of a dozen conversations in the background as I began to recall some of the unforgettable incidents of my 20 years in Liberia. Who could ever forget things like my voyage aboard the *Maritimos*, the mad taxi ride in Lisbon to clear my passport, the temperamental truck driver that took us from Bissau to Bathurst, first impressions of Liberia, my two treks with Mildred, the time we were washed out to sea in a stalled Lebanese motor launch, my first trip over the mountains to reach Fassama, our trek back to the coast during "flood time," the death of LaVerne, the shooting of Sharon Langham, the first time I saw Kubah, being struck by lightning then raised from the dead, the many souls I'd seen saved through the ministry of Fassama Mission, and. . . .

Here I was, almost 61 years old, returning to Africa for my fifth term. Something told me this would also be my final term. And, was it premonition, or just strong desire, that hinted that this would be my burying place in addition. I had left two years earlier with a job undone—I fully understood that now. I was returning to complete my task—however great or small. Then, I'd be ready to go. . . .

I was met at Roberts Field by Jack and Sandra Langham. After clearing customs and claiming my baggage, we drove to Bomi Hills where I spent the night. The next morning Brother Langham drove me into Monrovia to clear the government offices. Three days later I returned to Bomi Hills to begin my duties as the teacher of the Bible school that had just been established.

In addition to the Langhams, I would be joining Ena Hylton, who had been in Liberia for almost a year now. Jack and Sandra would be leaving on furlough shortly, and would be replaced by Valda, who was due to return to Liberia in a month or so. Samuel and Joyce Latta, newly-appointed missionaries, were scheduled to arrive shortly and replace the Cupples at Fassama. They would be joining Else Lund who was now assisting the Cupples.

Fassama was still the largest church in Liberia at this time, but Bomi Hills, with a student enrollment of better than 240, boasted the largest school. By adding the Bible school, with its dozen or so students, not to mention our efforts at evangelizing the neighboring villages, one could easily see that we had our hands full at Bomi Hills.

For the next few months there was seldom a spare moment, as I poured my entire self into the work of the

Bible school. At first I had honestly wondered if I could develop a real burden for Bomi Hills, with Fassama so close, and yet so far away. But, on the first day of class, as I looked out and saw several boys from the Fassama Mission, I experienced the instantaneous development of a burden. I knew of a surety that I was in the will of God—that I was in the process of completing my assigned task—putting the finishing touches on what I had started several years ago. Late in 1965 we had a three-week revival in Bomi Hills. From the very start it was a mightily anointed outpouring of God's spirit, and great conviction gripped the hearts of many of the villagers. As to be expected, the devil was not about to throw in the towel without a fight, and began doing all within his power to destroy what was happening.

One night in particular, about the middle of the second week, I could feel a heavy, ominous cloud of fear and superstition hovering over the mission. As time neared for service to begin I could sense the evil spirit intensifying its efforts. We had just started the song service when I began hearing the cries, screams, and agonizing moans of several village women as they paced up and down the road in front of the church building. Throughout the service they continued their ritual. Later that night we learned that these women, compelled by the powerful forces of Satan, had been attempting to appease the evil spirits in behalf of a newborn baby who was dying. They were convinced that if they did not prove obedient to these spirits, the baby, as well as some new mother in the village, would die by morning.

Shortly after the first of the year the Samuel Latta family arrived in Fassama to relieve the Cupples for furlough. Brother Latta, who was a trained pilot, became the

The End???

missions "chauffeur" and the plane remained based in Fassama.

A month or so after their arrival, in February of 1966, the annual missions conference was held in Bomi Hills. It was a real adventure for the fifteen or so native preachers and workers who were flown by Brother Latta to the meetings in Bomi Hills. I'm afraid that most of them proved to be better flyers than I.

The first night, a few moments after service had begun, we suddenly noticed a commotion in the rear of the building. Coming up the aisle was a young native couple carrying a tiny baby that looked as if it were dead. As they came closer I could see that the frail, limp figure was still breathing—but just barely. None of the missionaries or native workers could remember having ever seen the couple, but without a single word being uttered, everyone, including those in the congregation, knew what they wanted. Their baby was dying and they wanted the missionaries to pray for it.

Gathering closely around the feeble, almost-lifeless figure, we anointed the infant with oil and began to cry out to God. Suddenly, I felt that undeniable surge of faith take hold. I could sense that the others had experienced it also. There was absolutely no doubt in our minds—God was getting ready to honor His Word, His name, and our faith. A miracle was in progress!

While we were yet praying the miracle "began" and the baby started to stir. First one eye, then the other, opened. Next, it raised its skinny arms and began to cry a healthy cry. Moments later it was breathing normally, then fell into a restful sleep.

All eyes had been glued to that baby, and the miracle escaped the attention of no one. God, in His divine

I SURRENDER ALL

wisdom, mercy, love, compassion, and power, had challenged the forces of nature and caused a spark to ignite a fire that burned for the remainder of the services.

> *O the depth of the riches both of the wisdom and knowledge of God! how unsearchable are his judgments, and his ways past finding out! (Romans 11:33).*

In June of 1966 an accident occurred in the life of James Murphy which demands retelling. James, who had been trained on the Fassama Mission, had been conducting services in the village of Tavalata for almost two years. He had witnessed a steady growth of converts among the young people, but the older people, who were so steeped in tradition and superstition, were not being so easily persuaded.

In May of 1966, however, an elderly woman received the Holy Ghost, touching off a real revival in the village. Immediately, however, James and his wife became the victims of severe harassment at the hands of the Devil Bush. Their persecution reached a peak the Sunday they ordered James not to ring the church bell announcing the evening service. When church time came, James did the only thing his conscience would allow—he rang the bell as loudly as it would ring.

Almost immediately he found himself surrounded by an angry, practically insane band of Devil Bush members—bent on doing him great bodily harm—intending to teach him a lesson he would not soon forget. They knocked him down, tied his hands and feet, dragged him along the ground, and beat him until he almost lost consciousness. Then, they rounded up all the Christians they could find, including James' wife and baby, and brought them to the town kitchen. There, before the gathering crowd, they publicly taunted and humiliated them, calling them every low-down, filthy name imaginable.

Towards nightfall, one of the Christians managed to escape when his captors' backs were turned. All night long he ran through the deep, dark jungle. It was well into the next day when he finally reached Fassama. Going straight to the mission, he reported the incident to Brother Latta, who wasted no time in fueling the plane and flying to Tavalata. Upon arriving, Brother Latta discovered that James and his wife, along with several of the other Christians, had been taken by a group of the Devil Bush members to Bopolu, where the District Magistrate's office was located. Upon arriving they planned to falsely accuse James of teaching the villagers against paying the governmental head tax and hut tax.

Because of the plane, Brother Latta was able to arrive in Bopolu ahead of the Bush people and alert the judge as to what they were planning. After talking with the officials, Brother Latta was given a soldier to accompany him back to Tavalata. Upon arriving, the soldier arrested the responsible Bush members who had not made the trip to Bopolu. After arresting them, he marched them the ten hours back to Bopolu, where they joined their co-conspirators in standing trial. The trial lasted a full week—all day everyday. When it was over, God had given us the clear-cut victory over the devil and his cleverly-designed attempts at stopping the spreading of the Gospel.

In late July of 1966 Basil and Alberta Williams arrived in Liberia as newly-appointed missionaries. They would join Else Lund in Fassama, relieving the Cupples to go to Monrovia to begin a work. At this time the lineup looked like this: The Cupples in Monrovia; Else Lund and the Williams at Fassama; Ena, Valda, and I at Bomi Hills; and the Langhams on furlough and scheduled to return to Bomi Hills.

I had really never even come close to overcoming my extreme fear of flying in small planes, and I guess it had become sort of a standing joke among the other missionaries. I suppose it all went back to the time in 1953 when Brother Freeman and I were nearly wiped out while taking off in a small overloaded plane. But, I had accepted the fact that no matter how greatly I detested those little things, they had a lot more to offer than five-and-a-half day treks through the jungle, across swollen rivers, and over rugged mountains especially when I became a grandma in her sixties. Yet, even those who pretended to approach flying as they would a quick automobile trip to the corner grocery had to admit that there were real dangers involved.

It was just a week or so after the Williams' arrival that we had a near tragedy with the missions plane. Brother Latta was the pilot on this flight, and the Williams were his passengers. As they made their approach to land at the airstrip adjacent to the Bomi Hills Mission, the brake cable snapped. Needless to say, the plane was still traveling at a high rate of speed when they ran out of runway and began heading down the street of the village. It was only the divine intervention of God that kept the craft from striking a building or hitting a group of children that seemed to always be playing in the street.

A couple of years later Brother Williams was piloting our new plane, the Super Piper Cub, when the engine suddenly stalled. He began losing altitude quickly and immediately determined that his only hope was to find an

The End???

emergency landing spot. Finally, after what seemed like an eternity, he spotted a clearing that he thought *might* suffice and began to make his approach. In descending, however, one of the wings clipped a large tree, causing him to crash. Once again the blessings of God were upon us, and while the plane was severely damaged, Brother Williams was not seriously injured.

Easter Sunday of 1966 was a special day for Bomi Hills Mission, and one of the highlights of my 27 years in Liberia. It was that day that we had 604 in attendance for Sunday school. We were well aware that this would not make us anywhere near the top in the United Pentecostal Church, but we felt we might have a good chance of making the top ten. Not bad, I figured, for a struggling congregation that wasn't really into the bus ministry that heavily.

For the last year or so of their previous tour Sandra Langham had been troubled somewhat with a skin allergy. Upon arriving in the States it had disappeared almost immediately, so she had seen no need for seeking medical attention. Soon after returning to Liberia, however, it had once more appeared, seeming to intensify with each passing day.

Several trips to the Bomi Hills Mining Hospital failed to provide relief, or for that matter, even hint at a possible cause. In early October of 1967, after several months of intense suffering, it became apparent that for some reason God was not going to heal her at that time and that she would have to return to the States. Brother Langham would join her in a few months.

Soon after she left I was admitted into the Bomi Hills hospital to have "bunion surgery." The great toe on my left foot had gotten to the point that for days at a time I could not stand to wear a shoe. During the operation it was discovered that the condition had advanced to the point that part of the bone would have to be removed and a bone fusion performed. As a result of the surgery I was forced to wear a cast for several months.

A few weeks after being released from the hospital word was received from the Missions Department that Else Lund should plan on taking her furlough in a few short weeks. Because of her furlough and the Langhams being forced to return to the States it would be necessary to make some personnel changes. The plan called for the Williams to come to Bomi Hills to work with Valda, and for Ena and me to take over the work in Fassama. The Lattas would remain with the newly-established work in Monrovia. Needless to say, this arrangement had me shouting for joy. I would have danced a hallelujah jig had it not been for my cast.

It was a grand homecoming, indeed, when I arrived at Fassama. In my heart I knew that this would be the only place on the face of the earth where I could have a legitimate homecoming. I would be made to feel even more at home by living in the house that Jean and I had built for ourselves some 15 years earlier. Ena would be occupying the home Brother Cupples had built for his family.

The work had progressed tremendously in my four-and-a-half year absence, and the native preachers and workers were now pretty well taking care of the evangelistic outreach of the mission. Our primary responsibility would be the oversight of the mission, as well as assisting the natives in becoming even more self-sufficient. Our goal was full nationalization of the work within three years.

On paper our duties seemed light enough—little more

The End???

than coordinating the activities of a few native preachers. In reality, however, it was just as it had always been—seldom, if ever, a spare moment.

The first few months we were at Fassama I functioned as the general contractor for a new church building. When we had finished, we had an edifice we could be rightfully proud of, complete with cement floor, zinc roof, and plasterboard ceiling.

In the summer of 1969 I traveled by automobile with the Williams to attend a missions conference held in Kumasi, Ghana, a city of some 200,000 located about 170 miles from Accra. The first night of the conference I was presented to the huge crowd by Brother Williams. In his glowing and gracious introduction he asked the Ghanians to pay tribute to me for almost 27 years of love and service to the Continent of Africa. For several long minutes there was a thunderous roar of applause, accompanied by the beating of drums and tambourines.

I felt very small and insignificant as I nervously stepped forward to greet the people. In my heart I was still the little girl who had heard the voice of God underneath the shade tree. It was at times like this that I was made to wonder why in the world God had chosen me to be used of Him and honored in such a way by my fellow man.

I was asked to give my testimony in the six o'clock service Friday night. The power of God began to fall over the entire congregation as I described victory after victory over the enemy forces. The crowd seemed to take special delight in my description of encounters with the notorious and much-feared Devil Bush. Saturday evening there were in excess of 3,000 present when I stepped to the pulpit to preach through an interpreter. I chose a very simple message—the only one we are commissioned to preach—"The Result of the Crucifixion."

In the summer of 1970 Denzil and Evelyn Bolton arrived in Liberia to relieve Basil and Alberta Williams who had been serving in Monrovia. Brother Bolton had been appointed to succeed Brother Williams as superintendent of the work in Liberia. Shortly after their arrival, Brother Bolton decided that due to personnel shortages it would be necessary to jump ahead of schedule and fully nationalize the work in Fassama. Valda was scheduled to leave on furlough, and we had just learned that instead of returning to Liberia, Else Lund was being transferred to Ghana to work with Robert and Evangeline Rodenbush. Ena would devote her efforts towards evangelizing among the unreached villages, and I would spend the remaining few months of my tour as overseer of the Bomi Hills Mission.

Shortly after my arrival in Bomi Hills I received a letter from T. F. Tenney, recently-elected Director of Foreign Missions, "reminding" me that I had been in Liberia for almost six years on this tour, and that it was past time for a furlough. His letter went on to state that the Missions Board would be convening in St. Louis in the month of June and that I should make plans to meet with them.

He didn't come right out and say it, but then, he didn't have to. From the tone of his letter I could tell something was up. In times past I had not bothered to meet with any Foreign Missions officials until General Conference. Why were they so anxious to meet with me in June? I had my ideas, yet it *could* be that the new Director had instituted these immediate debriefing sessions as a matter of policy. Then again, my original idea was probably closer to the truth—at least in my case.

I had to admit that my health wasn't what it had been

The End???

in earlier years, and age and long hours *had seemed* to begin catching up with me as of late. But, what was I to do if they told me this was it—that they were terribly sorry, but I just could not return—that they sympathized completely with the way I felt, but that for my own good they were not going to reappoint me? What would I do?

I had tried to leave on my own some seven years earlier, and it hadn't worked out—hadn't even come close. Why would this time be any different? Why? Why didn't the burden leave when age caught up and the body began to slow down?

I decided that the best course of action, at least for the present, was to ignore Brother Tenney's letter—just pretend it wasn't there. Perhaps it would go away if I waited long enough. Later, however, conscience and common sense got a grip on me and I answered the letter, assuring him that I would be there in St. Louis on the appointed date in June.

In the spring of 1971, a couple of months before I was scheduled to leave for the States, we held our annual Missions Conference in Monrovia. In addition to the missionaries and the Liberian preachers, we were greatly honored with the presence of Else Lund, who was on her way to Ghana, and Robert and Evangeline Rodenbush, who had driven over to pick her up.

During the first evening service the missionaries and native preachers surprised me with a special tribute for my years of service to Liberia. It was touching, indeed, to hear some of the men who had come to Fassama as young boys stand before the assembly, and with the powerful anointing of God tell of their burden for the lost, then thank me for devoting my life to loving them and teaching them about Jesus. I felt deeply honored, yet totally undeserving, of the praise they insisted on giving me. All I could say was, "To God Be The Glory!"

Without a doubt the highlight of the entire conference for me was the ordination of Teacher Konah into the ministry. For several years this devoted and dependable Gola tribesman had been our right hand at Fassama Mission. It was a real treat to be able to attend and participate in his ordination service.

One afternoon between services, as the missionaries were sitting around catching up on all the church "news" from around the world, Brother Rodenbush asked me what my immediate plans were. When I told him I'd be leaving for the States in about eight weeks, he and his wife invited me to return to Ghana with them and leave from there. He was certain that Brother Bolton would be more than happy to see that my heavy baggage was properly shipped back to the States.

I really didn't know why, but at the time his proposal sounded particularly appealing. It would mean leaving my beloved Liberia eight weeks sooner than I had to, but something inside told me this was the thing to do. So, two days later saw me in the car with the Rodenbushes and Else Lund, headed back for Accra, the capital city of Ghana.

Accra, with its almost 500,000 people, was far more westernized and advanced than Monrovia. It was here that the Rodenbushes had chosen to make their home, establish their base of operations, and build a Bible school.

I stayed in Accra almost six weeks, teaching a few classes in the Bible school, and preaching a time or two. Also, upon the insistence of Brother Rodenbush, I began assembling my memoirs, hoping that someday a book might possibly be written. Who knew—stranger things had happened in this old world. I also spent considerable time remembering, dreading, and trying my best to relax.

We were sitting around the supper table one evening, when I casually mentioned the fact that I had always wanted to visit Europe, especially Germany. Oh, I had made brief stops in Portugal and the Azores, but this didn't really count. With the mention of Germany, I could sense the wheels beginning to turn in Brother Rodenbush's head. I could tell from the twinkle in his eye that he had an idea.

"Why don't I drop a line to Wayne Nigh, our missionary in Germany? I'm sure he and Esther would just be tickled to have you as a house guest and show you around Germany for a week or so. You could fly from Accra to Frankfurt, then from Frankfurt on to New York."

A couple of weeks later we received a reply from the Nighs, assuring us that they would be happy to have me spend some time with them, and promising to do their very best to show me the sights.

My stay in Germany was a dream come true—actually visiting the places and seeing the sights I had heretofore only read about or seen in magazines. I had never met the Nighs, but within hours of my arrival in Germany, they had become very special people.

All too soon the time allotted had expired, and it was time for me to once again change hats—time to quit being Pauline Gruse, world traveler, and re-enter the drab, unexciting world of Pauline Gruse, the soon-to-be exmissionary—the one who was being forced to return to the strange land of America—the one who was being put out to pasture.

The flight from Frankfurt to New York's Kennedy airport took a little less than eight hours. Upon arriving, I

I SURRENDER ALL

was met by John Korlatowitz, a very unique man who had made a ministry out of meeting outgoing and returning missionaries and seeing to their needs while they were in the New York City area. After spending a few days in New York, it was on to Cleveland for a brief visit with my brother, Leland.

From Cleveland I flew to St. Louis for my much-dreaded meeting with the Foreign Missions Board. I was met at Lambert Field by Brother and Sister Tenney and J. C. Cole, a member of the Foreign Missions Board. From the airport we went to the Howard Johnsons about a mile up the road from the new headquarters building. It had been a tiring day, so I excused myself from their invitation for supper, and told Brother Tenney I'd see them in the morning.

"We'll have someone pick you up about 10:00, Sister Gruse. You'll have time to take a grand tour of the World Evangelism Center before you meet the Board."

I was up bright and early the next morning. After getting dressed, I read a few chapters, then spent some time in prayer, earnestly seeking for the strength and courage to meet the challenges of the day. About 8:00 I decided to walk to the coffee shop next door to try to eat some breakfast. Actually, food was probably the thing farthest from my mind, but I had no idea when I'd have another chance to eat, and if my meeting went anything like I expected it to go, I'd feel even less like eating later in the day.

After playing around with my scrambled eggs and sausage for awhile, I finished off my second cup of coffee, paid the check, and returned to the room. It was still early, but already I could tell it was going to be another typically hot St. Louis day. Kinda reminded one of the weather in Liberia.

The End???

About 9:45 there was a light knock on the door, followed by a "Sister Gruse, I'm here to pick you up." Grabbing my purse, I walked to the car for my last ride as a missionary. I almost wished I could walk—anything to delay the agony.

I was amazed, as we pulled onto the lot, at the size of the headquarters office. I had seen pictures of the World Evangelism Center, but for some reason it had never dawned on me just how large and modern-looking it really was.

I arrived a few minutes before 10:00, just in time for the next tour of the building. By the end of the tour, some thirty minutes later, amazement had turned into stunned amazement. I had never dreamed of such spacious, well-appointed offices, such well-equipped secretarial areas, such modern printing equipment, and such a well-stocked Christian bookstore where one could easily spend an entire day just browsing. I had visited the previous headquarters building in South St. Louis, and there was just no comparison. Without a doubt, Pentecost had moved across the tracks. One could only hope that we'd always remember our store front, brush arbor heritage.

Upon finishing the tour, we arrived back at the receptionist's desk where we had started.

"Are you Sister Gruse?" she asked me.

"Yes, I am," I assured her.

"They want to see you in the board room," she told me.

After getting directions, I took the elevator to the second floor, walked down the hall, and knocked on the door I assumed was the board room.

I could feel the sweet, strengthening presence of God as I entered the room and took the seat Brother Tenney offered me. When I had mustered up enough courage I looked up into the faces of the men who composed the Foreign Missions Board. I could see their look of sincere compassion, love, and understanding, yet without a word being said, I could tell what the outcome of the meeting would be.

They cited my age, my health, and the possibility that my medicare would not be effective in Liberia. I really couldn't blame them—they had no choice. They were doing their job, and I would have arrived at exactly the same decision had I been in their shoes. Still, that didn't alter the fact that the burden remained, and would always be there.

After having prayer with the Board, I walked from the room and down the hall to the drinking fountain. I had fully expected this to happen for several months, yet I had still not been prepared for it. There was a lump in my throat, tears were forming in my eyes, and I felt kind of woozy as I leaned over to get a drink.

"Well, fancy meeting you here," I heard a familiar voice behind me say. Turning around I saw Bill and Frances Cupples, with whom I'd served in Liberia.

I did my best to keep up a good front as I told them about meeting the Board and their decision. I could sense, however, that they had known about the meeting and knew as well as I what the decision had to be. They tried to sympathize with me, assuring me that the Board had acted in my best interest, and was in no way showing disapproval in my past efforts.

They went on to tell me that they had driven up the night before to pick up Ruth Ann, who was a student at nearby Gateway College.

"Say, why don't you come back to Savannah with us and spend a few days? You aren't on a tight schedule are

The End???

you? We'll sit up 'til all hours of the night talking about the good ole days."

I started to decline their invitation, feeling that I'd prefer to have some time to myself. But, perhaps the company of good friends would be the best thing for me at this moment.

After visiting with the Cupples for several days, they drove me over to Memphis, where I caught a flight for Indianapolis. In Indianapolis I was met by a group of women from the Indiana Ladies Auxiliary. From the airport we drove to the Indiana campground, some 25 miles away. I was surprised, upon arriving, to discover that the Ladies had planned a "Homecoming Service" for me—my first in over 27 years as a missionary. To tell the truth, however, I really didn't feel that I'd come home. While words failed me when I tried to express my feelings to those assembled, I still didn't feel that I'd come home.

From the campground I went to Bloomington, where I spent several days with the Robert Johnsons. While I was there Brother Johnson told me that he had recently run into Johnny, my second husband. In their conversation Johnny had said: "Pauline just went crazy over the Lord, but I did do her wrong."

From Bloomington I traveled to South Bend for a short visit with the Klapps. While there, my sister, Helen, drove down from Monroe, Michigan and talked me into returning with her for a week or so.

Mother's death had caused Helen and me to go our separate ways some fifty years earlier. Time and distance had seen us drift farther and farther apart. Being able to spend some time with her, however, caused a renewed fondness and love to develop. I had fully intended, upon accepting Helen's invitation, to return after a week or so and settle somewhere in the South Bend area. It was the only logical thing to do. After all, my good friends, the Klapps, lived there. But by the end of the week I felt very strongly about finding a place to live in Monroe.

I had attended the church there, pastored by Brother James Hosch. He and his wife, along with the saints, had gone out of their way to make me feel welcome and a part of them. This, along with the company of Helen, made this my choice.

The first step was to find a place of my own. Helen had offered to let me live with her, but I was far too independent to feel comfortable doing this. My first residence was a small rented mobile home—we used to call them trailer houses. After spending a few months there, I moved into an apartment in the Monroe Manor. The church in Monroe assisted me in paying the rent on this place.

Soon after moving into the Monroe Manor, I heard of the River Park Plaza, a government subsidized high-rise apartment complex for senior citizens. The units were small, yet complete and comfortable. Best of all, the rent was very reasonable—based on the ability to pay. The only problem was the waiting list—it would take several years to get a unit. But I couldn't get away from the feeling that God wanted me to live there. So, by faith I went ahead and filled out an application. Well, the Word does say something about "one day with the Lord being as a thousand years." Perhaps this explains in part why I was able to move in within a few months.

Well, for the past seven years I've lived in my little apartment on the fifth floor at 20 North Roessler—going to church when weather and health permit, teaching the adult Sunday school class, speaking out occasionally, visiting relatives once in awhile, but mostly just dreaming of a land some 6,000 miles away—a land where there is a dark-skinned people who are short of stature—a people who have yet to hear the Gospel—a people who Jesus shed his precious blood for almost 2,000 years ago.

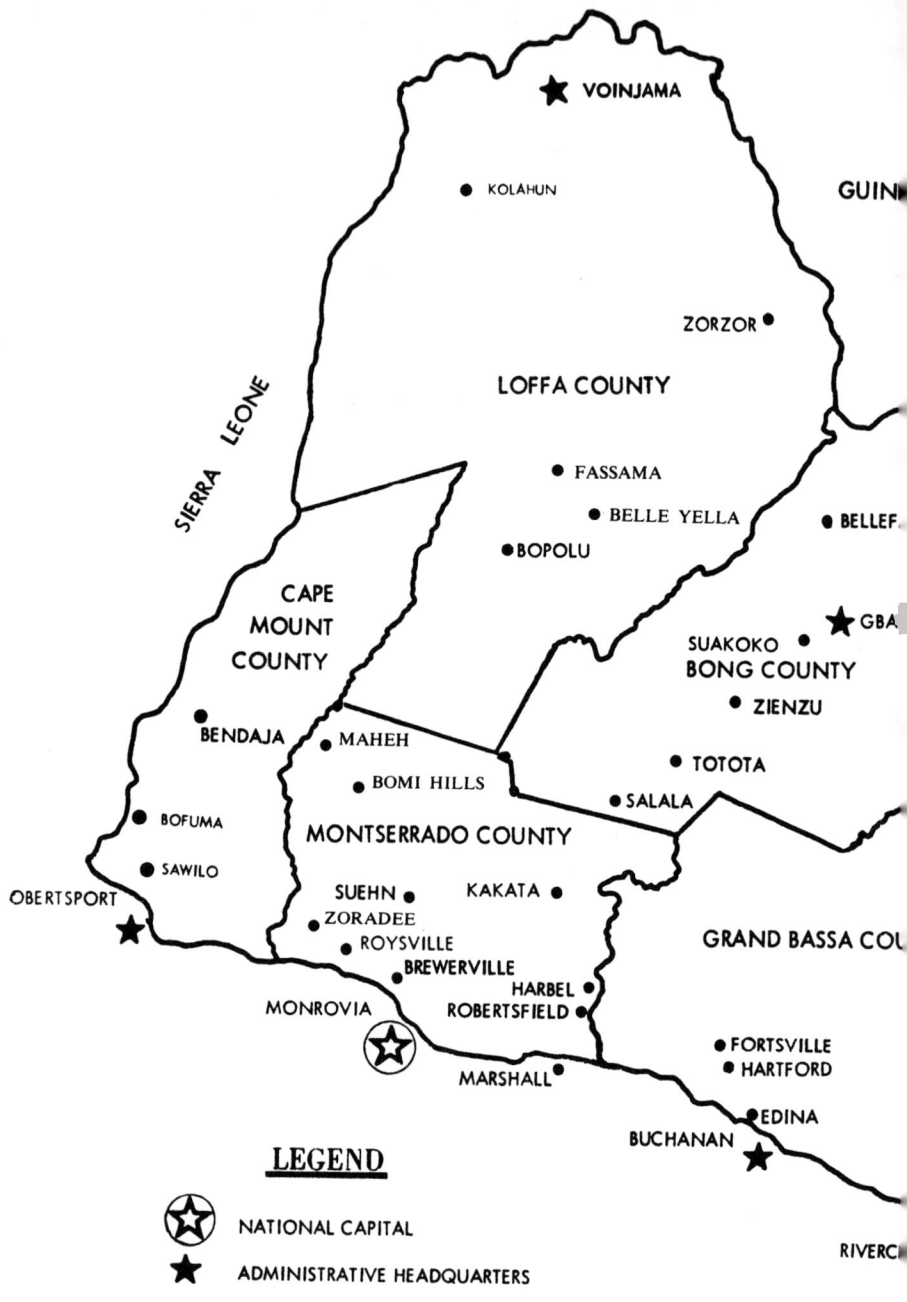

LIBERIA

POLITICAL MAP

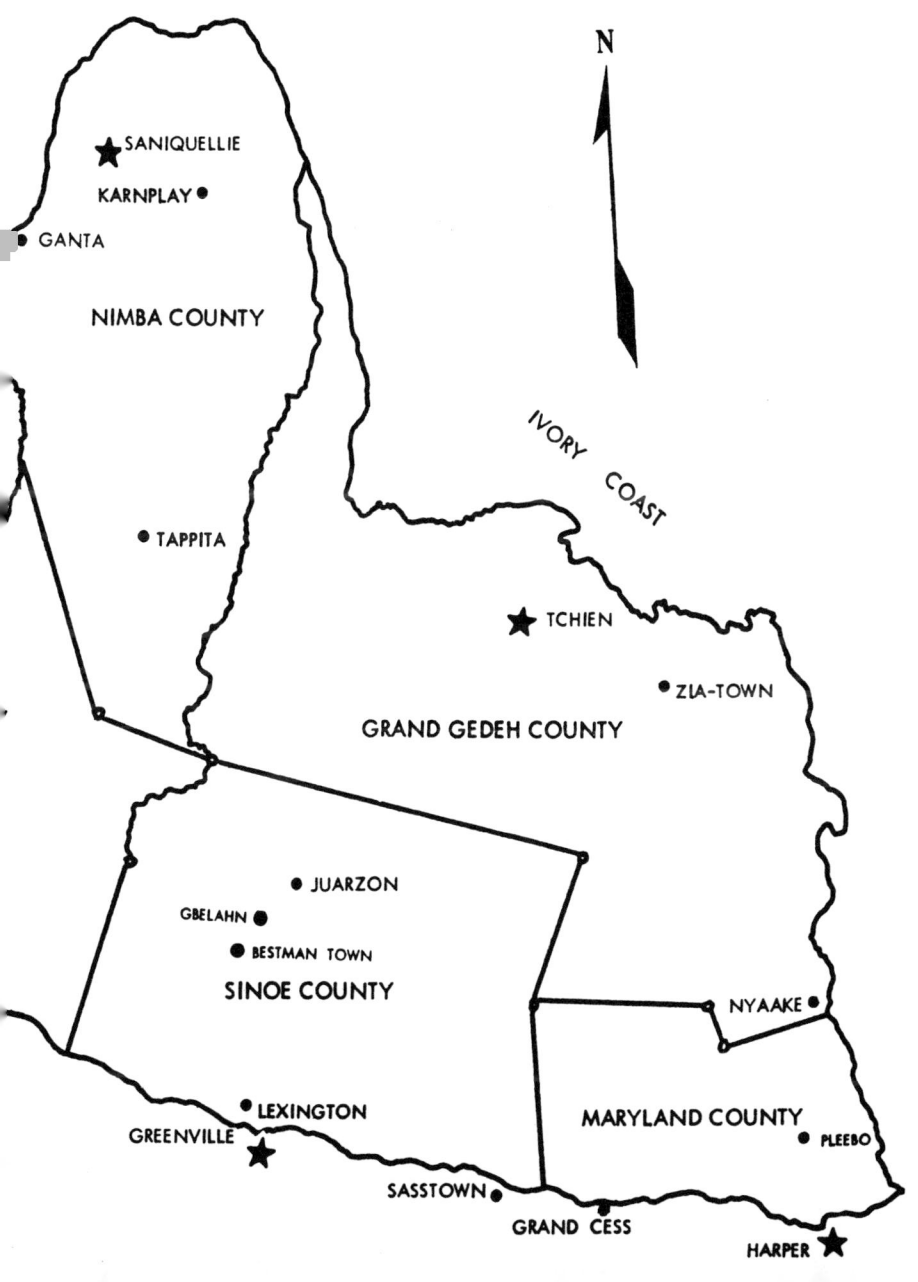

Epilogue

It was November of 1974 that I spent a week in Monroe, Michigan interviewing Pauline Gruse for *I Surrender All*. Each day, from mid-morning until late afternoon, I would pick her brain and push her overworked memory to its outer limits, as we sat in the tidy living room of her tiny apartment on the fifth floor of the River Park Plaza Apartments. Upon returning to St. Louis, I supplemented our 20 hours of tape with intensive research into the "Archives" of the United Pentecostal Church.

Sister Gruse continued to live in her apartment at 20 North Roessler Street until moving into the home of her pastor and longtime friend, James Hosch, and his wife in July, 1993. She remained with the Hosch family until ill health forced her into a nursing facility in July, 1994. Until the early part of 1993, she remained active in the ministry, filling the pulpit in her home church, as well as churches in the surrounding area.

She died on January 14, 1998 at the age of 93. Her funeral was held three days later at Apostolic Church in Monroe. Those officiating at her funeral were Harry Scism, Foreign Missions Director; Jerry Richardson, Regional Foreign Missions Director for Africa; Fred Kinzie, longtime friend; and James Hosch, pastor and friend.

For the last three years of her life, Sister Gruse was unable to communicate coherently, but the day before her

I SURRENDER ALL

death, she called for the nurses and attendants to gather about her. "Well, say goodbye to me. He's coming for me," she told them. The next evening, just hours before she died, she told Pastor Hosch and his wife, "He's coming!"

I will always feel richer for the 30 or so hours that I was privileged to spend with this great lady!

Charles E. Clanton
October 20, 1998

ORDER FORM

To order additional copies of *I Surrender All*, type or print the information below and mail your check or money order to:

        Heartland Press
        777 SW 19th
        Moore, OK 73160

Name _____

Address _____

City _____ State _____ Zip _____

____Copies of *I Surrender All* @ 12.99 each $ _____
        Postage and handling @ 1.50 each   _____
                Total amount enclosed $ _____

ORDER FORM

To order additional copies of *I Surrender All*, type or print the information below and mail your check or money order to:

        Heartland Press
        777 SW 19th
        Moore, OK 73160

Name _____

Address _____

City _____ State _____ Zip _____

____Copies of *I Surrender All* @ 12.99 each $ _____
        Postage and handling @ 1.50 each   _____
                Total amount enclosed $ _____